C000175945

Graeme Smith

A Captain's Diary 2007–2009

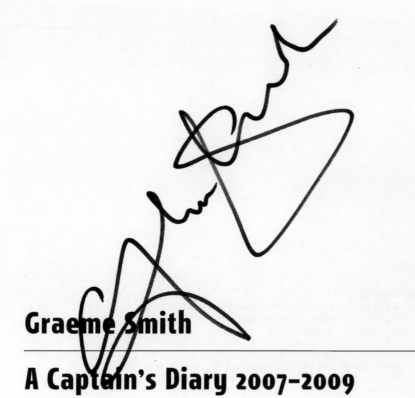

Graeme Smith

A Captain's Diary 2007–2009

Graeme Smith
with
Neil Manthorp

Jonathan Ball Publishers
JOHANNESBURG & CAPE TOWN

All rights reserved.
No part of this publication may be reproduced or transmitted,
in any form or by any means, without prior permission
from the publisher or copyright holder.

© Graeme Smith and Neil Manthorp, 2009
© The copyright holder for each photograph in the photo sections
is credited in the caption for each picture, unless it is part of the
private collection taken by Vinnie Barnes and Jeremy Snape.

Published in 2009 by
JONATHAN BALL PUBLISHERS (PTY) LTD
PO Box 33977
Jeppestown
2043

ISBN 978-1-86842-353-8

Cover design by Mr Design, Cape Town
Design, typesetting and reproduction of text and picture sections by
Triple M Design & Advertising, Johannesburg
Printed and bound by CTP Book Printers, Cape

Set in 10.5/14pt ITC Stone Serif Std

The authors would like to extend a special thank you to
Vinnie Barnes and Jeremy Snape for their dedication
to recording the events of the last eighteen months
on their digital cameras.

COVER PHOTOGRAPHS
FRONT COVER: Gallo Images
BACK COVER: Tall insert: Getty Images
All other images by Vinnie Barnes and Jeremy Snape

Contents

'The Moment ...'

Mickey Arthur

We were sitting at the back of the boat together, just the two of us, in Circular Quay just pulling out into Sydney Harbour to watch the New Year fireworks display. The last bits of orange from the sun were in the sky and the lights from the other boats on the water, and all the neon from the city centre, had already created quite a party atmosphere.

Graeme and I sipped a beer and gave each other a 'cheers'. There was absolutely nothing else in the world that we needed to say to each other. We instinctively knew exactly what the other was thinking at that second in time.

We had started this 18-month period with victory in Pakistan, beaten England in the middle of it and now just become the first South African team to win in Australia.

There had inevitably been times on the journey when the discomfort, sacrifice and emotional strain had worn us down, but right there – on a luxury boat with a cold beer and one of the most stunning views in the world – we would have put up with it all ten times over.

Graeme and I didn't chat about that moment until a long while later, but when we did, we realised that we had even more in common that we realised, because not only were we experiencing the greatest satisfaction of our respective careers, but we both regarded it as the first taste. The feeling of achievement was immense but, even on the boat at that moment, we were both already thinking ahead to how we could have this feeling again ... and again.

Foreword

Neil Manthorp

Mike Coward had just arrived in Perth from Sydney. Australia's most experienced cricket writer and broadcaster by some distance, Mike covered his first cricket tour back in the early 1970s and is one of the kindest and most astute people I have ever met.

'I can't see much changing, to be honest,' he said. 'They are undoubtedly a talented group of individuals, but I suspect that South Africa has tripped up so many times in Australia now, for so many years, that it's become ingrained. They just don't seem able to cope with being in Australia.'

It was a fair point, although he hadn't even seen the class of 2008! Still, I didn't say anything. Three times before I'd arrived in Perth as part of the travelling media and optimistically told my Australian colleagues that it would be different this time.

Later that afternoon Graeme Smith gave his traditional pre-match captain's press conference. Afterwards, Mike walked to the gates of the WACA ground with me to catch a cab back to his hotel.

'I think your boys might have a chance, you know. I really do.'

'What? Why the u-turn from a couple of hours earlier?'

'Because if Smith's demeanour is an accurate reflection of the mood of his team, then this is a Proteas team the like of which we have not encountered in Australia before.'

The funny thing is, the difference that Mike had noticed was the simplest of changes. Smith was, certainly for the first time on Australian soil, simply being himself. There was no particular strategy to his behaviour, he wasn't trying to convey an image or send a message. There was no sign of the defensive nervousness which has left previous touring teams twitching like flea-ridden cats when confronted with the Australian media. Smith was as relaxed as, I hate to say it, a senior Australian player.

And the media warmed to him almost immediately. I sensed that as surely as Mike had sensed the change in Smith. I hope that lesson doesn't need to be learned again in the future.

The Players

Yusuf Abdulla
Hashim Amla (Hash)
Gulam Bodi
Loots Bosman
Johan Botha (Botes)
Mark Boucher (Bouch)
AB de Villiers (AB)
J-P Duminy (J-P)
Herschelle Gibbs (Hersch)
Paul Harris (Harry)
Jacques Kallis (Jakes)
Justin Kemp
Imraan Khan
Rory Kleinveldt
Charl Langeveldt (Langers)
Johann Louw
Neil McKenzie (Mac/Mackie)
Albie Morkel

Morne Morkel
Andre Nel (Nella)
Makhaya Ntini (Makkie)
Justin Ontong
Wayne Parnell (Parnie)
Alviro Petersen
Robin Peterson (Robbie P)
Vernon Philander
Shaun Pollock (Polly)
Ashwell Prince (Ash)
Graeme Smith (Biff)
Dale Steyn (Steyntjie)
Lonwabo Tsotsobe (Lopsy)
Roelof van der Merwe
Vaughn van Jaarsveld
Morne van Wyk
Monde Zondeki

Introduction

Back in mid-2007 I needed to make some changes to the structure
and organisation of my life and to my game. I worked with Paddy
Upton, among others, and he suggested that I keep a batting diary.
It is all well and good to talk about tactics and approaches to certain bowlers, but theories quickly become forgotten unless you
have a way of anchoring them. The easiest and most obvious way
is to write them down.

I decided to keep notes on as many points of technique and
team discussion as possible. This notebook was never intended
to be to be published – and, to be honest, its contents would not
make interesting reading.

But as we came towards the end of 2008, it became obvious that
we were experiencing one of the greatest years in South African
cricket history. Several people, including team mates, suggested
that we should have a record of our trials, tribulations and suc-
cesses as a team.

For a while I regretted not having kept a tour diary. But then I remembered that my batting diary had actually become far more than just a record of my batting tactics and plans. I had been using it for so many things – notes for team meetings, observations about opposition and conditions, reminders about meetings and even the conclusions from meetings. I realised that it probably contained everything I needed to get the job done.

Much of what is recorded in this book is with the advantage of hindsight, but I couldn't help talking 'in the current' at various times, particularly when I was reliving some great victories and memorable moments – and making use of the notes in my batting notebook.

This resultant tour diary was never intended to be scientifically accurate or a precise, historical account of our time from Pakistan in October 2007 until Australia's departure from South Africa in April 2009. The intention was just to remember what an incredible journey it was and to share some of our memories and experiences with the people who had supported us so loyally, and hopefully still do.

Copies of my original 'batting diary' would only be useful for putting people to sleep, but it was a great reference point for all the critical moments before, during and after matches which helped me put this diary together.

In sport we talk all the time of implementing 'processes' and taking 'baby steps' to reach an ultimate target, no matter how high or far away that target is. Back in the middle of 2007 the thought of scoring over 1 600 Test runs in the next calendar year would have seemed a very high and far-away target! Our team goals were obviously to win all our series and finish what we knew would be an epic journey with a historical win in Australia. But like the entries in my diary, we knew we would have to take small but carefully considered steps in order to get there.

This is an account of several dreams which came true for many of us – often against the odds, but always requiring plenty of hard work and belief. I hope that message is clear.

It is far too early in this team's collective life to start talking about legacies – we are all still young and raring to go! – but if we made a difference to South African cricket with our success in 2008, I hope it is in the area of 'belief'.

In every match and every series I played against Australia, and other series I have seen Australia play in, their approach was always characterised by their confidence and self-belief. We would reduce them to 40-5, or reach 250-2, and their body language never changed. They simply believed in the impossible. And often they would make the impossible come true and recover to make 300, or bowl us out for 300.

In 2008 it was the Proteas' turn to believe. And we did. We didn't just talk about belief, we believed it. We won in England and then won in Australia, and one of our greatest weapons was our collective belief – in ourselves as individuals, in each other and in the strength of the team.

My greatest hope as a result of 2008 is that when Proteas teams in the future are faced with adversity and seemingly need a miracle, they will be able to say: 'Well, they did it back in 2008. Nothing's impossible.'

I hope you enjoy the read.

1.

'No Fear'

Pakistan: October 2007

TESTS
Karachi 1–5 October 2007
Lahore 8–12 October 2007

LIMITED OVERS
Lahore 18 October 2007
Lahore 20 October 2007
Faisalabad 23 October 2007
Multan 26 October 2007
Lahore 29 October 2007

Security. It dominated the build-up to the tour and, as always, the first port of call for me and the players was Tony Irish, the South African Cricketers' Association chief executive. We chatted through the situation and then met as soon as possible with Cricket South Africa and Bob Nichols and Rory Steyn, our security experts. The man we trusted most – simply because he was the man on tour with us – was Faisal Nagel, our 'personal' bodyguard, so we always liked to hear what he had to say. But Gerald Majola, as CSA chief executive, must take ultimate responsibility, and the players' relationship with him has grown immensely over the years. He has always shown that he has the players' interests at heart and has never compromised our safety so, although we were really concerned about touring, we also knew we were in good hands.

The most important thing from our perspective was that everybody shared the same priorities. Tony provided the 'bridge' between the players and the Board. The most important thing for us was that every piece of information that was available was passed on to us; we had to feel confident that we were being kept in the loop. If we had ever felt that something was being decided without our input I'm pretty sure it would have been disastrous in terms of some players choosing not to travel. But that never happened and the information from security reports in Pakistan was always shared with us. The biggest concerns, obviously, were the hotels we would be staying in and the travel arrangements between hotels and grounds.

The thought of going to Karachi was scary for all of us because we hadn't gone there on the previous tour when security was an issue and it seemed pretty obvious to all of us that the situation was just as tense, if not more so.

We organised a couple of meetings of the whole squad to discuss our feelings and decided, to my relief, that we would stand together, whatever decisions were made. Everybody had some concerns, but Jakes was certainly one of the most worried – the 'worst case scenario' affected him a lot. I tried hard not to allow emotions to cloud my judgement; I tried to handle the situation based on facts rather than emotion, even though I shared everyone's concerns. It was so important to get Bob and Tony in to talk to the players, to listen to their information and trust it. If they told us it was safe to go, and provided us with factual information to back it up, then, as far as I was concerned, it was our job to trust them. If they had told us it wasn't safe, then we would have found it even easier to trust that information, too!

It's one thing being clear in your own mind, but it became obvious that we needed to provide the same information and guarantees to players' families. If they were unhappy and worried because they didn't know the facts, that would affect the players. There were a lot of 'what ifs' raised by all of us, and we all had doubts, but the process was handled exceptionally well by all concerned.

We were the only team from outside the subcontinent to have toured for many months (and no major Test-playing nation went after us for over a year), so the feeling that we were being used as guinea pigs was inevitable, and that feeling still existed when we arrived. Even though we trusted the security people around us, there was still a major feeling of unease. I just told everyone that it was natural to be nervous.

When you arrive in Pakistan there are unique sensations that hit you in the first few hours. For me it's the pollution, the noise and the smells. And the crows! The number of crows and the noise they make can be overwhelming, and they are huge, too. In the evening we would almost inevitably order something with chicken, and the chicken pieces were always quite small. It did make you wonder …

The security situation hit us about 15 minutes after the plane touched down as a delegation of uniforms met us on board and escorted us through passport control to collect our bags. Normally on a tour of this length we'd have as many as five bags each, but this tour was different: there isn't quite the same need for casual clothes when you can't leave the hotel and barely leave your room after a day's play, so we were down to about three bags each.

As we walked out of the airport we entered a tunnel of security staff – police or army I'm not sure – and Faisal was waiting for us with his crew by the bus. The bags had already been whisked away from us and gone ahead on a truck. We drove away with a huge police and army escort, sirens blazing. It was a fairly obvious announcement that we had arrived.

One of the hardest things to get used to is the number of guns in your face. I know we have our problems with crime and violence in South Africa, but – unless you're very unlucky – you don't really see too many AK-47s or machine guns on a regular basis. But they are all around you in Pakistan. I'm sure I would have felt different if I'd done military service, but that was before my time. Pakistan's elite protection service was assigned to us for the tour and they travelled in vehicles either side of the bus. They were dressed all in black, from their paratrooper boots to their tight T-shirts with the words 'No Fear' emblazoned on the back. It was all very distracting. At times it felt like we were in a movie, not on a cricket tour.

The jeep which drove ahead of the bus was a constant worry (especially for me, Mickey Arthur and Vinnie Barnes, who always sit in the front of the bus). The 'No Fear' guys in the back of the jeep all rested their rifles on their knees with the barrels pointing towards us! As the bus bounced along the bumpy roads we were constantly joking about the reliability of the safety catches and asking each other to tell our loved ones how much we loved them in case we were hit by a stray bullet. And as always, there was an element of seriousness behind every joke.

*　*　*

The South African Embassy would normally have hosted us for a function at some stage, but security would have been a nightmare so the Embassy had to come to us. They held a welcoming function on the top floor of the hotel, which you had to get to in a glass lift backing out onto the city. It was a great view. Unfortunately, it wasn't great for Michael Owen-Smith, our media manager, who has such a profound fear of heights that he collapsed into a heap on the floor of the lift and couldn't move. The security guys had to pick him up, literally, and carry him to his room! We all hoped that this rescue act would be their most important contribution to the tour.

*　*　*

Shopping came to us! One of the great 'traditions' of touring Pakistan is the shopping for the magnificent carpets, rugs and leather jackets, among other things. If you were interested in something particular then you had to pass on that information to the security guys, who would then go out to certain recommended shops and relay the request. Then the shopowners would come to the team room with carpets, leather wallets, belts, jackets – and thousands of DVDs. We missed the 'real' experience of the shops and markets, of course, but it was certainly less hassle and, given our 'hotel arrest' status, at least we could still return home with gifts for family and friends.

*　*　*

When cricket finally became our priority, the first job was to get rid of travel stiffness and jet lag. The fitness and training staff took charge of the first couple of training sessions while we worked out the best way to tackle the cricket preparation. Fortunately we had a warm-up game before this series started, so Mick and I were constantly assessing the best way to approach that. You always have an idea of how to prepare but, equally, you need to be flexible. Some light work – volleyball, gym and pool – and some hard work, both cricket and fitness. It's easy to see when players need rest at the end of the season, but sometimes a planned hard session at the beginning of the season can also become the wrong thing to do. And sometimes, a planned rest day is better cancelled in favour of a tough session.

The first net session is just about finding your feet in the conditions – the heat, the low sun, the low bounce of the pitch, the grass burns, whatever it may be. Even if it's just the smells, or the bugs that fly in your face when you're bowling, or into your helmet when you're batting, you have to get used to it. There's no point in a guy diving for the first time in a Test match and ripping the skin off his elbows on the outfield – he's better off learning the hard way before the real thing.

Then we sit down as a team and discuss our goals and our experiences, before dividing up into batsmen and bowlers and doing the same thing again. Everyone has specific things to work on and it's important to share those thoughts and targets. We draw up a series of theoretical objectives before we even get to video analysis.

Reverse-swing was a key discussion amongst the batsmen, as was patience, the most important aspect of subcontinental cricket for both batsmen and bowlers. We had bowlers who had been there before – Andre Nel, Makhaya Ntini and Shaun Pollock, but there were also young guys on the tour – Morné Morkel, Dale Steyn and Paul Harris, who was on the tour for the first time as our spinner. There was a lot to talk about. We spoke about lengths and lines, how to attack and defend.

The warm-up game was just a couple of days away and we needed to start focusing on selection. Ideally, we wanted to play 12 or even 13 players in the game, and that was the way we were planning. But we also had our thoughts firmly planted on selection for the first Test, and it wasn't easy.

I arrived on tour believing that we needed to make some changes in our thinking on the way we played Test cricket. Not drastic changes, but drastic enough for the people we were going to select, and it took some convincing to get Mickey and Vinnie to hear my theory without thinking I had gone mad. It involved one of the hardest decisions I have ever had to face, because of the enormous respect I had for the man involved, not just as a cricketer but as a human being. Polly had become a senior statesman and one of the most respected cricketers in the world, if not the most.

I really believed that winning in Pakistan would require pace, and we needed to give the likes of a Dale or Morné the opportunity to really fly on flat wickets. I was completely convinced that Shoaib Akhtar had been the major difference between the two teams on the previous tour and my aim was to reproduce that 'edge'. His sheer pace through the air, and swing, enabled them to take key wickets and I knew we needed that advantage.

So we sat down and discussed everything, several times. It was so hard to contemplate leaving out a guy like Polly, for so many reasons. He provides your team with control, he is an extra batsman at number eight and, with his experience in the subcontinent, he's a great man for a captain to turn to when the pressure's on. There were also worries about whether Dale and Morné would have the control we would need – and just as worrying was the fact that they would give us one of the longest 'tails' in recent South African history. And if we weren't concerned enough ourselves, our travelling media representatives were making quite sure we knew the consequences if the gamble failed.

We were forced to drop a very big hint about our intentions before the warm-up game because the Pakistan authorities were insisting that it was played as a first-class game. What a load of rubbish. You get one warm-up game before a tour these days, if that, and it should be up to the touring team to decide how it should be played. I was furious and must admit that the word 'bullshit' was heard to escape my lips a few times during meetings about the issue. You arrive in a country with 14 players and need them all to be as sharp as possible, yet three guys face the possibility of not playing at all. Practice matches can only really benefit the squad when 12 or 13 people can play a role. Only 11 can bat and 11 can bowl and field, obviously, so it still resembles a proper match in that respect, but at least your 'first reserves' get a taste of match conditions. But they insisted, so we had to leave Polly out. Fortunately, the Pakistan media seemed to take the view that he was being rested.

The game went well – luckily everyone had a good work-out. But as we started final preparations for the Test, the subject of conversation remained the same. The topic still had not been finally resolved between the management and me.

The day before the Test, sitting downstairs in the lobby of Karachi hotel with Mickey, Vinnie and Ashwell, we were still talking about whether it was the right way to go. There was no doubt in my mind. I'm not a great reader of books, but there were some very influential ones I'd read over the years which had convinced me that you have to take calculated risks to be successful. I honestly believed that giving the responsibility of scoring the runs we needed to the top six, giving the responsibility to the bowlers to take the wickets, would bring the best out of each individual in the team. Instead of picking an all-rounder at eight, I said we needed extra pace.

Then fate played a role in selection, too. Morné had landed badly in a foot hole and the scan revealed a fracture. He would have to go home. There was almost an assumption that it was a reprieve for Polly and that we would revert to plan 'A'. But I had made my mind up, and tempting as it was to go the conservative route, I stuck to my guns. I felt that Jakes and Harry could do a good enough holding job in order for the other guys to attack. We could even use Makhaya in a more defensive role, if we needed to. It wasn't easy – and it wasn't easy telling Polly, either. Mickey took that responsibility and I know it wasn't a task he looked forward to. Everyone, including me, felt that Polly probably deserved better, but the team's interests had to come first.

When I look back now I can only be thankful to the team and the players for rising to the challenge and justifying the faith placed in them. It had been difficult to convince everyone of the merits of changing tactics but I am unbelievably grateful that I managed to convince everybody to go that way.

On a personal note, my Test form over the last year and a half hadn't been great, although my one-day form had been decent. I'd had a good World Cup with the bat and I'd made the most of the shorter formats of the game, but I had gone a bit wobbly in the Test format, for whatever reason. I had lost focus on how to score runs in Test cricket and I wanted to get back to the way I started my career. I made several big changes before the series.

After the World Cup I reviewed almost everything about my game, my 'brand' of cricket, and the way I wanted to play the game. One of the changes was in my batting diary. I compared myself at the start of my career – the way I used to think, what was important to me, planning and preparation, and the way I used to think when I was batting – and what had changed subsequently.

At the start of my international career, although I was very young, I knew my game so well. I was patient, I was prepared to work hard out in the middle, I probably had fewer shots available to me, but I was calm. I played the moment very well, concentration and mental strength were amongst my best strengths – and, crucially, I left the ball well. I was able to let the bowlers bowl at me and, if they bowled well, I was able to soak up the pressure and cash in afterwards when they tired or lost concentration. I was humble with my game and I knew my limitations. Having that single-minded approach at that stage in my career worked, but now it was different. There was a lot more to think about, my mind was busy and I was probably less patient. Basically, I had just had so much more going on in my life – and I wasn't always coping well with it all.

I realised I was looking to impress with the bat, and perhaps with captaincy, rather than to keep it simple and effective. My personality and life had changed. There were more stresses and worries and my answer was to try and dominate the game more. I hadn't balanced all of these things in my own mind – so, sitting down after the 2007 World Cup, I finally had the chance to take stock.

Working with Paddy Upton, I started with organising my life a lot more, so that when it came to batting, I could focus on just that. I was totally refreshed and determined in a different way than ever before. For the first time as a captain, my focus was on making a big impact with the bat, not just in Pakistan but for the next 18 months, culminating in the two series against Australia. I was disappointed that my Test form had faded away and I wanted to get back to what Graeme Smith was all about – and that was scoring runs, being strong at the top of the order, playing my own game and not being dictated to.

There was no doubt that scoring runs again would benefit my captaincy, so I allowed myself the time to prepare properly as a batsman without feeling guilty about missing some 'captaincy time'. Scoring runs would make everything possible, time with the team, tactical decisions, media commitments – they would all become easier and more successful if I was scoring. I did not want to go through another season of scraping 60s and 70s and being under pressure. No sportsman likes to feel that his place in the team is under pressure, but it's even worse as captain, because there is nowhere to hide.

As a result of all this, I was more nervous than usual in Pakistan, especially walking out to bat in the first Test. I felt calm as I had done my preparation, but I was nervous because I desperately wanted everything to work out. Having become more focused on my own personal preparation, and having started doing my own video analysis and writing down my thoughts in my batting diary, I wanted to make sure it all worked!

It's all well and good to talk about tactics against certain bowlers, but my work with Paddy has taught me that writing everything down helps reinforce your conclusions and commit them to memory. I wrote down the bowlers' names and how each was going to attack me.

Mohammed Asif's usual angle is away from me – so, what guard would I take, and what would be my general game plan towards him? Would I look to leave him, wait for a cut, wait for him to get too straight, be patient? I had worked out my general game plan towards all the Pakistani bowlers before the tour started in this way.

Sohail Tanvir – Hold my balance and my position as much as I could, watch the ball and look out for the ball I knew he would try to swing back in to me, be prepared for that.

Mohammed Asif – Stand outside my crease because he didn't use his bouncer very much. His main threat was the angle he created across me. So I batted more on middle stump, even slightly middle and off, to cover my off stump as much as possible.

Umar Gul – He worried me a little bit because he rushed batsmen at the crease and my concern was being trapped before getting into position. So I was conscious that my weight was moving forward and that I kept my balance and focused on hitting the ball back where it came from.

Danish Kaneria – Make sure I didn't fall over to the off-side. Obviously, the challenge with leg spinners is picking the ball out of his hand, but making sure that my balance was good and that I didn't go across the crease, and that I came at the ball, was just as important. If he bowled over the wicket I stood on middle stump and tried to work on my head going towards the ball. If he came around the wicket into the rough, I would bat on middle and off stump, almost trying to get my pads outside the line to take lbw out of play.

I tried to practise all these disciplines against net bowlers so they would become engrained in my memory, but writing them down in my diary helped just as much.

As a team we do team video analysis on the opposition and each bowler knows where he wants to bowl before the match starts, but as captain I've got to be as prepared as everybody else so I can help change tactics, if needed. A lot of the pre-match work can change, depending on the wicket and other conditions, but you generally have a plan for each batsman and an understanding of his strengths and weaknesses.

Salman Butt – The idea was to place square fields against him because we felt he couldn't score down the ground very well but scored a lot through cover point and square leg, so we wanted to block those areas. We thought the ball swinging in to him was something he struggled with and the angle we could create bowling round the wicket to him was also important.

Mohammad Hafeez – The idea was to bowl a bit wider to him and not get too straight. We felt that he flicked full length deliveries through the leg side quite well so we wanted to attack him at waist height. Back of a length, making sure we saw leg stump. Trap him between a cut and a push.

Younis Khan – He needs to start well, so we needed to give him no freebies. He was a key player. We believed we could attack him straight, early in his innings, and look for an lbw. And if he got 'in', maybe sit with a gully and a point in catching positions and see if we could get the ball swinging. Being in the middle order, he would probably be facing more spin, so Harry focused a lot on how to keep him quiet. With reverse swing at the other end, we were hopeful we could keep him under control.

Misbah-ul-Haq – We felt he wasn't great against the short ball and batted very deep in his crease. The aim was to mix up a lot of short balls with full and straight ones, and the occasional slower ball, because we thought that by taking such a big step backwards, he was making himself vulnerable to an lbw.

As subtle and complex as cricket can be, it's also very simple. The key elements of my team talk before any Test match remain consistent: patience, partnerships and pressure – the three P's. Build partnerships and pressure, and use patience to do it. You won't go too far wrong if you can do that.

I like to keep team meetings short and sweet. We've already done a lot of preparation by the final evening, video analysis, general meetings, training sessions and nets, so on the final evening I like to keep it simple with just three, four or maybe five key points. If it takes too long then everyone gets bored and no messages actually come across!

The Karachi Test

Before the Karachi Test we spoke about responsibility, about being clever, about maturity, and about reverse swing (and we left AB and Bouch in control of that). We knew that if we were going to be successful in Pakistan we had to adopt a 'when in Rome do as the Romans do' approach. That did not mean we were going to do anything illegal, however! Just be creative, within the laws ...

Thank goodness I won the toss because the wicket looked like a road and seemed certain to become dryer and dryer as the game went on. It was very flat on day one and I was absolutely obsessed with making the most of the first innings while we were batting. Herschelle and I got off to a good start and I started to feel comfortable. Just as I thought we were about to build something special, I was out for 42 just before lunch. It was very, very frustrating. There are plenty of times when you're not feeling good, or it's a bowler's pitch, and you can live with getting out cheaply. But when you feel good and conditions are in your favour, and then you get yourself out, that's the worst feeling.

But we reached 450, Jakes leading the way with a superb 155. All his experience and expertise against spin came to the fore. One of the things that has always amazed me is his composure when batting and how he sticks to his game plan and makes it work. It was great to watch. We were both excited and relieved about having the runs on the board because, as we all knew, we had a different bowling line-up and they didn't need the pressure of trying to defend a below-par score.

Steyn, Nel and Ntini were now free to attack, with Harry and Jakes doing the 'defensive' roles. It worked superbly. Harry proved that really good, tight defending can earn you wickets, too, and he finished with five as we bowled them out for 291. One of the biggest and most important lessons I have learned as a captain is to show faith in your spinner. It's a two-way relationship, of course – you can't just show faith in anybody just because he's your spinner! But Harry provided me with a lot of confidence, in terms of both control and attitude. I never expected him to bowl teams out and take nine for nothing, but he was consistent and he was confident in what he needed to do. You could set fields to him and you could control the game with him – but picking up five wickets in the first innings was a great bonus.

The Test was played during the month of Ramadan, which meant that two big milestones – Jakes's century and Harry getting his first five wicket haul (5-73) – went uncelebrated, at least with a beer. I think the medical staff didn't mind that – they were obviously keen for us to drink a lot of water and not much else in that heat. We normally wouldn't drink during a Test match, except to celebrate important milestones! Instead of a beer, our 'special' drink was a Pepsi – or for Jakes a Pepsi Lite. Another difference about Ramadan is that we had to leave the field and go to a tent for drinks breaks, which made a day's play feel quite different. It was as a sign of respect to those who were observing the sunrise-to-sunset fast that we drank out of their sight. From a purely cricketing perspective, however, it felt a bit like six sessions per day rather than three, and there were times when I felt we lost a bit of momentum.

* * *

After a while in Karachi we all had a bit of cabin fever, so when rumour reached us that there was actually a branch of Nando's in the city, we pleaded with Faisal to see if it would be possible for us to go after play. He went the day before to do a security check and, luckily for us, decided it was a 'low risk' venue. You wouldn't have thought so by the size of the army that escorted us there. They actually closed the restaurant to the public – no questions, no argument – just closed! We had all the staff cooking just for us. I actually felt very guilty, it must have cost the restaurant a fair bit of money. It was the only evening we got out of the hotel.

* * *

Having so many different cultures in our own team has helped us all to understand and respect the little things which set us apart. In fact, they set you apart but bind you together, too. I'm sure that is one of the reasons we have been able to grow together so much as a team. Everyone likes their little comforts after a game, whether it's a beer, a Coke or a toasted cheese sandwich: obviously, it's frustrating when you can't have those little things when you're away from home, but we were able to help each other get over it!

We added 264-7 before declaring and, once again, I got a start (25) before being dismissed. Aargh. So the target was set and we needed to bowl them out a second time. I didn't care who took the wickets, obviously, but I must admit that for Dale to take 5-56 was very special for me personally. To have made the selection decision and then to see it pay off so quickly was a massive relief and very satisfying.

I had known for some time that I wanted Dale in the team. He was confident, he had pace through the air as well as a skiddy bouncer and he could take key wickets. He might have gone for a few runs but, in these conditions, that was inevitable and acceptable. We set him attacking fields and allowed him the freedom to attack. It was a crucial aspect of the victory. Our mindset had changed from trying to squeeze batsmen to death, to getting the job done quickly and ruthlessly with pace and pressure – even from both ends when possible. It changed my captaincy completely and gave me far more options and variations, not just line and length from both ends.

Not only did Steyntjie bowl well and control the reverse-swing, but he showed that he had a real killer instinct. When he had a batsman rattled, or spotted a weakness, he really went for the kill and made it count.

The atmosphere in the change room afterwards was one of deep contentment and satisfaction. No wild celebrations or a party, just quiet smiles but deep happiness. It was my first win in a major subcontinent country and, given all the off-field stresses, it felt so good. Perhaps we were a bit subdued because of how ominous the rest of the season was looking. We had spoken so often about how this journey would take us to India, England and then finish with back-to-back series against Australia, that maybe we were too daunted to cheer.

Back at the hotel most of us gathered again in the team room to keep the winning spirit alive. Somebody had an i-pod, no doubt bought at the Dubai duty-free on the way, and then a couple of beers found their way into the room. Happy days! I'm not sure where they came from, but there are plenty of entrepreneurs in the world and a few US dollars often speak loudly in Pakistan. Even though we had done nothing illegal and were drinking in a private room, it somehow felt naughty, which made the beer taste even better. We spent a lot of time in the team room because we weren't allowed out of the hotel and the lobby was always jam-packed with autograph and photograph hunters. Sometimes it just felt a bit too much.

Maybe it was because we hadn't had a beer for two weeks, but after my second one I sat back and decided that it was the proudest victory of my career.

The Lahore Test

We arrived in Lahore really upbeat and excited – excited that we'd made it out of Karachi, first of all, and that security had done their job! But we were also one-nil up and Lahore had quite a few more attractions than Karachi, like the British Club right next to the stadium where you could buy a cold beer and order a steak and chips – without any hint of spice or curry! The hotel was amazing, too. Very large and grand, with superb rooms and facilities and a modern gym.

The Rugby World Cup was just starting to get interesting after the group matches and we were desperate to watch the matches and get into the tournament. Initially the hotel could only find certain matches on a French channel and, with respect, it was hard to enjoy. After a few days, however, they sent a technician up onto the roof with a screwdriver to have a fiddle with the satellite dish and – it worked! Our very own SuperSport was right there, on the flat-screen TVs in our hotel rooms! I'm pretty sure it wasn't an 'authorised' feed but that was the last thing any of us were worried about. The World Cup helped us through some quiet, long and hot afternoons. There are only so many DVDs you can watch, only so many times you can chat to each other or play putt-putt in the corridors.

The final, however, was very late at night and we were scheduled to be leaving Lahore the next morning at 6:30. It would have meant having about three hours' sleep – and less if the Boks won, of course. Somebody even asked whether we should record the final and watch it later. Everybody looked at him as if he was completely mad. What a ridiculous suggestion! Eventually, the management had to rearrange our travel plans the next day and changed the flight to a later one which meant we could sleep in until 9:00 am. Nothing really changed with regard to how much sleep we got, however, and when we finally emerged a bit groggy in the lobby, the hotel management presented us with a massive cream cake to say 'congratulations'! It was extremely kind, and typical of the hospitality which is a feature of the subcontinent, but I can't say there were too many volunteers to have a slice at that time in the morning. A couple of brave guys with a sweet tooth made an effort …

As far as the cricket was concerned, the biggest talking point, once again, was our selection policy and tactics. Did we bring Polly back now that we were one-nil up, or stick with the same team? I was keen to stay positive. I felt it would have been a defensive move and I have never liked the idea of trying to protect a lead, in any sport. Although the debate was healthy, our decision to stay with the same team was unanimous.

The state of the pitch might have prompted a rethink, but instead of gambling on a dry, dusty turner in order to try and level the series, it actually looked good. If anything, we thought it might have a bit more bounce in it than the Karachi pitch, which suited us perfectly.

The 'three Ps' dominated the team talk once again: patience, partnerships, pressure. I also made a couple of other points: good teams do the right things over and over again, Test after Test, and we really wanted to carry on the momentum we had earned and win the series. We hadn't won a major Test series on the subcontinent for a while and we wanted to begin this year-and-a-half journey with a significant trophy.

We needed to assess the wicket and then adapt to it as quickly as possible. If we could play calm, focused cricket for the first two or three days without ever letting them get their noses in front, we could put enough pressure on them to cause a few cracks and a bit of panic. Their media can be horribly critical, so that wouldn't help with their focus or morale.

The Test was dubbed 'The Inzimam Test' because he had been recalled for what was basically a testimonial match. There was a lot of talk about how his influence would affect their team, especially as he wasn't captain but remained such an imposing influence. I don't think he was fully fit and he didn't have much form to speak of, so it didn't seem right to me that he would use a Test match to bid farewell. It didn't seem to be in the team's best interests – but, having said that, we still very wary that he would rise to the occasion and do something special. He was still a great player, in every sense of the word. But he was also proving to be a distraction, especially in the media.

Fortunately we won the toss again, to my relief, and obviously batted first. A lot of us made a start but then failed to make it count and we were under a lot of pressure until Bouch and Harry put on 88 for the eighth wicket. It was another moment which was especially pleasing because, having shown that we might be able to survive without Polly in the bowling department, it was the first sign that we might, somehow, be able to get away with not having him batting at eight. Harry batted over three hours and took a few blows on the body. The next day he said he'd never been so stiff in his life. Batting makes a few more demands on your body than you might realise. Harry had a new respect for us batsmen after that.

That partnership took us to a total of 357, demoralising for a team which had their sights on replying to something closer to 275. We then dismissed them for 206. Apart from Inzi, they also had Mohammad Yousuf back in the middle order, so, along with Younus Khan, it was a formidable batting line-up. The bowlers had, once again, worked together and performed as a unit.

Then it was about making the lead count and, personally, it was fantastic. My innings of 133 proved everything to me, that I was correct to identify what had gone wrong in the last year and that I did have the patience, the grit and the determination required to score a hundred in the subcontinent. It wasn't easy. Facing Danish Kaneria for long periods with the ball turning and bouncing was a constant challenge, mentally as well as physically. I knew that I would have to be contributing regularly and significantly if we were going to realise our dreams over the next 18 months, and I'd done everything I could to prepare myself. Even so, my century came as a huge relief: I'd helped to make the series safe.

Then Jakes batted superbly well, yet again, to score his third hundred of the series, an incredible achievement. Just to survive for long periods of time in the attritional environment of a Test in Pakistan – the heat, everything – is impressive, but to score three hundreds and bowl the number of overs he did, I can honestly say I don't know how he does it sometimes. At the time I kept thinking to myself 'find out what makes him tick and learn from it'. I knew we were watching something very special. I reached the conclusion that his 'secret' was keeping things simple, making good starts count and being completely ruthless in terms of what he wanted to achieve; he was never satisfied. He reiterated in my own mind the goals and objectives for the season ahead, and how they should never be compromised.

When I started playing I used to have bets with Gary Kirsten on who would score the most hundreds in a season, which he often won, and I would have to take him out for dinner at the end of the season. The way Jakes was turning out hundreds I was glad that I had never made that bet with him.

We then had a huge lead and I wanted to declare and win the Test match, which was probably a bit risky. I would have been pretty much inconsolable if they had chased 480-odd to win the game, but the prospect of a two-nil series win was just too tempting. It was the image I wanted to present within our own team but also to the rest of the world, that we were positive cricketers and we played to win. That was the culture we wanted to breed within the guys coming through, the development of Steyn, De Villiers and Duminy. There were times on that last day when I was nervous, but we were able to pull things back when Pakistan were going well, and Harry bowled a huge number of overs with typical control. The draw meant we had won the series.

The one-day series
Lahore 18 October 2007
Lahore 20 October 2007
Faisalabad 23 October 2007
Multan 26 October 2007
Lahore 29 October 2007

The arrival of new faces for the one-dayers is always refreshing but, at the same time, there is some concern that you maintain the same successful attitude and work ethic.

The wickets were all spin-friendly and slow – we adapted well in the first game but not in the next two, so we faced the daunting prospect of having to win the final two matches to complete a rare 'double'.

We played the first two matches in Lahore and then lost a really tight game in Faisalabad on a pitch that turned square. Johan Botha was being groomed as our one-day spinner but he was still learning about bowling in the subcontinent and I felt that we really missed someone who could turn the ball away from the bat. Still, we probably deserved to be two-one down, to be honest.

It's hard enough trying to win a five match series from two-one down, but when the fourth match is scheduled for a place like Multan, it's even harder. The hotel was horrendous, terrible. Before the game, a day-nighter, I was woken up at 6:00 in the morning by the sound of running water ... in my room! It was flooded. I was on a floor two levels below the rest of the team; we had been split up because the hotel didn't have enough rooms on the same floor. The whole floor was flooded. There didn't seem to be much I could do so I lay in bed and turned the TV on. A few minutes later about ten guys with sponges came into my room, without knocking, and started sponging the water into buckets. Then they saw it was me and all stood up and stared at me, probably shocked to see me wearing my glasses. A lot of people don't know I wear contact lenses. Then they started taking pictures of me with their cell phones and asking me for my autograph. It was the morning of a must-win international, I was awake two hours before I wanted to be and there were a dozen strangers in my hotel room.

Breakfast was miserable. It wasn't the unfamiliarity of the food that bothered us, but it was cold, oily and generally unhealthy as well as being unrecognisable. Many times in Pakistan I was pleasantly surprised by new food which I hadn't tasted before, but this was not one of those occasions. I managed to find a piece of hard bread and put some jam on that, but it was an ordinary start to the day. Fortunately, the trusty Gulam Raja had organised a basic pasta meal for us at the ground so we managed to eat before the game.

All the other traffic on the way to the ground had been halted and all the other roads had been cordoned off. It was a lengthy drive, too – at least 10 kilometres – and the whole way there were people stacked on the side of the road trying to get a glimpse of the team coming past. It always amazes me ... just to catch a glimpse of the bus speeding past!

As far as the match was concerned, we had no idea how heavy the dew would be in the evening. We were lucky that Pakistan didn't either! It's one thing for the touring team to be unaware of conditions, but the home side should have known better. They won the toss and batted first – we bowled really well and then used Polly as a pinch-hitter. Both Herschelle and I made runs and we won the game quite comprehensively. After the match the guys took the mickey out of Mickey for not having come down to the stadium the evening before to see if dew would be a factor. He rarely makes a mistake so we rubbed this one in! The outfield was soaking wet.

Security once again became the focal issue after the attempted assassination of Benazir Bhutto, who had returned from exile and landed in Karachi. We were supposed to play the final match in Karachi and then fly home from there. The extent of the violence was frightening. Just watching the television pictures of the explosion and its aftermath was really unsettling. Once again, despite our personal fears, we trusted the people around us and left them to make the decision. But it was a huge relief to all of us when they vetoed a return to Karachi and insisted that the match either be cancelled or moved to Lahore. In the end we moved to Lahore.

The amazing thing about situations like this is the number of people who get involved from the comfort of their armchairs. How can anybody tell us whether to go to Karachi, or not, while they sit in Johannesburg? It was outrageous to hear people talking about the importance of 'sticking to the original itinerary' when our lives could have been at risk. The mood in the squad was not good! They had never even been to Pakistan before.

The same had happened when the team left Sri Lanka a couple of years earlier. It amazes me how people can call the players 'soft' for being reluctant to play cricket in countries with random bombs going off – and the even more terrifying prospect of actually being targeted by extremists. I fully understand the importance of maintaining good diplomatic relations with major cricket-playing nations, but you simply cannot make valid judgements unless you are there or have experience of the conditions. It affects the players; it's constantly on your mind. Every time you get on the bus you imagine what it might look like after driving over a bomb and what chance you would have. We were a high-profile target that would grab plenty of headlines for a terrorist group wanting to make a name for itself. [*Ed note:* This section was written before the 3 March attack on the Sri Lankan cricket team in Lahore.]

To be fair, we received plenty of support once again from Gerald Majola, and we knew that Faisal would do everything in his power not to put us in a compromising position. Logan Naidoo was the team manager and it was up to him to liaise with Cricket South Africa and the Pakistan Cricket Board. Meanwhile, the television pictures and photographs of the carnage of Bhutto's bus were everywhere, nobody could escape them – and the death toll figures rose with every report. It's fair to say that, even when the decision was made to go back to Lahore, the majority of us would have preferred to go straight home. We didn't like the idea of taking a 2:2 draw and leaving behind a series win, but our safety was more important than cricket results. Even the idea of flying back to Karachi just to catch our connection to Dubai didn't thrill us. It felt like we were in a country at war with itself.

A couple of newspaper articles and interviews with politicians staggered us with claims that we were doing their country a dis-service and being disrespectful by not wanting to play cricket there. That created an emotionally charged atmosphere within our squad, while the return of Shoaib Akhtar (once again) was creating a big stir in the local media. Suddenly, there seemed to be more at stake than just a match and a series. For the leadership group, myself, Mickey and Vinnie, managing the situation and trying to get the team to focus on the match was a real challenge. I haven't done much boundary fielding in my career but I can imagine what it must feel like standing close to the crowd with your back turned for half the day. Sitting duck. What could we say to the guys who regularly fielded on the rope? Not much except 'trust the security arrangements', which sounded pretty weak.

As usual, the team meeting before the match stressed the basics – every run scored, every run saved was going to be important, maybe even decisive. The pitch looked ugly and under-prepared – hardly a surprise, given that nobody was expecting a game. I stressed the need to work as a team, to back each other and show support. We had been through a hell of a lot, physically and emotionally, and this was our last hurdle. I asked everyone to imagine how satisfied they would feel if they could win both series. And I asked them to put all the other 'stuff' to one side – which was a very big ask!

I'd had a good series with the bat. After the hundred in the Lahore Test, I'd carried on batting well through the middle peri-ods of the one-day games and, although I hadn't scored a hun-dred, I had made some important runs and played my part. So I was comfortable and confident going into the last match and was determined to make an impact. I made nought.

I was pretty sure we didn't have enough runs and, sure enough, we were behind through most of the match. But the change of ball after 34 overs changed everything. I made the decision to give the ball to Albie Morkel because I thought it might swing, and he usually swings it. It was a risk because he pitches it up and can be costly, but the gamble paid off handsomely and Pakistan imploded on themselves with a couple of crazy shots and one great catch. I will never forget AB's effort in the outfield to get rid of Shadi Afridi. I still don't know how he got there – I can't think of anyone else who might have reached it, but he did. Then Sohail Tanvir came to the crease and our plan to him worked perfectly. We had discussed him being an lbw candidate and Albie hit him bang on the toe with a perfect yorker. Watching him limp off was doubly pleasing. After that the home side lost the plot in spectacular fashion.

We produced an incredible fight-back to win the game. The celebrations that night were fantastic: Ramadan was over and we had a few beers in the change room and a hilarious fines meeting, as we always do to celebrate a series win. We had won both series in Pakistan under the most trying conditions. The subcontinent is a tough place to win – but, dealing with the security in the mature way that everyone did was something we could justifiably feel proud about. I was absolutely convinced that we had the right people to make a success of the season ahead.

We were buzzing with excitement as we left. Anticipation about leaving Karachi, certainly, but it was only for a couple of hours. After the dreadful disappointment of being eliminated from the Twenty20 World Cup a month earlier after losing just one game, it was vital that we started the new season well. Whatever people have thought about me over the years, I have always been convinced that no team can succeed, ever, without the support of the public, and I hoped this would be the start of a long period where we could earn their respect and support.

*   *   *

It disturbed me how comfortable I had become with guns. For the first couple of weeks I was constantly shocked to walk out of the hotel room and bump (literally sometimes) into a soldier with a machine-gun and 'NO FEAR' on his shirt. As we started our journey home I did think, a couple of times, that I hoped it wouldn't be something that lasted.

*   *   *

2.

Building confidence

New Zealand: November – December 2007

TESTS
Johannesburg 8–11 November 2007
Centurion 16–18 November 2007

TWENTY20
Johannesburg 23 November 2007

LIMITED OVERS
Durban 25 November 2007
Port Elizabeth 30 November 2007
Cape Town 2 December 2007

Confidence was obviously buoyant when we arrived home and there was a deep satisfaction that our attempts to redefine our style of play had succeeded. The next challenge was presented by New Zealand and, in home conditions, we would have been very disappointed not to win – and comprehensively.

The first Test was at the Wanderers, which suits our style of play. New Zealand hadn't played much cricket for months and hadn't been involved in a Test series for over six months. We were itching to get started – but, first, there were more selection issues to discuss. Did we bring Polly back? He had always bowled brilliantly at the Wanderers and I had the feeling that he was expecting a recall after missing out in Pakistan.

Once again, we all sat down and discussed it; and, once again, there was bound to be emotion involved when you are talking about the career of one of the all-time great cricketers. Eventually we decided that we had made our choice to move forward and to stick with the way we had chosen to go. We had embraced a style of play and wanted to give it the best run. Several of the players we used in Pakistan had gained a lot of confidence and we wanted to continue building on that during the New Zealand series. We decided to stick with the same team going in to the series.

Far, far harder than making the actual decision, was telling Polly. He was very emotional about it. It made it even harder because he was obviously still passionate about playing and was adamant that he could still contribute match-winning performances. It wasn't a day that I enjoyed ... at all. In retrospect, it left me emotionally drained for a long time to see Polly as disappointed as he was, and understandably. It was a day a captain dreads. A hundred times I thought about taking the easy option and picking Polly, and no doubt he would never have let us down, but deep down inside me I remained convinced about the style of play we had chosen to pursue – and that couldn't change. We needed specialist bowlers who could take 20 wickets in conditions all over the world and a top six with the ability and desire to take the responsibility of scoring 300+ runs on a regular basis. Polly used to be more of a strike bowler but his greatest skill towards the end of his career was his accuracy and control, both of which were still brilliant, but we needed to be more incisive. I tried to console myself with the thought that it was all part and parcel of the game of being captain, but it didn't work.

The Johannesburg Test

It was vital that we started well. A two-match series is Test cricket's equivalent of a sprint, so we knew how important it would be to make a fast start. We felt they would battle to catch up if we could get ahead. My only concern was that we might still be in subcontinent mode – bowling too full or not expecting the ball to bounce! But it was only a minor concern.

The Wanderers pitch had changed a bit over the last couple of years. It used to be a really good batting track for the majority of the match before deteriorating naturally with sun and heat over the last day and a half. The cracks used to open up and make it more difficult to bat on, the further into the match you went. But in the previous couple of series the pitch had been damp on the first morning to such an extent that the ball was taking divots out of it. When the pitch hardened up the divots made the ball seam around at a quicker pace on days two and three but that was easier than the first day when it was damp. We had learned a harsh lesson against India previously when we'd misread the conditions, played terribly and lost the first Test.

Both sides struggled a bit in the first innings but the key to the match was Hashim and Jakes both making big hundreds in the second innings. Jakes simply carried on his incredible form from Pakistan, but for Hashim the innings was critical – he was still establishing himself and, like all opposition teams, the New Zealanders sensed that he was vulnerable.

I was batting with Hashim and I'll never forget Scott Styris saying to the fielders: 'Right, let's put an end to this bloke's career...' Hashim was dropped off the very next ball, but went on to make 176 not out and never looked back for the next year and a half.

The other highlight, obviously, was Dale. I couldn't believe that just a couple of months earlier we had been agonising over whether we should give him the new ball, whether we should back him and see where he could take us when he was full of confidence. He was swinging the ball and bowling with serious pace and aggression. Just as he did in Pakistan, he showed a real killer instinct which was fantastic to see. When he saw a gap, he kicked the door down and barged through.

There was a moment towards the end of the second innings when the wicket was playing a bit up-and-down and Brendon McCullum tried to counter-attack by being positive and using his feet and charging Dale. Dale didn't appreciate that and dropped in a short ball at extreme pace which hit McCullum extremely hard on the forearm. I was surprised it wasn't broken. But it epitomised what Dale had become in such a short space of time. He had confidence in his skills, he knew what he needed to do and when to do it – and he backed down from nobody. As a captain I felt empowered. I could only imagine what Clive Lloyd and Viv Richards must have felt like with four of these things at their disposal.

We won the Test easily with Dale picking up ten wickets and Harry having a very quiet Test – I suddenly thought I'd better give him a bit of work to do before they were bowled out in the second innings. He bowled six overs in total ... and took a wicket!

The Centurion Test

We were really starting to develop a collective confidence in our game now, having been so successful in Pakistan and following it up with such a convincing win against New Zealand. The Centurion Test, I believed, was likely to suit us even more than the Wanderers. Just as Dale had developed a killer instinct, I sensed that the whole team wanted to dominate the series. We might have drawn a Test a couple of months earlier to secure a series win, but not a single member of the squad would have accepted a draw now if it had been offered to them.

Once again, the team meeting concentrated on the basics: partnerships, patience and pressure. Let's really set up the Test match in the first three days. Day one: make an emphatic statement that will affect the rest of the match. Take responsibility – top six batsmen, four specialist bowlers, Bouch in the middle. Know your job and your role, and get the job done. Again we talked about maturity and responsibility. Just like at the Wanderers, the wicket looked as if it would do a bit for the bowlers, which meant we would have to work hard and earn the series win. We knew it would be hard work from a batting perspective, especially against the new ball, but I was also concerned that the bowlers didn't relax and just expect things to happen. I wanted them to prepare as though it was a flat wicket and be prepared to bowl a lot of overs at top pace.

Neil McKenzie was placed on stand-by for the Test match, a situation which had been a long time in the making. I had been talking to the selectors for months about Neil as a possible opener. I felt strongly that he had a really good technique against seam bowling, he had never stopped working at his game and, of course, there was the extra dimension he would bring to the team, his maturity and experience. His personality commands the respect of everyone he plays with or against and I knew, as a captain, what a good ally he would be with tours to India, England and Australia coming up. As a ready-made 'senior player', you couldn't ask for a better man. The main problems he'd had in the first part of his international career had been against spin, so that was another good reason to get him out of the middle order and up to the top so he could score some runs against the seamers! It made logical sense to me.

Every time I mentioned it, the selectors were reluctant. They had a hundred excuses for not doing it, but once again, I was sure it would be the right thing to do. The fact that he'd been scoring lots of runs domestically certainly helped. By the time he was finally placed on stand-by, it had been a six-month discussion.

For Dale to take another ten wickets in the game was fantastic. He burst into tears in the team huddle after the match, he was so emotional. Here was this humble, small-town guy suddenly at the centre of the cricket-playing world and struggling to believe that all his boyhood dreams were starting to come true. He's such a quiet and modest person off the field ... very different to his on-field persona, especially with a ball in his hand. Everything was just rolling right for him. The boys were holding onto their catches, he was swinging it, finding lots of edges, and his short ball was also becoming more and more dangerous – as one man found out.

Craig Cummins had enjoyed a bit of luck, especially early on, but as a fellow opener I certainly didn't begrudge him that and I actually admired his dogged determination. Steyntjie had given him a pretty decent working over with the short ball and, although he looked a bit pale at times, he'd ducked well enough and managed to stay out of the way during the new ball spell. But when Dale came back for another spell just before lunch, Cummins decided to hook. It was horrible. I walked from slip to see if he was okay and the blood was just pouring out of his face on to the wicket. He just lay there, motionless. No batsman likes to see that, it was a graphic reminder of the dangers of cricket when the ball is bowled at that pace. I don't think many openers spend any significant time pondering potential injuries. It wouldn't do you any good. I try to focus on things I can control – which, in that case, would have been getting out of the way of the ball. Hopefully.

Obviously word reached us at the end of the day that the injury was even worse than it had appeared. We all knew immediately that there would have to be surgery, but it was still a shock to be told that Cummins had had six or seven plates inserted in order to reset the cheekbone and nose. Dale handled it very well, both on and off the field. He will always be an emotional guy, and that's one of his most endearing characteristics, but he also accepted that injuries like this were part of his job and didn't become involved on the field. After the day's play, however, he got the number for the hospital and called Cummins to make sure he was OK and wish him all the best.

It was also Stephen Fleming's 100th Test. When I was first appointed Flem was one of the most experienced captains in the world. He is an astute reader of people as well as the game and he put me under a lot of pressure a few years earlier when we toured New Zealand. I was very young and, having been appointed young himself, he knew all too well where I would be vulnerable and when I would be feeling under pressure.

After the Test had finished we sat together for a long time in the change room chatting about life. He was coming to the end of his career and I suppose I was somewhere near the middle of mine. He said he could see what I was trying to do with the team and really felt that I was starting to make moves in my captaincy career – he could see what steps I had tried to take and the direction we were heading in as a team. He didn't need to say those things but I was very grateful and appreciative that he did. It was an important and valuable endorsement to me because I wasn't alone in respecting his style of captaincy. I didn't need a pat on the back but it was good to chat about tactics, leadership skills – and batting – and to feel that I was on the right track. Flem had been through much of what I had been through, and was still heading for, so I listened hard. He is a good man.

Hash and Jakes added another hundred each to the ones they scored at the Wanderers, which was fantastic because the culture of the 'top six club' was as strong as ever and we all shared in the success of each other. Just when I thought I couldn't be more amazed by Jakes, he stepped up to yet another level. Five hundreds in four Test matches ... the mental, physical and emotional

drain of doing something like that is huge. It's hard to comprehend the number of runs and centuries, and then you add in the
wickets, and the catches. At moments like that I sometimes wondered what it would be like captaining a team without him in it
and it sent a shiver down my spine.

Hash built beautifully on his last hundred. Sometimes you worry about a 'new' Test cricketer going through a bit of a dip after a
century, but here he was, business as usual, rising to the challenge.
He was hungry for success, keen to take responsibility – and never
satisfied with his performances. Like the rest of the young guys,
he always felt that he could have done something better.

The only disappointing aspect of the New Zealand series was
my own form. I'd had a really good time in Pakistan and was full
of optimism. A Test century in Lahore and then a good one-day
series on difficult pitches ... I was raring to go. Even though the
wickets at the Wanderers and Centurion had been awkward to
bat on, especially against the new ball, the truth was I had been
tentative and not as decisive as I could have been. I knew that,
and I knew I needed to take responsibility rather than make
excuses. Confidence is normally the key to anyone's batting;
it affects everything from foot movement to calmness and decision-making. It was really important for me to find a way to
'discover' my confidence during my preparation process before
a game.

I had started a new preparation routine before the series in
Pakistan and there were several new things which I'd been developing and was keen to build on. I felt the pressure was on me
once again to perform; perhaps some of it was self-induced, but
certainly not all. Opening the batting is a key position, I was a key
player and I was captain. That was all very well understood. But
there was certainly some pressure from the public and the media
and I'm no different to any other sportsman in the way that I felt
about that. While I understood the frustration, I was also disappointed occasionally with some of the things that were said and
written. I'd had a good tour of Pakistan, but two Test matches after
my last hundred there were people speculating about whether I
was worth my place!

The one-day series
Durban 25 November 2007
Port Elizabeth 30 November 2007
Cape Town 2 December 2007

The one-dayers were always going to be a harder proposition against New Zealand, who have always been a really good one-day team. They are a hard team to get on top of and tough to dominate – they have clever game plans and they stick to them well and play to their strengths. But they had lost the experience of Fleming and had a new captain in Dan Vettori, so we were all interested to see if he made many changes or had any different ideas. Their 'bits and pieces' cricketers were always far better equipped to make an impact in the shorter version of the game and just about everybody could bat and bowl. Just when you thought you'd faced everyone, somebody else would come on and you'd have to start rethinking game plans all over again.

Durban was a horribly tight game, which, if we're honest, we should probably have lost. Chasing a total of 248-6, we ended up needing 10 off the last three balls – and got them! It would have been a decent achievement for a recognised batsman, but it was, in fact, Nella who scored the critical couple of boundaries to get us home. A couple of things stood out for me after that game – the first was team confidence. It is infectious, it breeds more and more among the players. Whereas heads might start to droop in other teams, a winning team has a deep belief, even in the impossible. You can't always explain it – but something seems to happen just when you need it most. The second thing was the attitude of the tail-enders to the responsibility we had given them towards batting. Polly, in particular, had taken Nella under his wing and worked with him a lot. It was no longer acceptable to just walk out there and have a swing, just because you were a bowler. We all had to chip in and take responsibility. Maybe Nella was just lucky enough to get two balls in his hitting zone, but I preferred to think otherwise. I was sure there was more to it.

It was also my 100th ODI as captain. One hundred ODIs as captain ... it was incredible and a milestone I was hugely proud of although it had snuck up on me. I had been so focused on where we were going as a team, and on developing myself and my own skills, that I had no idea until a day before the game. It's probably not something that I will look back on as greatly significant at the end of my career but, at the time, it was a huge milestone. I thought how much energy and preparation had gone in to every game – people may think that one-dayers come and go, but that's not the case as a player – and it was amazing to reflect on the fact that I'd captained a hundred of them.

So confidence was very high, once again, as we headed to Port Elizabeth for the next game. Which we lost! Kyle Mills bowled exceptionally well with the new ball and had us in early trouble. There was an unusually high amount of dew in the evening, which pretty much changed the whole game. The ball didn't do as much as it had done during the day, it was skidding on to the bat and we were beaten in conditions that we hadn't really expected – but, obviously, we didn't play well enough. So no excuses there. Absolutely none.

The decider was at Newlands, and we didn't just want to win, we wanted to make a big statement. We had won the Test series emphatically and we felt strongly that we were also the better one-day team. The idea that we could actually lose the series was terrible – a bad hour, or couple of hours, and we could end the tour losing the ODIs and a lot of positive energy.

We bowled superbly, led by Steyntjie, but everybody chipped in. A total of 238 at Newlands was reasonable, particularly in a day game. Fair but certainly not daunting. Hersch was simply awesome. Every shot he played came off, and it was great just to stand at the other end. He made 119. It was fantastic to see him flowing like that and to be playing with such confidence. I must have looked very stodgy and uncoordinated scraping my way to a 50 at the other end. I was just trying to get in to a rhythm, to find some form and confidence. I needed a decent score.

For all the times we argue against statistics and the fact that they don't tell the full story, cricket remains a game which is ruled and judged by numbers. If a batsman is playing beautifully but has a run of 7, 2, 0, 9 and 4, then he is officially out of form. And when an out-of-form batsman scratches together a 50, he is officially back in form! It even works for us. I knew that I needed to see a 50 ... But I was the supporting act and I loved it. Hersch took all the pressure off me with one of the greatest one-day knocks I've ever seen. We dominated a key game and I was convinced that it was another important step towards our goals for the next year.

3.

Polly's farewell

West Indies: December 2007 – February 2008

TESTS
Port Elizabeth 26–29 December 2007
Cape Town 2–5 January 2008
Durban 10–12 January 2008

LIMITED OVERS
Centurion 20 January 2008
Cape Town 25 January 2008
Port Elizabeth 27 January 2008
Durban 1 February 2008
Johannesburg 3 February 2008

TWENTY20
Port Elizabeth 16 December 2007
Johannesburg 18 January 2008

My preparation for the visit of the West Indies centred around two weeks away on holiday in Knysna. I still hadn't shaken off a nasty stomach bug that I'd picked up in Pakistan and that had affected me during the New Zealand series. I kept playing through it but I was tired and felt nauseous for long periods of time – the break did me the world of good. I just did some low-key physical training and switched off for two weeks, so by the time we gathered for the series I was feeling really fresh and alert.

A number of the senior players missed the first Twenty20, in which we were beaten comprehensively. The only highlight was an amazing spell from Dale that gave the tourists early notice that his form was as good as ever and that he would be a handful.

He took four wickets and very briefly threatened to keep us in the game, a near impossible task after we'd been reduced to 12-6 at one stage before 'recovering' to 58-8 in a game reduced to 13 overs each. It was the first time just about anybody had played in a game reduced down from 20 overs – nobody really had a clue how to approach it!

The Port Elizabeth Test

We assembled in Port Elizabeth three days before the first Test and lost about 90 per cent of our training time to rain. We were badly under-prepared as a result – although, with good reason given our recent results, we were still confident. But with the benefit of hindsight I know we should have got together earlier. Obviously we thought we had sufficient time to prepare, but that wasn't the case. So much of the preparation required for a Test match is mental, but on this occasion, it was the physical work that we needed. A great deal of credit must go to the West Indies, however, and the determination they showed. We were outperformed all round. Chris Gayle got off to a flyer in the first innings and we bowled poorly in the first innings. We lacked rhythm and we looked under-prepared. It definitely wasn't a 408 wicket, but that's what they scored.

Once again, we stressed the importance of the three Ps before the match: patience, partnerships and pressure. Having had our preparation so badly affected, we needed to make sure our basics were strong. We also felt that the West Indies were inexperienced and impatient with both bat and ball, and we felt that we could gain an advantage in those areas. We needed to draw on all our experience and the confidence we had built up as a team – we believed we could draw them into playing loosely. And absolutely none of that happened!

We were under pressure immediately, with Gayle smashing 60 in no time, and before we knew it they had 408 on a wicket that had dried out a little bit and had quickened up a bit as the game went on.

Marlon Samuels made 94 and Shiv Chanderpaul 104; he is a key batsman for them and he started the series well, which was unfortunate for us. We replied with 195 in the first innings, which just wasn't good enough. A couple of guys were dismissed by genuine, good fast bowling, and it was obvious that we would be playing catch-up for the rest of the Test match. It was especially disappointing to fall behind from the first day, because we had discussed how much of a 'confidence team' the West Indies are. They rely on momentum more than any other side – and if you can deny them that, they generally struggle to come back.

We managed a small fight-back in the second innings – we bowled them out for 175, but then we were bowled out for 260 and the West Indies had their first victory on tour. A major victory – the first Test match. It hurt a lot. We sat in the changing room after the game and had a real heart-to-heart about how we had let ourselves down. Retrospect and hindsight is one thing, but even at the time I thought how encouraging it was to see and hear how open and honest the guys were with each other. The senior players led it, but everyone agreed and accepted that it simply wasn't good enough. It was encouraging that the guys took responsibility for it and we all put our hands up. We sat in the dressing room for quite a while; we didn't rush off to the hotel and hide away. We had a quiet beer with each other and then, slowly, began to come to terms with our own individual disappointment. Even before we finally left, we had started the build-up to the next Test.

A final point to mention about the Boxing Day Test match was that we had Christmas in Port Elizabeth – highly unusual because most Boxing Days are either in Melbourne or Durban. We had a Christmas dinner with a large number of family members and kids, it was fantastic! We always get a Father Christmas to come in and hand out presents to the kids while the squad members are designated a fellow team mate to buy a present for. It can't be too expensive – somewhere between R100 and R150 – which makes for some creative shopping. It was a lovely evening. I was stuck at the 'singles' table ... which suits me for the moment, but I don't want to be there for ever!

The Cape Town Test

We arrived in Cape Town in a good frame of mind, a very determined frame of mind. Whatever anger still remained had been channelled in absolutely the right direction. We've always played well at Newlands; we all love it, and it was a good place to be. I had a very good feeling.

I will admit that there are very, very rare exceptions, but in general Test matches are highly pressurised, every session feels vital, every day is critical and the level of emotional strain is constantly high. After five days you feel absolutely drained. Being one-nil down makes everything seem twice as emotional and important. We needed to ensure that we remained absolutely focused – that we didn't allow our determination to win to overtake us.

We bowled reasonably well in the first innings, bowling them out for 243. Dale looked good again, taking 4-60. Our 321 was all right (you can never be too far ahead, however!) – and a well-played 98 from Ash ensured that we did, at least, have a bit of a lead. We were hoping for more, but 78 was still reasonable. But we needed to make it count with the new ball in the second innings. Dale was nursing a slight hamstring twinge, but we thought he was able to bowl within himself and concentrate on getting the ball swing.

We had the game well under control until the 10th wicket when Chanderpaul was still at the crease. He was like a tick under your skin, eating away at you and drinking your blood while you're not even aware! He sucks away at your patience from some dark corner of your body and just keeps sucking – his resilience was infuriating. You end up almost ignoring him and concentrating on the other batsman, that's how he was on the whole tour. Gayle came out at number 11 with a broken thumb and, as always, he cashed in against an old ball that wasn't swinging. Our bowlers had worked so hard to put us in a winning position and then, just when we all thought the job was done, they put on 70. It transformed our fourth innings target from a simple one to one that was potentially very tricky.

To be fair, we didn't bowl well at Chris and we undoubtedly got caught up in our own emotions. We'd been working so hard at staying calm, focusing on the job rather than the man, but he 'got' to us, again. Nella, especially, got tangled up in the emotions of bowling to Chris and we started leaking boundaries all over the place. I sympathise with fast bowlers who put so much effort into their work only for a bloke with a broken thumb to smash them back over their heads, it's rude and insulting! But we needed to focus on the basics, calmly deciding on where to bowl the ball and what field to set rather than becoming embroiled in a contest of bravado, one that Gayle will win just about every time. He's one of the coolest customers around. Eventually we knocked them over and we needed 185 to win.

As we walked off I was acutely aware that we had lost momentum quite badly with the Gayle–Chanderpaul partnership. After two failures in the first Test, my head was full of thoughts. I really needed to take control of my own game. All the things that I had spoken about in the first few series were still there. I was preparing well and needed to find confidence in my own game. I was aware that early wickets would give the Windies belief and momentum. That couldn't happen.

With Fidel Edwards having injured a hamstring they were a bowler light, but I always thought 150 and over was going to be difficult to chase. As I padded up I was desperate to swing the momentum our way early on, almost immediately. I knew that the only way I was going to find confidence was to find it for myself. I had prepared well, I was mentally ready, I knew what I needed to do. I had been feeling good in the nets, my game felt good, my balance felt good: I went out and I was positive. I backed my shot selection, I used my brain and I targeted my bowler. Dwayne Bravo had bowled a huge number of overs in the first innings, and bowled them well, so he was one that I decided to put under pressure.

Jerome Taylor had bowled successfully at left-handers. He had a really good delivery that left the left-handers off the wicket and also a good change of pace, so he was going to be the danger man. As for the others, I felt I could put them under pressure with positive body language and by making them feel that, if they made a mistake, they were going to be punished. Obviously the new ball was the key. If we got through that, it would be difficult for them as they didn't have a spinner who could win the game on the last day, or the fourth evening in this case. There was rain forecast for the fifth day so we didn't want to get into that situation. I never had a negative thought. I never contemplated the possibility that my aggressive approach might result in early wickets, that I would be endangering the team. I was completely focused on what would happen, not on what wouldn't happen. I took control of my career again on that day. It was a huge turning point for me in my season, and it was the first game of 2008.

When I walked off the ground with 85 I was deeply satisfied. It would have been good to finish the job, but the game was as good as won and it was just a case of the guys finishing the job. What a feeling, levelling the series! The way we handled the pressure was good. There were obviously still lots of things we could improve on but we could move on to Durban with confidence completely restored and with the West Indies now under pressure. They had their captain injured; Fidel had hurt his hamstring, and our only major worry was Dale, who had also twinged a hamstring but still managed to bowl. Things were right back on track.

I must mention the impact of Neil Mac coming in to the side for that Test. I'd been searching for confidence myself, and it was painful seeing how Hersch was battling after he got out in the second innings. He looked blown away by the amount of pressure that he was under to perform. He had been struggling for a lengthy period of time in Test cricket, without much success. He was crying out for time away from the pressures of having to try and score runs and needed to go back and get some runs in domestic cricket, or just some time away from the game. I won't forget the conversation that Mickey and I had with selector Shafiek Abrahams on the staircase outside the PE change rooms – it was the only quiet place we could find at that stage! The decision needed to be made quickly, and it was.

The selectors consulted and made a decision – Neil Mac was brought in for the Newlands Test match. CSA president Norman Arendse kicked up a huge amount of fuss about that. After the disappointment of the Twenty20 World Cup, where he had played a huge role in selection, he seemed keen to get his teeth stuck in again. He changed his tune a few times on the issue of my opening partner. First, he said that Herschelle and Neil should both be picked in the squad. Then, when he realised that once the squad of 14 or 13 was selected, Mickey and I chose the starting XI, he tried to have Neil removed from the squad so that only Herschelle was there. The selectors had made a decision that he tried to change.

After the embarrassing confusion of Jacques' omission from the Twenty20 World Cup squad, the situation had arisen again with Norman and selection. His manipulation of the rules governing selection was becoming untenable. Despite everything he said, it was obvious that he had a personal opinion, or agenda, regarding who played. He was interfering with things that he shouldn't have been interfering with. It was the first real taste I had of it. In the end he lost out and common sense prevailed, with Neil Mac playing at Newlands. He made a good start but unfortunately tore a calf muscle on what was a ridiculous outfield. The grass was so long it was more suited to sheep and cattle than cricket. I was deeply disappointed in Newlands. It was a place I'd grown to love; it was the place where, to all intents and purposes, I started my career. I'd been given my opportunity there and it was a wonderful place to play.

But the way the stadium had deteriorated generally over the last two or three years really upset me. It looked dirty and unpainted, the pitch, the nets ... everything had started to look run-down. It was disappointing, to say the least, and I was desperate for someone to take control of the place and return it to the way it was in earlier years. It's an icon of South African cricket and it's vital that we are all able to feel proud of it.

The Durban Test

Anyway, we moved to Durban and had a couple of really hard training sessions in intense heat and humidity, which I took as a very good sign. There was an intense determination to be ruthless and emphatic. We also had a couple of important selection issues to address before the game. We came back to selecting Hersch, because of Neil's injury, which I wasn't too happy about. Once we had made the decision to give him time away from the game I felt it was important to stick with that decision, but the selectors felt differently and they brought him back into the squad. The other change was to leave out the spinner and bring Polly back into the team. Although it represented a change of policy and, to some degree, a reversal of the way we had been trying to play, we all felt that it was the right thing to do for the final Test of the series. Besides, nobody in the country knew the ground as well as Shaun, and nobody had the slightest doubt that he would be able to add value to the XI.

Apart from the three Ps, patience, partnerships and pressure, my only messages to the team were to back our collective ability, believe in our talent and to challenge ourselves to become better. I asked the guys how, within our core values and responsibilities, we could become a better team and better players. I reminded everyone, including myself, that one of the secrets of becoming a great player and a great team was the ability to repeat successful things and not just correct mistakes. We needed to repeat the things we had done well at Newlands!

We won the toss and put them in to bat. There is always a bit of a knot in your stomach when you do that, but the pitch looked like it might have a bit in it and there was also plenty of cloud cover that morning. I needn't have worried – we bowled them out for 139, with Polly picking up some key wickets at the top of the order. He more than played his part and it looked like the all-seam attack decision had worked. You almost had to feel sorry for the West Indies, because the sun came out straight after lunch and the wicket changed from 'lively' to 'flat' in the space of about half an hour. I felt completely comfortable with every aspect of my game and flowed as well as I've ever done in making 147. Now I really knew that my game had come back. You never, ever feel 'ho-hum' about scoring a Test hundred, but that one was especially satisfying and a little emotional. I had taken control of regaining my own confidence back in Cape Town during the second innings there, and then I had really built on it in Durban. It was my second hundred of the season, and although you should never take anything for granted in a Test match, let alone after just two days, it seemed likely that it helped set up a platform for victory.

All the preparation and the mental 'stuff' that I had committed myself to doing had now started to pay off. It certainly hadn't happened overnight, but I had persevered with it and had been determined to get it right – and now it felt like I was starting to reap the rewards. I had regained the awareness of how to make a big moment really count. It requires a special focus and I was excited about having it again. I was very aware of all my feelings and tried to mentally log them so I could reproduce them again when the next 'big moment' came along!

But the first thing I will always remember in years to come was not my hundred but what happened on the second morning. I had no inkling of what was about to happen when we arrived at the ground and started getting ready for warm-ups. Polly called me and Mickey into the back room of the changing room and told us that he felt it was the right time for him to retire. He said he had already made the decision after discussing it with his family and that there was no going back.

I must admit it didn't come as a huge shock in terms of the Test side, because it had come a long way in a short space of time. He said he could see how the bowlers had developed and it was obvious in what direction our Test cricket was moving. But it was a huge surprise that he wanted to retire from one-day cricket as well. I still felt very strongly that he had a significant period of time in which he could remain at the top of the game and continue to be very, very successful. He was still one of the first names written on every team sheet, and as much as I had started the process of life without Polly in Test cricket, I had not even contemplated the process of rebuilding the ODI team without him. It was a very big surprise indeed.

The whole day was very emotional for me ... for all of us, in fact. I have a huge amount of respect for Polly – his professionalism as a cricketer is one thing, but he also happens to be one of the most decent men in the game, and was a great ally for me to have within both squads. My head was spinning at various times during the day. We were in the middle of a Test match, but I couldn't help thinking about how much his experience would be missed, especially in the one-day format of the game.

Ashwell (123) and AB (100) scored hundreds which put us firmly in control of the game – there was no way back for the tourists. It was just a case of finishing them off. Steyntjie bowled unbelievably well again – 6 for 72. It was exceptionally hot and the boys toiled hard all day. There was a bit of drama right at the end concerning the light. The West Indies were trying to get off the field and playing it up quite a bit, pretending they couldn't see anything, but Dale knocked over the final wicket with a beautiful delivery which seemed to knock all three stumps out of the ground and that was that. We'd won the series.

It had been a great fight-back during which we had become stronger and stronger playing the kind of cricket we knew we were capable of. We cost ourselves in PE by being under-prepared and not planning as well as we could have done. Mickey and I both knew we had to take responsibility for that and learn from our mistakes. It was unfortunate that it rained for three days in the build-up to the first Test, but that was no excuse. Perhaps we should have been more aware of that possibility and had a contingency plan. In the end it all worked out fine and we learned a few valuable lessons – although we still hadn't come to terms with the surprise of Polly's decision. Personally, however, my game was starting to feel good again and the team was once again taking good steps forward. Now for the one-day series.

THE ONE-DAY SERIES
Centurion 20 January 2008
Cape Town 25 January 2008
Port Elizabeth 27 January 2008
Durban 1 February 2008
Johannesburg 3 February 2008

To be honest, I was concerned. Not in a bad or negative way, but I was worried about keeping everyone on an even keel. I was completely comfortable with the fact that the five-match series would be all about Polly's farewell, but my worry was that it would become such a distraction that we might not do him, or ourselves, justice. He deserved the best send-off possible. I said that repeatedly in my press conferences. A man with his record deserved a proper send-off and recognition for everything he had done for his country, both as a cricketer and as an ambassador. He represented our game with so much dignity and competitive spirit throughout his career and it was important to provide him with the appropriate stage to say goodbye. And the worst thing we could have done was to under-perform and start losing games! The crowd at every ground had come to bid farewell to a popular hero and I felt a particular responsibility to make sure everybody was concentrating on their cricket rather than being distracted by the emotion. That's why I was worried. Imagine if we had lost the 'Polly Farewell' series ...

All five matches were memorable, but the Kingsmead game stood out well above the others. Just before he bowled his last ball I saw a tear, or two, in his eyes. The whole of the over had been very emotional, with the crowd cheering every ball. I was standing at mid-off before the final delivery, looking at him with the ball in his hand, not really knowing what to say, just trying to keep him as calm as possible. The emotions of the whole day had obviously got to him. He ran in to bowl the ball, probably blind as a bat and struggling to breathe, and managed to land it on a good line and length. A dot ball! How absolutely, totally, typically Polly! Every aspect of his action, every facet of his job, was totally ingrained. He could probably have bowled maidens in international cricket with a blindfold on. All the hard work he had done throughout his career, the muscle memory he had created, had come through, even in such a turmoil of emotion.

We moved to the Wanderers for the last game four–nil up. By now we were so proud of ourselves for making Polly's last series memorable that the determination to complete a clean-sweep was almost overpowering. We were probably even more determined to win the last game than we had been to win the first. Shaun, however, seemed so drained by everything that had happened and the attention he was receiving at every ground that he was just looking forward to some quiet time. It was clear that it was going to take him a bit of time to recover from the emotional roller-coaster that he had been on throughout the one-day series.

Personally the series was immensely satisfying, because I was able to carry my form throughout with three half-centuries and continued to strike the ball well. It was just about the perfect ending to Shaun's career – although Norman Arendse giving his daughter a happy birthday message during Polly's final farewell presentation was a bit peculiar! But everything went according to plan, and Polly left in the most incredible manner. I don't think a player of his calibre could have asked for anything better and there was a deep feeling of satisfaction amongst all of us. We gave Polly the chance to conduct the fines meeting in the dressing room afterwards. Being a non-drinker, he took the opportunity to make sure he gave everyone else a few 'down-downs' without fear of reciprocation! Most of us ended up having strawberry milkshake, which is one of his favourite drinks! We all had to down one in honour of Polly. It was something a bit different, but I don't think it mixed too well with the Castles after the game. It all curdled nicely ... but there may have been a few boys feeling a bit queasy later that night.

I'm pretty sure Polly was just as satisfied with the way it had all ended. A little while later there were several of us who reflected on the value of calling it a day when the time is right, at the top rather than when the slide downwards has started. It was a lesson that we all learned – and will hopefully remember when the time comes. Do it in a satisfying and graceful way, just as Shaun did. It was just wonderful to be a part of that.

4.

Adapting to the subcontinent

Bangladesh: February – March 2008

TESTS
Mirpur 22–25 February 2008
Chittagong 29 February–3 March 2008

LIMITED OVERS
Chittagong 9 March 2008
Mirpur 12 March 2008
Mirpur 14 March 2008

Strange as it may sound, this was a tough tour in so many ways. Our last tour to the country was my first as captain, so it was a full circle coming back to Bangladesh this time, although I felt that I was a very different man. In many ways it was satisfying to go back, even though some of the memories of the last tour, certainly in terms of 'lifestyle' aspects – hotels, etc – were extremely 'testing', so I wasn't looking forward to that side of life.

We were all very well aware of the fact that the tour was the start of a long period away from home, with the India tour following almost immediately and then, for some of us, the Indian Premier League (IPL) following straight after that. I was amongst several players looking at three straight months in the subcontinent. The glass is always half-full or half-empty, depending on your personality, but I was determined to prepare well by concentrating on the positive aspects of life on the subcontinent.

It didn't start particularly well with the news that Harry had an abscess on his backside and would miss the tour because he had to have it removed. Like everything in cricket, the more awkward and painful something is, the funnier it seems to everyone else.

It was even funnier to the rest of the team because Harry has a reputation for having the worst bum in the team. But amidst the hilarity, the reality was that we would be preparing for a major tour of India without our frontline spinner, which was extremely frustrating. But, as always with injuries, rain and all the other un-controllables, you quickly come to terms with it and move on. Besides, it offered another opportunity to Robby P and Botes to stake a claim and that became my focus.

I thought I was prepared for the traffic in Dhaka. I thought I had remembered everything ... but I reckon the volume had doubled in the five years since our first trip. It was staggering. It took us ages to get from the airport to the hotel, hours – even with the police escort which seemed pretty pointless at times. We were all tired from the flight and the drive seemed to last even longer as a result. All the time I was thinking: 'if the roads have deteriorated this much, what's the hotel going to be like?' But my first thought on arrival was how much it had improved and developed, it felt so much more modern. Suddenly I was feeling a lot more comfort-able and less nervous about conditions.

As usual, we started with a fitness session. What was unusual, however, was that it was a full-blown 'bleep test', which was a tricky assignment given that we were tired, a bit stiff and jet-lagged after the journey. The bleep test is designed to push you to your aerobic maximum by sprinting between set markers at a gradu-ally increasing pace. You have to keep going until you physically drop. It's not everybody's favourite. Also, it was held in a dusty old indoor centre. But everyone came through fine, with a bit of coughing and spluttering.

The Mirpur Test

The first thing that stood out for me at the Dhaka ground was how black the wicket looked. I have never seen a black wicket before, never encountered soil like that anywhere before. Even days before the Test started, it looked very dry and flat – hard work for all concerned.

We had a warm-up game before the Test which involved a sig-nificant drive each day from the hotel, which was fascinating and pretty moving too, because we travelled through a lot of the poverty-stricken areas and got to see the real Bangladesh. It wasn't the first time most of us had seen the way the majority of people live on the subcontinent, but every journey is different. Mothers and children washing themselves from puddles of water in the street, dogs and goats drinking from the same place, it will never cease to amaze me and remind me of all the things I take for granted. I still moan about some things I shouldn't, but far less than I used to. And when I remind myself of how little people in India and Bangladesh complain about anything, then I tend to keep my mouth closed. About anything.

We drove past flea markets, dogs skulking all over the place, with goat legs and chickens hanging off meat hooks, mixed with clothes and spices, cheap shoes ... anything and everything. It was so densely populated you couldn't help feeling the claustrophobic atmosphere even from the sanctity of the bus. The water in the ditches beside the roads stinks like hell and there are crows flying in and out of everything, all over the place. You shouldn't think about it all, to be honest. We talk about 'adapting' but that's easier said than done. It's obviously not a very healthy environment and it's difficult to just 'go with the flow'. The smells are probably harder than anything! The noise, constant as it is, also gets to you but the smells easily outrank all other surprises. Just when you think you can't cope any longer, you bump into a rookie team-mate who has turned green – literally – and is convulsing over the balcony. That's absolutely hilarious, you can't stop laughing ... suddenly all the perspective returns and you feel great again as he turns away to find a toilet...

We played the game on a pretty flat wicket, which didn't upset anyone because that's what we were expecting for the Test match, and besides, we had long ago given up pretending that warm-up games were about the result – the only thing that mattered was how much preparation we could get out of it. It was all about spending time in the middle and adapting our game to the local conditions, all the same things that I had talked about before for the Pakistan tour. Reverse swing, getting our batting channels right (positioning more 'inside' the ball rather than getting on to off stump as you do in South Africa) and just adapting to the weather, the heat and the rough outfield.

And it all went pretty well!

We felt it was futile to pretend that we weren't regarding the tour of Bangladesh as a critical part of our preparation for the subsequent tour of India. We felt we could be open about that without being disrespectful to the Bangladesh players or administrators. Besides, we also felt it would be dishonest and sound ridiculous to suggest that we were worried about losing, considering that they had won one Test match in the 60-odd they'd played since Test admission.

Having said that, I was also concerned that nobody got ahead of themselves and became complacent or tried to finish things off too quickly. We may have been up against a weaker team, but that did not mean we would not respect them, their conditions and their home advantage. I was very determined about that. Having lost an ODI at the World Cup to Bangladesh, I wasn't about to let anyone take any chances. If you don't take care of the little things in cricket, then it's the big things which bite you.

So it was important that we were all certain of what the process is and the way to go about achieving our goal. The emphasis was on taking personal responsibility and not leaving someone else to do the job. It was about being patient, being prepared to have to earn the win rather than just expecting it to happen. Basically, the message was to treat the Test as we would any other, not to even think about the fact that it was Bangladesh and not India. All the little one-percenters that are so important in deciding the outcome between two evenly matched teams ... we had to concentrate on giving them as much attention as we would against anyone else.

Although we started poorly with the bat, I wasn't concerned about our attitude at all and we fought back for a win. We were given a little scare but never wobbled in our approach or belief. It was an interesting wicket – very weird in terms of the colour, but it played very typically, low, slow and with very little bounce!

The DVD shopping in Dhaka, and the evenings, provided more lasting memories for me than the Test match, to be honest. The hotel had a massive DVD store downstairs to which the guys gave their full and frequent attention. At night, after supper, there were three Thai lady singers and one Thai man who provided the entertainment next to the restaurant. No disrespect intended at all, but they were probably best viewed for the comedy value rather than the music. They performed in a dark and dingy room and inspired some extraordinary dancing styles from the Bangladeshi people who were obviously frequent guests. Or perhaps they always danced like that, I'm not sure, but we hadn't seen much to compare before. There weren't too many other options after dinner and the boys spent a few evenings chilling out and having fun trying to recognise which song the band were singing a version of. It was infinitely better than sitting in your room, and we always left in a good mood.

The Chittagong Test

The second Test was played in Chittagong and I was dreading going back because of my memories of the truly horrendous hotel we stayed in the last time. I am sensitive to different cultures and very different economies, and I have become even more so as the years have gone by. You can forgive anything when people are trying hard in difficult circumstances. But as the years have gone by, I still remember that hotel as being something out of a horror movie. Dirt, cockroaches, leaking pipes, rats, terrible smells, food that was frightening to look at never mind eat – and staff who really didn't seem to care.

So imagine my relief when we arrived to discover that Chittagong had built a new hotel! Not only was it very pleasant but there was a Pizza Hut just across the road, which gave us the welcome option of mixing up the standard 'chicken breast and pasta' meal every night. Actually, the guys thrived on the pizza. It's a very social meal, especially in the environment of the team room with a good DVD to watch. And we had about 35 000 to choose from.

Obviously the most significant memory of the Test match was of Neil Mac and me breaking the world record 1st wicket partnership. We both went to the same school, King Edward VIII in Johannesburg, and to bat with him was always special. It was obviously a great wicket for batting, but the most satisfying thing was how much I felt in control of my game. The feeling you have when you make a really big score is so special, so deeply satisfying.

Yes, it was against Bangladesh, but just to score a double hundred again was special. The way I was applying my mind and preparing myself for each delivery, and the time between them, was all coming to fruition. Equally satisfying, and I really mean that, was Mac's double hundred. It put a permanent stamp on his selection and meant that he could concentrate on playing his natural game and relaxing without certain people saying that he had to prove himself. It meant that, barring a huge loss of form, he knew that he would be a part of the massive series still to come. It was a vital innings with regard to the success of 2008.

The world record – 415. Like your best golf score, it was made because we didn't know about it or think about it. It never occurred to either of us at any stage on the first day. We just batted, kept hitting fairways and making putts. Obviously we were told at the end of the day that we were close and that was when we started getting a bit nervous, a feeling that got worse and worse. By the time we took strike again the next morning I was a gibbering wreck! Having got this close it would have been a pity to cock it up, but nonetheless, my nerves were totally out of proportion to the occasion. I was looking forward to Mac facing a lot of the strike but, as it turned out, I don't think he faced a ball until we passed the record. Even when I tried to block the last ball of the over I nicked it past slip for a single!

Of all the heroic dreams you have as a boy, I can honestly say I never thought about breaking that record. I won the World Cup loads of times and beat Australia in every second dream, but this was a new experience. It was very special to share the record with someone like Neil whom I respected so much and who meant so much to the team. Having under-achieved in the first phase of his international career, he had worked tirelessly and waited over five years for a second chance. Now he had something to show for all the hard work. It was a feather in both our caps. It also made a fair number of KES old boys pretty proud, too, judging by the number of messages of congratulation we received.

At the end of the first day, just before we climbed into a couple of ice baths, Morne was joking around about the way that Jacques had spent his day waiting to come in to bat. Morne had never seen Jakes in one of his more focused moods – and certainly not for six straight hours. He couldn't believe how Jakes could sit in one place all day staring at a cupboard in front of him without flinching or getting bored or getting involved in any conversations. Cricket superstition dictates that the next batsman in doesn't move from his chosen seat in case it leads to the fall of a wicket. But it really freaked Morne out, he couldn't handle it all. But it just epitomised Jakes's personality when he enters 'the zone' before he bats, he goes into another world and just seems to drift off … he has an amazing ability to keep himself occupied, or not occupied, for long periods of time. But it bothered Morne immensely and he didn't know quite how to work it out. It was very funny listening to the stories at the end of the day.

We had large cans of bug spray in the changing room because of the swarms of mosquitoes and all manner of other bugs. We spent every morning after arriving at the ground rushing to get to the bug spray first, guys fighting over the bug spray to clean their corner out first. Otherwise you ran the risk of being nailed by mosquitoes or other midges throughout the day's play. The rush for the bug spray at the start of the day became an integral part of the warm-up.

We won the series two-nil but, just as importantly, I was certain that we had all benefited from some quality preparation time.

The one-day series
Chittagong 9 March 2008
Mirpur 12 March 2008
Mirpur 14 March 2008

As far as the one-day series was concerned, we decided to bring in a bunch of new guys and to give a rest to those who were going to play a crucial role in India. It was also designed to test our depth and to give some international exposure to the next generation. It felt very unusual having a large number of guys leaving the Test squad, normally it's just two or three. From a captaincy point of view it meant starting from scratch to some degree because we had done so much work on role definition within the squad.

There was a little carrot dangling in front of us with the prospect of the number one ranking if we could win the series three-nil. It was a good line for the media and far more of a talking point out-side the team than it was for us because one of our mottos all year had been 'take care of the little things and the big things will take care of themselves'. As it turned out, we did win three-nil, but per-sonally it felt a bit hollow because all three games were played on dreadful pitches and I was very aware of the complete lack of enter-tainment we were providing. The surfaces were so dry and slow that hitting the ball was virtually impossible and with no pace from the bowlers, it was just a case of pushing and taking singles. It was ter-rible to watch and not much better to play. If Bangladesh are going to develop as a cricket nation they have got to explore their play-ing options and prepare a few wickets that are more conducive to learning and improving. I got the impression they had read media reports somewhere that we don't play well on terrible pitches ... who does? The irony is that we probably handled conditions better than they did. We played spin a lot better than they did throughout the Test and one-day series and, if anything, it looked like we had grown up in those conditions rather than them.

There is clearly a lot of cricketing talent and ability in Bangladesh, and heaps of enthusiasm, but they will never become a serious force in world cricket unless they commit themselves to adapting to all conditions. There isn't much point in being one-dimension-al at home if you still end up losing in that dimension.

The toughest part of the tour was off the field – the day the squad was announced for the tour of India. The Test squad had been together for the best part of six months and felt very settled. But that didn't count for much with the CSA president, who was becoming more and more involved in every facet of the game. I think, at various times, he wanted to be captain, coach, CEO, president and convenor of selectors, which became very frustrat-ing. My role in selection at that stage was merely as an advisor – I would tell Mickey what I thought and Mickey would go in to se-lection meetings and use his vote to try and get what we believed was the best possible team.

The issue of Nella's omission and Langers' selection, based on race, was well documented. The squad was actually announced the evening before the second one-day game and I spent a lot of time in both players' rooms and didn't get much sleep at all. I have always had the utmost respect for Langers – he is a sharp guy and saw immediately what was going on. He hadn't been part of the Test squad for quite a while and Nella had been there all along. It didn't add up to him and he was very unhappy about it. Nella was very emotional about it and there were plenty of tears, tears of anger and frustration.

When I told Langers: 'You're going to India,' there was no smile, no celebration – he just looked at me and said: 'But why?' He was very taken aback by his selection and he took the fax and put a red line through his name. I found myself in a very difficult position as captain, caught between the political side and the cricket side, not wanting to take sides on any of these issues and just trying to make sure both players were in a decent frame of mind for the next day, which was an international.

I had always felt very strongly about administrators who make decisions from behind a desk in an office without any idea of the impact they have on real people with real emotions and careers to think about, and this was one of the worst examples. It is impossible for players of our generation, from all backgrounds, to fully appreciate the pain and anger caused by the divisions in sport and society. None of us ever have a desire to be disrespectful to our predecessors and particularly to those who were denied the opportunity that we have enjoyed. But it was a very disappointing night and I hardly got any sleep. The next day on the bus there was a lot of tension in the air and it was very quiet; everybody kept their heads down and nobody spoke. It was a terrible environment.

It is an enormous credit to the team that we managed to remain successful throughout the Arendse presidency, because this wasn't the only curve ball he threw in our direction. He threatened players, one-on-one, for not doing what he wanted. When we arrived back home after the tour I got a phone call from Langers saying that Norman had been distinctly unpleasant towards him for saying that he was withdrawing from the squad. It was a huge power struggle for him, he wanted to dominate the players and he seemed to quite enjoy the conflict.

It was a very tough period for me, I felt caught in the middle of a rock-throwing fight. I believed I knew what was right and wrong, but I wasn't always sure of the right way to handle things, what to say – and when to say it. Obviously it would have been better to keep things private, but that wasn't always possible. Sometimes there was no choice but to respond. I tried to be as neutral as possible and tried to avoid taking sides between Gerald Majola and Norman Arendse, who were clearly now destined for a head-on collision. I tried to focus all my energy on the players, who are ultimately my responsibility, and make sure they were in a decent frame of mind, not allowing all the rubbish to poison their cricket. It was all that I could control. I couldn't control any of the other stuff, I didn't have a role to play, that was Mickey's job!

Mickey never took a backward step or backed down. He knew what he had to stand up for and did exactly that, even when it seemed like his job would be on the line. He gained a huge amount of respect in the country and, in fact, the cricketing world – and certainly amongst the players.

As irony would have it, Nella took a handful of wickets and was named man-of-the-match. He was still angry and pretty tearful so he didn't feel up to going and collecting his award. I went and took it on his behalf which felt really wrong. It left us all feeling very exposed and with questions to answer that we could really have done without, especially with a huge tour to India starting a week later.

In the end Langers made the decision to stand down, which was incredibly brave. It wasn't a knee-jerk decision; he considered all the implications and effects and then calmly made the announcement. Ultimately it led to the abolition of the presidential 'veto' on selection, which was ludicrously out-dated and irrelevant anyway. A few months later the selectors were free to do their job without fear of reprisal or being over-ruled, and future generations of players should always offer a quiet word of thanks to Langers for the part he played in making that possible.

I desperately hope that those who fought so hard during the struggle years for equality don't feel let down by Langers. He thought about his decision but I suspect it was based on instinct. Mickey, too, thought long and hard about the stand he was taking and did so with the support of all the players.

5.

There's nowhere more special!

India: March – April 2008

TESTS
Chennai 26–30 March 2008
Ahmedabad 3–5 April 2008
Kanpur 11–13 April 2008

The big talking point on arrival in India was the fact that we had cancelled our scheduled warm-up game to give the guys a little bit more rest time between tours. There was only a week between tours and we felt that the time spent in Bangladesh had given us sufficient subcontinent preparation: having everyone mentally and emotionally fresh would be better option than a three-day net session against uninterested opposition. Three or four net sessions in Chennai would be enough, we were confident of that. We'd just spent a month in Bangladesh. There was plenty of criticism in the media about the decision, and it was understandably described as a 'gamble', but we felt in control.

Landing in Chennai was great: I love going back to India. As a cricketer, there is nowhere in the world more special than India. From the moment you encounter the first customs official or policeman, you are instantly reminded of how big the game is in the country and how much you are welcome. The excitement starts to build minutes after you set foot in the country and hardly ever relents. It can be exhausting, but you'd rather have it that way than playing in front of 25 people and a dog. Perhaps it will feel a bit different in future, following the terrorist bombings, but this tour was still in cricket's 'age of innocence' and the police were purely there to stop us being mobbed by autograph hunters. At least, that's how we felt.

There are at least three or four people fighting to help you collect your bags off the carousel, you can't turn around without bumping into someone. Our bags were probably heavier than most of the men wanting to carry them, but they always managed without apparent difficulty. The crush of people can get a bit much after a while, the constant invasion of your personal space, but that's India – if you can't get used to it, or learn how to cope, you'll be a very bad tourist.

Chennai is one of the hottest places I have been to in my entire life. The heat and humidity hit you hard from the moment you arrive – it was the height of summer and suddenly the prospect of five days of Test cricket didn't seem quite so exciting! We had four days to acclimatise ...

We started immediately with the normal routines which included, mercifully, a pool session very early on and stretches to get over the flight. It's vital to get straight into good sleeping and eating habits, too. The time difference is only three and a half hours, but it still needs to be addressed so that you aren't missing any rest – it's one of those 'one percenters'.

As far as diet is concerned, conditions have changed dramatically in recent years and the majority of hotels we stay in now are very, very good – as good as anywhere in the world. But everyone still needs to find a comfort zone as far as eating is concerned, a couple of items in a restaurant or on the room-service menu that you enjoy and that can be relied upon! You don't want to be 'experimenting' with your food during a Test match in India – not that there would be anything unhealthy or wrong with the food, but it may contain spices or ingredients that you are not familiar with and that could be dangerous.

It is a good idea to eat some local food, however, even if you're not a fan of the spices and flavours, because you can't avoid it all the time and it helps to build up some resistance. Over the time I've toured India I have really grown to enjoy spicy curries, breyanis and dahls. Like many people I battled on my first couple of tours and craved a plain piece of toast and marmite, but I gradually introduced myself to more and more until I was completely comfortable with the heat. It still feels a bit odd seeing all the curries at the breakfast buffet, but I tend to stick to eggs and cereal at that time of the morning!

The Chennai Test

So much of the speculation before the Test centred on Gary Kirsten, who had just started full-time as coach after spending some time with the Indian team on their previous tour to Australia. I wish I could have played more cricket with Gary. The times we did play together were always amongst my happiest and I loved everything about him, from technical to tactical and sense of humour. One of the most professional people I ever played with or against, but also one of the most humble. He was also one of the calmest people under pressure I had ever met and I was very wary of how good India might be if he was able to apply that characteristic to the team. He obviously knew a lot about certain players – me, Jacques, Bouch, Makhaya – but I wasn't too concerned about that. He hadn't been involved for four years and we had all evolved a bit in that time.

It was great to see Gazza again, but obviously times were a bit different now and we both needed to just get on with our work and make sure we were well prepared going in to the series, without getting too caught up in our situation. There were moments when it did feel a bit odd, I must admit, seeing him in Indian kit and sitting in the 'wrong' changing room. But we soon got used to it.

Preparation is the key to 90 per cent of sporting success, but now it felt more crucial than ever. We had general chats about how we wanted to bat and bowl in the conditions and we discussed the 'three Ps' once again. But we also spent a lot of time on reverse swing and discussing ways of coping with the heat and maintaining concentration. Basic things like maintaining hydration would be crucial. If a player loses concentration because he is dehydrated, he isn't just endangering himself – he's letting down another ten people. Or 20, if you include the whole squad.

We did our usual video analysis preparation for batsmen and bowlers and we all had our game plans worked out. Then we took the plans to the nets and systematically worked on implementing them, whether it was to bat on off stump against Harbhajan or to bowl full and straight at a certain batsman – whatever it was, we practised it. We also discussed what the Indian batsmen and bowlers would be trying to do to us and worked on strategies to counter that. There's nothing more pointless in cricket than going through the motions in a net session

The amount of sweat that comes off you in those training sessions is incredible. You wouldn't believe that your body could sweat that much, there isn't a dry spot on your body or your clothes. The helmet feels like instrument of torture – a portable sweatbox. The best thing about Chennai, in the circumstances, is the air conditioner in the change room – it is most definitely needed.

All things considered, we were as well prepared as we could have hoped before the Test, but you're never quite sure until the action starts. You absolutely have to make a good start in India. If you fall behind early on and give the home team the chance to control proceedings, you will find it very, very hard to catch up. But with success in both Pakistan and Bangladesh, we felt we had as good a chance as any team.

The best possible start on a wicket like that one is to win the toss – which I did, thankfully. Mac and I had a good opening stand, Hash played beautifully for 159 and we put 540 on the board. Ha! Take that, India!

Oh dear.

Our plan to put India under pressure ran into a glitch by the name of Virender Sehwag, who played one of the best knocks that I have ever seen in my life. Everything about his game is just perfectly set up to succeed on subcontinental pitches. He's always been an aggressive batsman, but the tempo of this innings, and the length of time he kept it up, was unbelievable – literally, at times. I was standing there thinking 'this isn't actually happening, it can't be.'

He played some staggering shots off every bowler in our attack. I know this will sound a bit crazy, but our game plans were pretty sound to him and we set good fields, too! He hit Harry over extra cover with the ball pitching in the rough outside his leg stump, and then reverse swept him over point ... he was sweeping him all the time, and middling it constantly. I kept thinking 'this is high-risk cricket, it can't last.' He hit it just over the fielder's head on countless occasions – I'm not saying he was lucky, because it was far too brilliant to be lucky – but during any of the 'iconic' innings you'll find that a batsman has a few things go his way. He played like a millionaire, backing his skills one hundred per cent, and he committed himself to everything, no half measures. Whatever luck he had, he made for himself.

There was an unforgettable moment just before tea on day three after he'd been smashing us to all parts of the ground and I had no choice but to set very defensive fields. But with two balls of the over left, I suggested to Makhaya that we brought the fielders up to see what his response would be. I doubted that he would take Makkie on two balls before tea. The next ball disappeared for six over extra cover. Makkie and I looked at each with blank faces for a moment and then burst out laughing. It was hilarious. What could we do? Sometimes you have to applaud great batsmanship.

The other amazing thing about 'Viru' is his willingness to take a risk by going 'over the top' when approaching a milestone. I didn't make a note of it but I'm pretty sure he went to his 100 and 200 with sixes. He's the original 'free spirit' when he bats. I kept saying to the bowlers 'we must keep going, keep bowling in the right place and he'll mess up'. And I was right, too. On 319 he nicked one to slip. Neil Mac caught a good catch, we really made that ball count for us. He could have scored 500 if Mac had dropped it ...

We reviewed our whole approach to preparation during the Test match. We decided that traditional 'warm-ups' on the outfield did more harm than good in that heat so we actually did our stretching in the swimming pool before we arrived at the ground to make sure we didn't lose too much fluid before the day's play had even started. We arrived at the ground already stretched and would go straight into the 'skills routines'.

The new routine worked very well on the fourth morning as Makhaya bowled beautifully and knocked over Sehwag and Sachin inside the first half hour. If only we could have played the whole game in the pool I think we would have hammered them.

The ball lost its shape at some point and we managed to persuade the umpires to change it. After a few overs we managed to get it to reverse swing, which was something that both teams had struggled to do throughout the Test, for some reason. The surface was slow and flat, but with the amount of sweat that you have on your body, on your hands, it was very difficult to get the ball to do anything because you just soaked it every time you picked it up. The new ball became soft after about ten overs and then it deteriorated into a soft, soggy marshmallow after another hour. It wasn't easy for any of the bowlers. Steyntjie went wicketless for about two days but never, ever gave up and then suddenly cleaned up the tail in his seventh or eighth spell to finish with 4-103. Harry did his job, too. He went for 203 but bowled about 1 000 overs and finished with three wickets. I was very proud of both of them. Actually, I was very proud of the whole team for the way they stuck to the task and never gave up, even when we thought we were hallucinating in the heat when Viru was going wild.

At one stage we were contemplating a very awkward second innings – if they'd scored 700 we would have been under pressure – but we finished the Test solidly with Mac getting 105 to add to his first innings 94, and Hashim making 81. We finished the Test on a real high. The draw wasn't as good as a win, but we had bowled with discipline (seriously!) and batted with great composure and skill under pressure. We played their spinners particularly well. We were confident afterwards. We didn't feel as though we had 'escaped', far from it. We had been hit by a freak storm in Viru, but we had weathered it well.

We were settled afterwards, but it was obvious that India weren't. Sachin was injured, they were unsure of their selection, and the inaugural season of the IPL, due to begin just days after the third Test, was creating a massive distraction. On to the second Test.

The Ahmedabad Test

Ahmedabad. Not our favourite destination. It was an interesting journey, too. Travelling between cities is always an experience, although made much easier for us by having Goolam Raja controlling the movement of our luggage and doing everything possible to ensure that our airport time is kept to a minimum. Airports in India unnerve me, as does airline travel in general.

I am a little bit of a nervous person, to be honest, particularly in unfamiliar territory. I simply believe that the majority of rules and regulations are put in place for a good reason, and therefore

I like to abide by them. Perhaps there are a few more than necessary in Australia, but by and large I like to 'stick to the rules'
which society has determined are appropriate – and I like to see
other people do the same, too. So it really upsets my equilibrium
on Indian flights when half the passengers keep their cell phones
turned on. Mostly it's so they can take photographs of the players,
but I hated it. I would often ask people to switch them off, but it
had little effect. I admit I was partly motivated by getting some
peace and quiet on the flight but mostly it was the thought that
we might crash and die for the sake of a bloody photograph ... a
bit dramatic, I admit, but there must be a good reason why they
ask us to turn our phones off.

In every squad there are the 'brave' guys who sample the food
on the plane, but I'm not one of them. Once again, it's not because I think there's something wrong with it, it's just that I'm
not good at eating things that are unidentifiable. I've had stomach
bugs in India and it's not a friendly experience, so I try and stay
away from things that I think might affect me.

The other thing about Ahmedabad is that it is a 'dry' city – no
alcohol. You can sign a form as a foreigner and be given a permit
allowing you to buy a certain number of beers per week, but most
of us felt too awkward to do that. It's just easier to adopt the 'when
in Rome' attitude, although there inevitably comes the time when
you really feel like popping down to the bar for a beer at the end
of a long day ... and have to make do with a Pepsi. Or a Thumbs
Up!

The hotel was different to the one we had stayed in for ten long,
sometimes tortuous days during the ICC Champions Trophy,
and there were hundreds of people waiting outside when we arrived. Everyone seemed to have a camera – the popular, unpaid
paparazzi.

It was a relatively modern hotel, but the lift seemed to have
been borrowed from one a hundred years earlier. It was unbelievably creaky and, needless to say, we were staying on the top floor.
There was always a thought about whether we would actually
make it to the top whenever we climbed aboard. But it was comfortable and we had a really good few days there. Before the Test
our team dinner was a braai with prawns and chicken – it was

excellent. I made a point of thanking the chefs for looking after us so well.

If anything, Ahmedabad was even hotter than Chennai, but much drier and less humid, for which we were deeply thankful. The training sessions were genuinely productive and there was a big swimming pool at the ground in which we spent a lot of time after nets doing some recovery exercises.

The ground held terrible memories for me from during the Champions Trophy, because from the changing rooms we had to walk through the kitchen to get to the nets. It became one of the worst experiences in my career. There were dogs lying all over the place and it was filthy. The smell of old oil and rotting meat was unbearable: nobody ate anything at the ground. We lived on bread, meal replacement sachets and energy bars during that game. No one ate anything else.

This time we had planned ahead and had asked the chefs to make pasta and grill chicken where we could see them. I don't mean to sound ungrateful, but it made a huge difference to our confidence and, to be honest, the chefs enjoyed being involved and appreciated the interaction. They loved having us around and sharing in their work. We needed the guys to be eating properly and being physically prepared. Once again, we made a difference by spending time on preparation.

People often ask me why we don't take our own chef on tour. I don't like the idea at all. If you ask a local chef to prepare a specific meal, or to look after you in a particular way, he is much more likely to succeed than a foreigner who knows nothing about local ingredients and where to find things. Some of my favourite match-day meals have been cooked by Indian chefs who have taken pride in producing what we really want rather than what they thought we might be impressed by.

The wicket had a little bit more grass on it than we expected and there seemed to be plenty of hype in the media about it being fast and pacey. The head groundsman seemed to be an incredibly proud and stubborn man and we heard and read many accounts of his confrontation with Anil before the game. Anil wanted him to shave all the grass off the pitch but he said it was too hot to play cricket at that time of the year and the pitch would crumble to dust by day three if he did that. So he refused. A pitch crumbling to dust would have suited Anil Kumble just fine, I thought. No wonder he was so pissed off. It was all very interesting for us.

I lost the toss and just about everybody's heads dropped. Yes, the pitch looked like it might 'do a bit', but this was still the subcontinent; you bat first.

In the days before the Test a couple of senior players had been chatting with Mickey about Sehwag and how we were going to approach him. We decided to feed the voracious Indian media with a line about 'targeting' Viru with the short ball. Not that we thought he was particularly weak against it, but we thought we might be able to create a little bit of doubt – at the very least it might annoy him and cause a distraction. Having scored 319 off 305 balls the week before, we were prepared to try anything.

Besides, we had the pace in our attack and we wanted everyone to know that we were prepared to use it. We weren't going to be scared off by a couple of flat wickets without much bounce.

So we walked out to bowl and all of this was swimming around in my head. Would Viru counter-attack? Should we bounce him straight away? We were hoping to get him to lose his 'shape' and technique at the crease, perhaps make him get his weight going forward rather than be as balanced as he had been in Chennai.

Dale did it superbly. The first ball of the match was a fabulous bouncer – Sehwag hooked and it went for six! But we knew he was a bit late on the shot and we also knew it was a slight top edge. He had been lucky, and he knew it, too. There was an intensity of combat in the middle straight away, which I loved – it was fantastic. Everyone got involved, too, with a word or two here and there. You could just feel that everyone was pulling in the same direction, determined to make the game plan work and put Sehwag under pressure. He chopped a delivery onto his stumps in that first over, which started the rot.

The intensity with which we had started the game, and our little press campaign had worked. Sometimes it can be better to start a Test quietly and build towards a big finish, but we started at 100 miles an hour and never looked back. After Sehwag's dismissal I caught Wasim Jaffer low to my left at slip, which is the hardest catch, because you're never sure whose catch it is, whether the 'keeper is going for it or not.

We bowled impressively all morning and the Indians played some loose shots – but, nonetheless, to bowl them out for 76 in exactly 20 overs was inexplicable. We walked in to lunch completely bewildered; none of us could quite believe what had happened. We'd all seen a few low totals in first class matches over the years, but not the first morning of a Test match.

Dale's 5-23 was important for us and very important for him personally because there had been a lot of hype around him and, once again, he'd been able to respond. But the way that Makhaya and Morne bowled was also fantastic. They were a mean trio that morning.

I must admit that Mac and I walked out to bat with a few nerves. Although we hadn't seen too much to scare us in the pitch, a Test team with one of the best batting orders of all time had just been bowled out for 76, so the pitch must have played a role. Surely?

Well, there was a little bit of seam movement, but there certainly wasn't much pace in it. Actually, it was a slow pitch.

We had India on the ropes straight away. A couple of loose deliveries when you're defending 76 soon cost you, and before we knew it the teams were level well before tea and we hadn't lost a wicket. It was ridiculous.

I made a good start but gave it away in the 30s. My personal disappointment, however, very quickly disappeared as I settled down to watch the AB and Jakes show. They had a huge partnership which played the hosts completely out of the game. It was Jakes' 30th Test hundred ... 30! There have been many moments over the years when I've been reminded of what a truly great cricketer he is, and this was yet another. Think of the players who have passed 30 hundreds ... Rahul, Ricky Ponting, Brian Lara, Steve Waugh, Sachin, Matthew Hayden. And how many of them could also be called upon to break a vital partnership with the ball, or open the bowling, or bowl a spell of 10 overs under pressure, let alone take over 250 wickets? It was a great day for him, but also one on which several of us could celebrate just being able to play so much cricket in the same team as him.

AB's innings was the most mature of his career. He stuck to his game plans, never lost concentration and never got too far ahead of himself, which had been his tendency in the past. He controlled the game virtually from the moment he arrived at the crease and finished with a double century batting at number six, which was only the sixth or seventh time that had ever happened in Test cricket.

When AB was on 217 there was the biggest thunderstorm anyone had ever seen in Ahmedabad. It hadn't rained for about six months and, apparently, it hadn't rained at that time of year for about a century. But there it was, thunder, lightning, windows being blown out of the pavilion and flash floods. It cost AB 250 and, the way he was playing, probably the South African record of 277. I can't wait to see that broken. I would love someone in my team to score 300 with a Proteas badge on their chest. I'm as sure as you can be in cricket that he would have done it that day, but the rain cost us an entire session and, although I wondered about batting on the following morning, the moisture in the wicket meant I had to declare. We had a huge lead, and a Test victory is always more important than personal goals.

It was a long, hot day and we had to work as hard as ever before to wrap up the win. It took its toll on the boys but, as ever, the reward was made all the more special because we had really earned it.

The ball was soft for most of the day and we couldn't do much with it. For long periods of the day I was just focused on stopping the flow of runs. Rahul is the exception – he has the patience to grind away for weeks – but the others all like to see the scoreboard moving and they can become frustrated when they're bogged down. We showed admirable discipline, right up until the end when it felt (and looked) like some of the guys were becoming a bit 'dreamy' and hallucinating in the heat. Makhaya dropped a catch off Sreesanth after six hours in the field and the ball hit him on the head. I wanted to laugh, everyone wanted to laugh actually, but we were too buggered to raise the energy. We just wanted it to end.

Just when it seemed the game would stretch into the next day, I begged the bowlers for one last effort. They were all cramping and exhausted but they responded superbly and we finally knocked the tail over. It was one of the happiest moments of my career – to win on the subcontinent, to win against India in India. It is one of the toughest challenges you can face in your career and we had done it with a couple of key players who didn't have much experience of the conditions. We did have plenty of experience too, of course, but guys like Dale and Harry hadn't spent much time in India and they had been key players. Sure, the pitch hadn't been typically Indian, but ultimately we had still outplayed a very, very good Indian team in their own backyard.

There's no such thing as the 'perfect Test', but for the first time in my life I was left wondering what we could have done better! It had been so comprehensive, so overwhelming that it was quite hard to comprehend. And as much as India had made mistakes, I knew in my heart of hearts that we had played brilliant cricket. I was hugely satisfied.

All the pressure would be on the home team for the final Test and they had problems. Kumble was out, injured, and Dhoni would be making his debut as captain. The media were turning on the team and there was tension in the air. Much has been written and said about the media in India so let me just say that you never get used to facing 20 TV cameras and 50 journalists at a press conference. Not even a guy like Anil Kumble, who'd been around for 16 or 17 years – even he became grumpy during press conference time. The questions aren't as tough as you might get from the Aussie or English media, but the sheer weight of numbers can still wear you down. Especially when you have to answer the same question 80 times on tour. But I have genuine sympathy and respect for the Indian media, I really do. I would hate to be in a position where I was competing for a story with 100 other guys, having pressure placed on me to find an 'exclusive'. I would not cope well with that.

We had a wonderful time together after the win. It wasn't a huge celebration. A couple of beers found their way to the changing room, but literally a couple. It was one of those days where you could sit in your chair in the changing room and feel the 'high' of achievement and the warmth of team spirit. Every single one of us could look each other in the eye and see and acknowledge that we had all given 100 per cent for each other, and that we were totally committed. Jeez, it was a terrific day.

We had a couple of days off before we travelled again, with the Test having finished early, so we decided to visit a shopping mall that had been recommended to us rather than sitting around in our rooms all day. Although that was a tempting option too, given how tired we felt. This was a really interesting day.

It was a clean and modern mall with a fascinating mixture of shops varying from clothing to electronic gadgets and much in between. The boys love the 'gadget' shops. I was milling around a clothing shop minding my own business and looking for a couple of shirts when I turned around to see 20 or 30 people with their faces pressed up close to the shop window. I suddenly felt like a fish in an aquarium. Security had prevented them from entering the shop while I was in there, which didn't seem right, but it would have been chaos if we'd all been in there together. That's India for you. Cricket is so massive and international cricketers are placed on such a pedestal it can be uncomfortable. But it can also put a big smile on your face and make you laugh.

Three or four of us went into a supermarket in the shopping mall to buy a couple of essentials – shaving cream, deodorant, some fruit and nuts, that sort of thing. But we weren't able to buy anything because of the throng of people who had gathered around us. We'd only been in the mall for a total of, perhaps 20 minutes, and despite our best efforts and those of the security guys, it was over. It was completely unmanageable. I reckon I posed for 40 cell phone pictures in those 20 minutes.

We went back to the team bus and, to be honest, I was full of regrets. I had tried to go out and experience India, because I love the country, but it was obvious that the more successful you are, the more recognised you are and the more people mob you. But it's important to keep things in perspective. Gary told me that when Sachin and his wife want to go shopping they have to fly to London.

The Kanpur Test

We'd been joking for several days that the groundsman's preparation of the Kanpur pitch would involve a rake rather than a mower in order to guarantee that it turned square. We laughed about it but we probably didn't believe how prophetic our jokes would be.

There is only one hotel of acceptable international standards in Kanpur and – I'm not sure I should say this – but it's like something out of a 1970s 'adult' movie with its purple bedding and strange mirrors. It's been there for a good couple of decades and hasn't been subjected to very many refurbishments in that time. If any.

There aren't too many entertainment options in the city and home comforts are in short supply. There is a ten-pin bowling alley in the hotel but, with 10 000 teenagers also looking for a bit of fun in the evening, it wasn't a realistic option. The drive from the airport lasted about an hour. By now it must be obvious that I am sensitive to strong smells and my heart sank a little deeper with every kilometre as we approached the city and my nostrils burned a little more. Industrial pollution is a serious problem in the city and, being the leather-tanning capital of the country, the overwhelming odour is of sulphur. You can be as polite as you like, but the truth is – it smells like the biggest fart ever produced in the world.

We had expected the worst from the pitch and we weren't disappointed when we saw it. It was horribly under-prepared and would clearly disintegrate quickly once the match began. It most certainly wasn't going to last five days. The toss would be very, very important.

In most hotels I'm given a slightly bigger room than the other guys, usually with a little lounge area so that we can have team chats with a group of players or management. This one was bigger than average and seemed a bit spooky, to be honest, with lots of little dark nooks and crannies. I made the mistake of mentioning this to some of the boys before the Test.

AB's room was next door with a balcony between the two which, if you were brave or stupid enough, you could use to get from one room to the other. After the final training session before the Test, a couple of guys asked to come for a chat. Without me noticing, they opened up the window to my room so they could climb through. That evening when I went to bed I locked the door to the lounge part of the room and climbed in to bed. Suddenly the light turned on in the lounge! So I quickly got out of bed and turned the light off and went to bed again wondering what the hell was going on. I started watching TV and again the same thing happened, the light went on. So I got out of bed again and this time a chair had been moved in front of the door. I wasn't happy – I kept thinking 'jeepers, what the hell is going on?'

When it happened for a third time I moved more quickly into the room and caught AB and Dale climbing back out through the window. It was really very funny!

But AB wasn't finished with his pranks. We often leave our hotel room doors open because we are all on the same floor and next to each other. It's good to be able to wander into each other's rooms for a chat. Then, as the evening draws to a close, we shut our doors and prepare for the next day. We usually have a favourite TV programme we plan to watch before bedtime.

But AB decided to hide under Harry's bed with the remote control. So Harry was lying on his bed watching TV and the channel kept changing, usually at crucial times. We were aware of the joke and Harry hadn't actually closed his door so we were able to see him hammering the TV, unplugging it and plugging in again, freaking out and swearing at his TV while AB was giggling underneath the bed.

It's fair to say we were in good spirits before the final Test.

When we won the toss it seemed even better. Gary had said it was the worst first-day pitch he had ever seen for a Test, and he'd seen a few. Unfortunately we didn't make as many runs as we should have and were bowled out for 265. I would have been happy with 300. I played well but fell to a good delivery from Yuvraj which bounced more than normal and I was caught at short leg.

We were in a decent position at lunch but never managed to capitalise on it. India replied with 325 and I felt that we had lacked patience with the ball for the first time in the series. We were desperate to take wickets because of the nature of the pitch and, consequently, never built up the natural pressure that would have come through just bowling in the right place and letting the pitch do its work. Sourav scored a brilliant 87. I don't want to take anything away from the quality of his innings, but I'm naturally inclined to see things from my perspective and I know we got our plans wrong against him. He scored quickly because we tried to bowl him out rather than being patient and letting conditions take care of things.

India opened the bowling with Harbhajan in the second innings and times were tough! Some people criticised us for not scoring quickly enough and going into our shell but it wasn't easy to manage things. The ball was bouncing out of the rough to me and they had a ring field around the bat – I started thinking to myself: 'Where the hell am I going to get a run?'

The only viable option I had was the sweep. I often laugh in South Africa when guys who have never toured the subcontinent say you should never sweep, you should always hit the ball straight down the ground. If you don't have a sweep shot available to you sometimes in the subcontinent it's almost impossible to score. You have to learn to adapt your game. Maybe we should have taken a few more risks and tried to score quicker, perhaps that is a valid point, but it was increasingly difficult with the ball turning and bouncing from the spinners.

In the end we had a feeble 64-run lead. It played in to Sehwag's hands perfectly and he blazed away without any pressure. The wicket was substandard and not conducive to good Test cricket, but that was what we had expected from a desperate Indian team which simply could not contemplate the prospect of losing the series. In many ways I could not help admiring the gamble they took in producing a pitch like that. If we'd played 10 per cent better they would have lost 2-0. But their gamble paid off, and good on them for that.

It wasn't perfect, but we were all aware of the value of a 1-1 draw in India. It wasn't what we wanted, but it was good. The XI, and the squad, had developed enormously and we were all firmly focused on the England tour ahead. It would involve very different conditions, but we had come up against one of the major nations and handled ourselves with great aplomb – with pride and skill.

AB had made enormous strides, Neil Mac had cemented his

place as an opening batsman, Hashim Amla had a great tour and all the bowlers had done what was needed. Harry was a bit frustrated that he didn't pick up more wickets, but it was his first tour to India and, having chatted to Warney, it is a very difficult place to succeed on a first visit.

* * *

During the Kanpur Test there was plenty of stress and confusion caused by haggling and counter-haggling concerning participation in the IPL by those players who had been bought by an Indian franchise at the auction.

Our domestic Pro20 competition was coming to an end back home during the first 10 days of the IPL, so obviously there was a potential conflict of interest. Every single one of us, however, knew that our first loyalties and priorities lay at home despite the huge amount of money that we would lose by missing between three and five matches in India.

The Titans guys were very clearly wanted back by their franchise because they would definitely be playing a part in the semi-finals and would be pushing for a place in the final with the incentive of a place in the inaugural Champions League.

But in terms of the Cobras players, it felt a little like we were disposable commodities which could be bargained off to make a quick buck. The Cobras felt that they could win the tournament without certain of the international guys and still make money on the side by selling us to our Indian franchises for that period of time.

Gerald Majola stood his ground and made it perfectly clear that South African cricket came first, which is absolutely right. The IPL was a major bonus in all of our careers, but it would never have happened unless we had a career with South Africa first. There was plenty of tension and unhappiness when it emerged that the Cobras had only picked me and J-P for the semi-final and 'allowed' Jacques and Bouch to stay in India, even though they would have preferred to contribute to the Cobras' cause. The Cobras even announced their team six days before the match, before the Proteas had even left India. Six days! I've never, ever heard of a team being announced six days before a match.

I think that Andre Odendaal (Cobras chief executive) believed he could get some financial compensation from the Indians, but it ended up costing the Cobras a place in the final, because they messed up a tense run chase which would have suited Bouch absolutely perfectly. It all felt like a bit of a mess, to be honest, with everybody having a sour taste in their mouths.

I've always said that, no matter who you are, South African cricket has got to come first. It's a principle I have always been strong about, right from the early days and throughout my captaincy. We all have a responsibility to the game, whether it's media, administrators or sponsors, to ensure that the game is going from strength to strength in our country.

It was a disappointing way to end what had been a pretty solid tour. Actually, it was a crap way for it to end. The whole thing could have been handled so much better if people had thought about the long term rather than becoming sidetracked by what was in the deal for them.

Ultimately, however, Gerald and CSA handled themselves well, but I believe Norman had once again been acting a little deviously behind the scenes and trying to bargain and broker deals. Still, Gerald proved his strength by putting South African cricket first and that was comforting although the squad had to split up in India with some guys staying behind and some travelling home to play in the semi-finals before returning to India for the remainder of the IPL.

* * *

6.

Groot balles

England: July – September 2008

TESTS
Lord's 10–14 July 2008
Leeds 18–21 July 2008
Birmingham 30 July–2 August 2008
The Oval 7–11 August 2008

TWENTY20
Chester-le-Street 20 August 2008

LIMITED OVERS
Leeds 22 August 2008
Nottingham 26 August 2008
The Oval 29 August 2008
Lord's 31 August 2008
Cardiff 3 September 2008

A tour of England is a highlight in any player's career, and to make a success of it as a player or captain, you need to plan and prepare well. Although some of the guys had spent a few weeks at home, most of us had either been involved in the IPL or playing a bit of county cricket in order to acclimatise to English conditions. I had torn my hamstring in the IPL semi-finals so I was doing a lot of rehab and recovery in the short break between that and the start of the England tour. Mickey and I decided to take the guys on a camp before the tour – a camp with a difference. There wasn't a single piece of cricket kit in sight.

We believed that quality time spent together, having a bit of fun and talking cricket rather than playing it, would be of enormous benefit. There would be more than enough time in England, with two warm-up matches and a lengthy period of time in Taunton to prepare our cricket skills.

We travelled to the Pezula resort in Knysna, which was an awesome experience. I have a personal sponsorship relationship with Pezula but I haven't stayed in the five star hotel very much before – it was a real treat, very luxurious. We used our time wisely – fitness tests, team bonding, playing golf, war games (which became a little scary for some – it was a bit of a concern to see what happened to a couple of the guys when you put a gun in their hands!) and we had good chats about touring England, on and off the field.

One of the many issues to address was the English media. We had addressed the subject before, most notably before previous tours to England and Australia, but probably from a defensive point of view rather than a positive and constructive one. Rather than concentrating on 'coping' with the media, we tried to understand their requirements and provide helpful and considered answers. That hasn't always been a strength of South African teams abroad.

Our media officer, Michael Owen-Smith, presented a host of questions and topics for everyone to think about and prepare answers to. We also discussed the particular subjects which made us uncomfortable and Michael suggested ways we could answer questions without getting tangled up in 'difficulties' but while also providing a valuable and genuine answer to the question. Common themes included Zimbabwe, the 'quota' system and the way South Africa has transformed and developed over the years. We also spoke a little bit about Hansie – although, to be honest, there were only a couple of guys left in the team who really knew him and they were very comfortable anyway with their thoughts and emotions concerning him. By the end of it we were all very comfortable that we weren't about to accidentally cause a scandal or controversy at our first press conference before a ball had even been bowled. It was the first of many little boxes to tick.

We discussed just about everything – our strengths and weaknesses as a team, as individuals, how we wanted to play, how we needed to play and how we needed to stick together through thick and thin.

Francois Hugo, who is actually an industrial psychologist by trade but who has worked with us before, held sessions with the whole squad. We also had team sessions in which we would pass around a sheet of paper with four columns covering where we were good, as a cricketer and a person, where we needed to improve and things we must keep doing. Each guy would then write in the four columns and we would then discuss it. That could be an awkward process in a group which didn't know each other well, but we'd developed so well together and we were happy to be honest and open. There were a few wobbly moments, for sure, but there was a lot of laughter and humour, too.

The golf afternoon was very popular, as always – except for Makhaya, who's never really taken to the game. We actually have to keep him off the course because his etiquette leaves a lot to be desired. I don't think they would ever have allowed us back at Pezula if we'd let Makkie drive around the course in a buggy.

The war games afternoon was exciting ... sort of. It was very well organised, but I can assure anybody who has never tried that paintballs bloody well hurt. We dressed up in overalls and had various obstacles to hide behind while we trying to kill each other. I was not one of the bravest – I don't think I would have done very well in a war. I was OK at providing 'cover fire' at the back for the more adventurous guys taking the bullets, but otherwise I was happy to fire off the odd 'sniper' shot, which was fun. I hit the target occasionally, too! There were some hilarious moments. Dale emerged as the madman – you definitely wanted him on your team. At one stage I don't think he even had his overall on, he was just running around in his shorts and taking bullets. Rambo.

We had some great braais in the evening, just quiet time for the team for four or five days with no outside influences or distractions. We focused very much on what we wanted to achieve but in a relaxed and pressure-free environment. The prospect of becoming the first team to win in England, post-isolation, was a huge incentive. I was so proud of the way everyone bought into the camp.

We picked a squad of 15 rather than 14, partly because of the lesson I learned in 2003 about mental fatigue: England tours are longer than most. We played five Tests in 2003, preceded by a triangular one-day series plus county games. This time it was 'only' four Tests, but we still took an extra bowler to help us through three county games and to make sure everyone had a chance of staying mentally fresh.

The itinerary was perfect: we moved straight from Heathrow to Taunton, a small town in a lovely part of the country where I'd played county cricket and made many friends and very fond memories. It was a fantastic place to start the tour and the ground staff and everyone else at Somerset looked after us so well. We had great facilities to train on, the nets were always in good condition and it allowed everyone to work hard on their cricket skills, just as Mickey and I had planned and hoped for.

After intensive rehab with Shane Jabaar on my hammy, I'd started to bat again before the first warm-up game and was facing the stark reality that my tennis elbow condition was far worse than I had imagined. I'd picked it up during the IPL with so many games close together on top of the South African tour before that. It's a wear-and-tear condition which normally sneaks up on you and becomes serious before you even begin to take it seriously.

It meant that I was basically doing my own 'quiet' work alongside the guys in the nets – there wasn't much I could actually do with a dodgy hammy and a dicky elbow! So Dale and I both rested for the first warm-up game against Somerset, but we chatted a lot during the three days because I and the team needed him to be in the perfect 'space' before the first Test.

The game went well. Sadly, from a spectator's point of view, it wasn't a contest and was never going to be one on a flat batting wicket. But from our point of view the batsmen all spent quality time in the middle and the bowlers had to work hard which was exciting for me because it meant that their skills were going to have to improve. If you start a tour on a green seamer, the bowlers get away with murder and are often under-cooked for the 'real thing.'

Another challenge we had was getting used to the Duke ball. Our bowlers needed to learn about the differences to the Kookaburra ball and we spent a lot of time talking about that. Talking is one thing – the bowlers had to do the actual work. But everyone had a theory, and some guys had more experience than others, and we passed on our knowledge to each other.

The exciting stage of the tour started when we moved to London after the Somerset match. The tour bus was awesome; it's one of the best parts about touring England. We all had tables and comfortable seats which allowed us to play Uno or other card games. There was a DVD player as well, which was extremely unusual in our lives. Normally the thought of a three- or four-hour road trip in heavy traffic would be a nightmare, but in a bus like that, with a fridge, toilets, comfortable seats, music and video, it was actually a pleasure.

London has its drawbacks after a while, but there is no mistaking the excitement as you drive in for the first time on tour. The hustle and bustle, the sights and attractions, you are instantly reminded of all the things there are to see and do, the different cultures ... it's impossible not to be excited that you have arrived in one of the world's premier destinations.

We arrived at the Royal Gardens Hotel, a fantastic location close to the centre of the city with a massive park right next to it. The only thing about English hotels is the size of the rooms. We have five bags each, large bags. Two sets of pads, four sets of boots, running shoes, casual shoes, bats, helmets, casual clothes ... it all takes up a lot of space. Finding a system to fit everything takes time, it's a challenge. Some guys can cope quite easily in a state of chaos, but I need to know where everything is, all of the time.

It's at times like this that I appreciate being captain – a slightly bigger room comes with the job – worth hanging on to, then! I must admit I have become used to the extra space to organise my things and sometimes don't appreciate how much difference a small annexe can make, but I'm constantly reminded about it – with a bit of abuse – when the other guys come around for a one-on-one chat.

The second warm-up was against Middlesex at Uxbridge. It was a lengthy drive out there every day but, thanks to the bus and the fact that I was actually playing again after so long off, it was exciting for me. And besides, the prospect of Lord's was looming large and nothing quite gets the taste buds going so much as a game at 'headquarters'.

We batted first and I spent at least three hours in the middle making 35. I certainly wasn't at my best (and didn't care) but I genuinely felt that I had achieved so much from being at the crease. I started to feel my batting 'shape' return, feet moving well, recognising my lines, leaving the ball well. It was good. I read the *Daily Telegraph* the next day and Derek Pringle was scathing about how rusty I looked, how terrible I looked. I honestly felt very different to that. He is an experienced cricketer, and an accomplished writer, but I felt so different about it. It was a little test for me, actually. I'm not one of those players who pretend to ignore media and never read papers. But I took on board what Pringle had observed, digested it, and then decided that it's what you feel personally, deeply, that counts for more. I felt I'd had a good work-out. I felt good. That was the important thing. Sorry if I looked a bit ordinary.

Dale played in this game as well – and wished he hadn't! A terrible cold wind blew throughout and the bowlers never ever gained any rhythm. It was wretched. Given that tourist warm-up matches have long since ceased to be 'contests', I reckon they should be confined to two days rather than three. The only people who turn up to watch are complete aficionados and gurus, or autograph hunters, so let's be honest about the 'entertainment' value. Two days to see Dale Steyn, Morne Morkel and AB de Villiers in action – that's what they want. They don't expect to see teams 'making a game of it' with sporting declarations any more.

The Lord's Test

We had three days before the first Test. My main worry concerned the bowlers and whether they had done enough work. Along with Makhaya, Bouch and Jacques, I was acutely aware of the impact that a Lord's Test can have on people experiencing it for the first time. We had planned and trained according to a strategy which allowed the whole squad to breathe in the Lord's experience as much as possible before we played, but that was another plan compromised by the weather!

Unfortunately we didn't complete a single training session because of rain. The nets were flooded and our preparations were confined to indoors. The bowlers were able to bowl on a little strip outside, close to the middle, but the batsmen faced net bowlers in the indoor nets, which is never ideal.

I was worried about that, but also about how much our pace attack – particularly Dale and Morne – had been hyped in the English media. Both of them were still young and it was their first major tour to the UK. Makhaya had obviously been before, with great success, but getting his overs up had been difficult. He's always bowled better with plenty of overs under his belt and I was concerned that he might be underdone.

Dale and Morne are both down-to-earth, humble guys from small towns and now they'd been hysterically hyped up to be the fiercest, fastest bowlers in the world. One paper devoted the whole back page to the pace attack and compared them to the West Indies quartet of the 1980s. It was ridiculous – it would have been funny if it wasn't so silly.

The English media can be harsh in terms of building people up and then breaking them down again – with a quick turnaround time in between. It certainly affected Dale and Morne's performance during the match and they both admitted as much afterwards. I think Dale's words were something like: 'I can't believe I actually started believing that crap they wrote about us…!'

The pre-Test match referee's meeting with Michael Vaughan went well and the playing conditions for the series were all clear – no doubts, no confusion. We had a photo session with the series trophy and I felt relaxed and calm. We'd prepared as well as we could, in the circumstances, now it was just up to each individual to make sure he was ready for the challenges that lay ahead.

The team meeting was straightforward. By now everyone knew the 'three Ps' speech off by heart! I talked about our lack of time on grass in the days before the Test and how it would be crucial to think on our feet in order to adapt. We needed to commit 100 per cent to everything that we did, batting or bowling. And finally, I spoke about not becoming caught up in the hype around Lord's, to take ownership of the stadium and the occasion. We'd all seen Lord's empty – I told those who hadn't seen it full that they were in for a treat.

I arrived at the ground early in the morning and there was a lot of moisture around. Lord's has an incredible drainage system and

I was amazed how firm the outfield was given all the rain that had fallen in the last 48 hours. When I walked through the Long Room I was surprised by how vivid the memories were of 2003 and my double hundred. And when I saw my name on the Honours Board it was almost like I could hear the applause again. The hair stood up on the back of my neck. All the new guys commented on the atmosphere in the ground on the first morning, it's unlike anything else in the cricket-playing world. Almost like a loud humming rather than buzzing!

I was really battling with a decision if I won the toss, it was definitely a good one to lose. There was so much moisture around, and the wicket felt cold when you touched it, which the bowlers enjoy, but it looked like a belter to me! The recent history of Lord's suggested that it got better and better to bat on after offering the bowlers something on the first day, or day and a half. Inevitably, because I didn't want to, I won the toss. We chose to bowl and, true to my team talk, I committed to the decision and gave a rousing speech about how we were going to put England under early pressure, etc etc.

It was the wrong decision, and felt more and more wrong as they started heading towards 400. When they declared on 593-8, it felt like one of the most wrong decisions of my career! We didn't bowl well. My personal conviction that the pitch was a 'belter' was absolutely right and, to make matters worse, the ball wasn't swinging either. Nonetheless, we lacked one of the Ps when we needed it most – patience. Ian Bell (199) and Kevin Pietersen (152) both played superbly and took the game away from us. The only, tiny consolation I had in my mind was that they had, perhaps, batted too long. They'd given us a glimmer of safety.

I thought I handled myself pretty well through two days of pain, all things considered, apart from one incident when I was very upset, and justifiably so.

There was bad light and drizzle around at one stage so we trouped off to the change room, followed by the umpires. The England batsmen could see that it would clear up soon, so they stayed on the field. Quite soon Billy Bowden gave us a message that play would start again in 15 minutes – and then carried straight on down to the field with his partner, Daryl Harper! So the sun came

Nothing tastes quite like a hundred. (AP Photo/K M Chaudary PictureNet Africa)

Top left: Stephan Botha – undercover security consultant. Dressing in official team kit was the best and most obvious 'disguise' there was.

Top right: Inzamam ul Haq and Mohammed Yusuf – legends of Pakistani and world cricket. Fortunately we didn't run in to them in the prime of their form.

Above: Jakes makes a bold attempt at the Inzamam look but clearly needs several more months' growth to get there. In the meantime, he's happy to be as close as possible to our head of security, Faisal Nagel.

Above: 'Coach talk'. Mickey may have had his share of boardroom issues to deal with, but they were nothing compared to Geoff 'Henry' Lawson's off-field burdens. What is the average life-span of a Pakistan coach?

Left: Faisal enjoys his share of the trophy, but hopefully his real reward was the fact that he kept all of us out of harm's way for 38 consecutive days.

Vinnie keeps a close eye on one of 'his' souvenir stumps. Polly does the honours with his signature.

Harry celebrates his first Test 'five-for' by signing the Karachi match ball – which looks like it has done 100 days of throw-and-fetch with the family dog rather than 100 overs of Test cricket.

Polly – legend of the game and inspiration to everyone he ever played with, right to the end.

Top: Team meeting: 'Who's in favour of NOT going back to Karachi for the final one-dayer?'

Above: Faisal holds an impromptu inspection of our elite security unit's weaponry, much to their approval, it seems.

Right: It's part of the game, but that doesn't make it any easier when a fellow opening batsman is hurt as badly as New Zealand's Craig Cumming was when Dale Steyn shattered his cheek bone. (AFP Getty Images)

Below: Dale was a teddy bear when he started, but he toughened up a lot. You can take the 'care' out of a fast bowler, but not out of a person. Dale is a caring person, and that won't change. (AFP Getty Images)

A world record is exactly that. Scoring 400+ against England at Lord's would undoubtedly be harder, but the record stands. And Mac and I worked hard for it. (Getty Images)

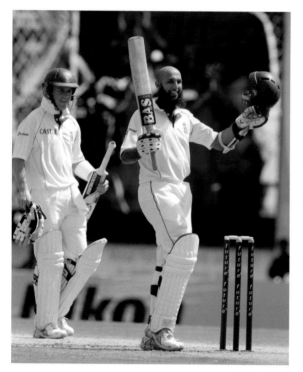

Top left: The quiet but confident man. Hash probably influences the team more than he realises. People look to him when they need reassurance. He is a special person. (Getty Images)

Top right: Virender Sehwag. Two triple centuries in Test cricket mark him down as one of the greatest ever. We always felt in control of him on our pitches, but we were helpless on 'flat' wickets in India. (AFP Getty Images)

Above: Sometimes you simply have to accept your fate. Rahul Dravid leads India off the field after their victory in Kanpur. They gambled with a terrible pitch, and it paid off. No complaints. (Getty Images)

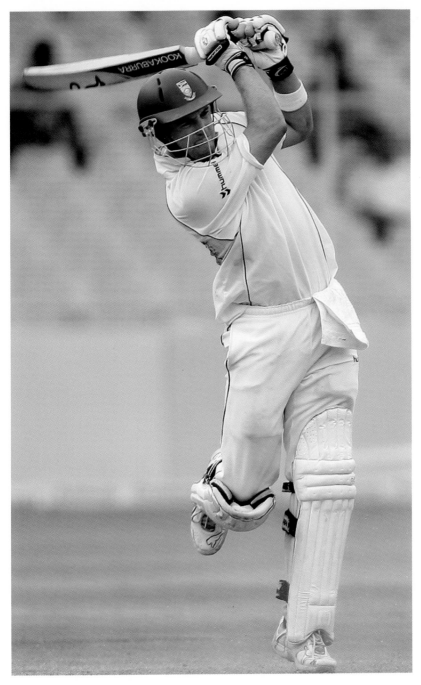

AB – a giant in the team. Already establishing himself as one of the 'greats' of his
generation, he has the ability to become one of the greats of any generation.
(AFP Getty Images)

Above left: The English countryside glides by … slowly … from our team bus.

Above right: The games of 'Uno' became highly competitive as the tour progressed. Hash, Neil Mac, J-P and Shane Jabaar are embroiled in the heat of competition.

Left and below: Impossible not to be excited about being in London: Roger Federer won again at Wimbledon, and the view from the hotel was great!

Below and bottom: Lord's changing room – one of the more comfortable on the world circuit.

Right: A century is a century – you'll be proud of it for the rest of your life. But there was still more important work to be done. (Getty Images)

Top: If ever I needed a picture to remind me of the joy of victory, this may be the one. It brings a lump to my throat. (Getty Images)

Above left: Interview with Michael Atherton – a wonderful challenge. Captain for 54 Tests, smart, intelligent and fearless, Athers keeps you on your toes, fair but firm. He won't accept platitudes.

Above right: We couldn't wait to see the real thing: SAB's Rob Fleming and I bask in the glory of the Lord's honours board.

Left: Neil Mac dons the 'Fines Committee Crown' after the series win at Edgbaston. With that on his head, we dared not disobey his orders or instructions.

'Who thinks Graeme should drink another down-down?' At least Snapey appears to be asking for an update on the scoreboard before voting.

Left: Many of the greatest sportsmen are only fully appreciated when their careers are over. I hope Jacques will be an exception. People are finally beginning to realise what a phenomenon he is. Great friend, too.

Above: There was much emotion after the win at Edgbaston – here Nella engulfs me after the series win. (Getty Images)

Left: Freddie Flintoff – the man who has represented the spirit of fair play and respect amongst opposing teams more than anyone in recent years. Plays harder than most, gives everything, but subscribes to the 'nobody died' theory when you lose. (Getty Images)

Top: Accepting the trophy at The Oval – iconic gas holders in the background.

Left: Two trophies, actually. The sponsors' trophy and the Basil D'Oliveira trophy first presented to England in 2005 – on our soil. That hurt. But for Ashwell and Vinnie it made this victory even sweeter.

Bottom: There are exceptions, but most English changing rooms are not spacious …

Above, clockwise from top left: John Paul Getty's private ground at Wormsley in the Buckinghamshire countryside. The fixture was against an England PCA XI to raise money for the Cricketers Association. But it was more about the Pimms and prawns than the cricket. Sunbathing … English style! Cold and grey, but a swimming pool and sunbeds still deserve some attention. An early morning walk with AB: 'One day, young man, all this could be yours.' Anyone for croquet? There seems to be a rules dispute.

Above right: Trent Bridge, scene of the worst result in the entire 18 months.

Above: In the back of a London cab. A pair of Morkels, a Botha and a Steyn, complete with tongue stud. It didn't last long.

Left: The Lord's 'Long Room'. An austere place when empty, it can be intimidating to walk through – either to or from the changing room And the members aren't always as gentlemanly as you might expect!

out and a packed Lord's saw two batsmen, two umpires … and no fielding side. I can understand them turning on us, but I was genuinely surprised at how nasty it became.

There were chants about 'Pakistan', in reference to their refusal to come onto the field during the Oval Test a a couple of years earlier, and lots of boos and abusive shouts from the Members Stand. Then, when we walked through the Long Room – right on time, just as we had been told to do – some of the comments from the 'Gentlemen' sitting there should have been a deep source of embarrassment. So much for 'tradition' and old-fashioned respect! It left a bitter taste in our mouths, but on the bright side, I'm certain it contributed to us saving the match. I had quite an argument with Billy about his lack of communication, or miscommunication. I told him that it was his fault that we were being seen as the 'bad guys' and that it was his responsibility to get a message on the tannoy informing the crowd of what had happened. He didn't.

The declaration left us with just a handful of overs to bat on the second evening. I knew how important that little period was but I was also very clear in my mind about what I needed to do. I knew exactly how England would attack me – full and straight and swinging into my pads. It was how Matthew Hoggard had been successful against South Africa a couple of years earlier when I was going through a bad patch. The first ball it happened, I was in position and it thudded into the middle of the bat. I felt good for the rest of the evening and there were no alarms.

The next day was overcast. In England the overhead conditions can play a big part in how the match unfolds, and I was concerned. One delivery bounced more than expected off a good length and dented the shoulder of the bat. I still have the bat today. I was caught in the gulley and it started a bad slide. We lost too many early wickets until Ashwell and AB resurrected things, briefly. AB chipped one from Monty Panesar to long on just as we were beginning to get ourselves back in the game. Ash made a tremendous hundred under pressure to get us to a total of 247, but we were still following on, a mile behind.

The game has changed to such a degree in the last decade that the follow-on has almost become outdated. One of the reasons

England had little choice this time, however, was because of the length of time they batted in the first innings. Now they needed all the bowling time they could get. The light was poor on the third evening so Mac and I just faced a couple of overs from Panesar and Pietersen before play ended.

After play, I had a proper heart-to-heart with the guys. I made it very clear that the rest of the series could be decided by the way we defined ourselves over the remaining two days. I actually singled one or two players out and told them to wake up and take more responsibility. I tried to avoid doing that in front of the team, but there were two reasons for doing it. The first was that they needed to hear it. The second was selfish: if you do that as a captain, you bloody well better perform yourself or you can really look like an idiot. So I put more pressure on myself, which I was happy to take. I tend to do all right under pressure.

The bus ride back to the hotel was pretty quiet. Everyone was very down about the way we had played and the situation that we now found ourselves in. I had room-service that night and lay quietly in my room, just having two or three chats on the phone with guys who I knew needed to have a bit of a 'pick-me-up' before they went to sleep. I watched a light-hearted DVD, just something silly, to take the sting out of my mood. It did help me relax and get a decent night's sleep. If the next day went well for us I knew it wouldn't be memorable from a headlines point of view, but it could be vital in defining many of our careers.

The bus ride back to the ground was pretty quiet, too! But I was in a really good space – a bit nervous, but in a good space. My preparation was simple. Hit some balls, stretch, run, hit some more balls. Ready. Pad up. It was a good, sunny day – even better. I had honestly never hoped for rain. Batsmen want to bat, and bat in good conditions. Given a choice between saving a game by batting for 10 hours under a hot sun or sitting in a cold change room while it rained for two days, I'd take the former every time. Well, almost every time.

Mac and I started well and then just kept going, and going and going. And going. We kept each other focused. We concentrated on what was important in the moment, we heard the crowd sledging us for scoring slowly but it didn't change a thing. Neither did Pietersen's comments to Mac that we should bring Herschelle back so the crowd could at least get some value for money. We knew what our job was and we were making damn sure we did it properly.

When we walked off together at lunch I had only one regret – when we're still batting at lunchtime during a Test match it's our policy not to eat anything solid and, at Lord's, that's almost criminal. Lord's lunches are the best in the world, bar none. Everybody says so. The most incredible prawns I have ever had remain a highlight – although you are given a choice of five or six main course meals, so everybody has a slightly different food experience. Team management gain 2–3 kilograms each during the Lord's Test. It's not just the lunches, but a constant supply of sandwiches, biscuits, cream cakes … there is always something delicious within arm's reach. But the meal replacement drink tasted fine in the knowledge that I was still batting.

There wasn't much conventional swing for any of England's bowlers at any stage of the day. A little bit of reverse swing, but not dangerous. As a left-hander I had to be careful against Panesar, who was getting a little bit of turn from the rough outside my off stump, but I just had to concentrate. The biggest threat, however, would come from me. I felt strongly that my destiny was in my own hands. And if the rest of the top order felt the same way, we would save the game.

I stuck strictly to my game plan against Panesar; he was bowling on a worn wicket so I needed to be really strong. I took a middle-and-off guard to get myself outside the line and take lbw out of the equation in case anything really misbehaved out of the rough. Then I worked with the spin as much as possible and tucked a lot of deliveries off my legs, looking for gaps on the leg side. I swept a couple, too, just to mix up his line and length. I hardly drove the ball at all – it had to be virtually a full toss before I considered the shot. Not much was happening for him and I wasn't about to give him even half a chance. Mac played him very well; we all did, to be honest. His figures – 0-116 in 60 – overs must have left him feeling as mentally sore as he was physically.

We kept England in the field for 167 overs. We'd chatted about the repercussions later in the series if we could keep them in the field for a long time – and, with the second Test just three days later, there is no doubt that they paid a high price for not being able to bowl us out.

When I was on 99 the memories of 2003 started coming back. I remember being quite overwhelmed by the reaction and atmosphere when I reached three figures five years earlier. Now here I was again – and I wanted to experience that feeling again! Vaughan took his time, as you do when an opposing batsman has 99. He moved short fine leg a little squarer, maybe three or four metres. When Panesar finally bowled the next ball it was a tiny bit too straight and I tickled past the left hand of the man Vaughan had just moved.

Neil ran as fast as I've seen him on those creaky legs of his and we came back for three. The feeling was the same as it had been five years earlier. They might have been booing us a couple of days earlier and calling me names, but the Lord's crowd appreciate success and now they were applauding. It was a special feeling, naturally, but I was still very focused. We'd made a damn good start, but the Test match was still losable. We still had a lot of work to do.

Unfortunately, I was out to the second new ball fairly soon afterwards, and it wasn't a great shot either. Still, I knew I'd made a difference and led from the front. Neil Mac was still out there, and I saw a look of great belief in Hashim's eyes as he walked past me. The change room was buzzing again. There was a lot of belief around the camp once again.

When we finally drew the match we shared a deep sense of achievement. No, it did not feel like a victory – not in any way, because we'd played so poorly for the first three days – but now we'd saved the game, restored our reputations, England were exhausted and their trump card bowler had got absolutely nothing to show for a marathon workload.

After the game we spent some quiet but high quality time together in the change room, just chatting and sipping a couple of cold beers. Rob Fleming, sponsorship manager of Castle, brought a couple of people up to meet us and it was obvious how much it meant to them to be at Lord's. They were also quite emotional about how we'd saved the game, which was a perfect reminder – not that we really needed one – that we play this game for millions of South Africans, not just ourselves.

Some of our family members came up to see us, too, but just the men because females aren't allowed to threaten the sanctity of Lord's. Silly, very silly. My Dad came up with a family friend and we took pictures and soaked up the atmosphere. We'd stuck three strips of masking tape on the Honours Board with the names of Smith, McKenzie and Amla on them because we couldn't wait to see the real thing. So there I was, twice. It gave me goosebumps to see, even thought the second one was scrawled in Koki pen. It meant so much to both of us to share the moment with my Dad.

Later that evening I was still deep in thought about all the cricketing punches that had been thrown, where we'd gone wrong and what we'd done well. I knew we would have to improve with the ball. I was convinced there would be a result on the seamer-friendly pitch at Headingley, and we weren't going to win the game if we bowled like we had at Lord's.

The Leeds Test

An accident on the highway between London and Leeds forced us to take some back roads and made the journey last five or six hours. Normally that would have been a nightmare but, thanks our magic tour bus, it just gave us a chance to see some English countryside and little villages. Any longer and it might have been a problem – we were pretty stiff when we arrived.

I'd had plenty of time to chat to Dale and Morne, as Mickey did, but they certainly didn't need to be told that they hadn't done themselves justice at Lord's. They were desperate to make amends. The biggest concern was that they were too desperate and wouldn't be able to relax.

Headingley is a very strange ground to adapt to, even for the non-bowlers. Television flattens everything out so you can't see them, but the slopes at Headingley are everywhere. It slopes most noticeably towards the football ground end, but it also has a lot of 'bumps' and 'dips' in it which take a lot of getting used to for the quick bowlers. Everyone talks about the famous Lord's slope, but it's Headingley they should visit to see an international ground with hills in it!

And it's not just the outfield that takes some getting used to. There is no greater contrast to the comfort and tradition of Lord's than the cold, cramped concrete of Headingley. The changing rooms are tiny underground bunkers with no view of the ground. The benches are barely wide enough to sit on and there's so little room that three or four of our squad had to set up their 'corner' in the showers. People thought it strange that we left the ground straight after our warm-downs – we didn't have any choice, we couldn't get to the showers.

The hotel was comfortable, however, but obviously with a very different feel to London. Leeds may have a bit of a 'working class' reputation but it's quite a vibey town with plenty of good restaurants and lots of choice. It's probably a bit rougher around the edges and certainly a bit more football crowd orientated, but it's fun – I enjoyed it.

My folks had always planned to be with the tour for the first two Tests and they also enjoyed Leeds, having had a couple of small reservations beforehand! They went to Lord's and Edgbaston on the first tour, so they're gradually ticking off England's Test venues.

The only thing Headingley has going for it, from a preparation point of view, is that the nets are on the edge of the outfield, so you spend two or three days close to the middle getting used to all the idiosyncrasies of the ground.

Andrew Flintoff was recalled to the England squad, which would significantly change the balance of the team but also immediately created a media circus which happily took a lot of the attention away from us. We were far more concerned with Fred as a bowler than a batsman ... at least, I was! He bowls brilliantly to left-handers and has bowled some of the best deliveries I've ever faced. He can angle the ball into a left hander and then make it nip away, pretty much unplayable. But was he really fully fit?

Naturally, being Leeds, one of our practice sessions was affected by rain and we went indoors, but at least it was only one. The pre-match press conference was also straightforward (which is actually a relief in England. You never quite know what trick question someone may have up their sleeve!) I said simply that I believed the pressure had been transferred from us to England by our second innings batting display and that they had to make the running now. But most of the questions I was asked concerned the England team. Ryan Sidebottom was a casualty of the bowling marathon at Lord's and there was a serious question mark about whether Flintoff would bat at six or seven. But I couldn't see the point in asking me about that!

One of the themes of the team meeting before the Test was dealing with the uncontrollables. There is a very hostile crowd at Leeds, especially the Western terraces, which are wild with a bizarre mixture of crude humour and aggression. We needed to make sure we didn't allow them to affect our play and get caught up in the emotion. We needed to play with our coolest heads and make good, clear decisions. Overhead conditions would be crucial, too.

Oh, and the three Ps made their customary appearance, too. Patience, partnerships and pressure! We also needed the ball to swing far more than it had at Lord's, so we appointed AB and Bouch to take specific control of the condition of the ball. Nothing 'unnatural' and certainly nothing illegal, but the ball needs to be very carefully maintained and its natural deterioration must be controlled, as far as possible.

Although we like to concentrate on our own preparation, we also spoke about what we had learned about the England camp and the issues they had going on. Tim Tremlett had been travelling around with the team for months, even before we got there during the New Zealand series. He'd been 12th man at Lord's and now he was here again at Headingley. But then they brought in Darren Pattinson, who'd played a few games for Victoria but had made his biggest impression in half a dozen games for Nottinghamshire in the county championship.

We didn't know a lot about him. Actually, we hardly knew anything. I phoned a few people in Australia and got a little bit of information on him, but it was a surprise to us that this was all going on, seemingly out of nowhere. They had picked their squad and suddenly a 'nobody' had arrived out of left field because of Sidebottom's injury. We discussed Pattinson, but it wasn't a long chat! We didn't really expect him to play – and besides, our performances would be more important than any of England's.

On the morning of the match it wasn't only the pitch that felt cold – we all did! It was overcast but chilly ... would it swing? Probably not. But it would certainly seam about. My gut feeling was to bowl first again but, obviously, the scars after doing that at Lord's were still fresh and painful.

Luckily I won the toss and, even more fortunately, I was brave enough to make that decision again. One of the reasons I had the courage of my convictions was because I'd seen Vaughan and coach Peter Moores in a heated discussion an hour or so before the game, obviously about their team selection. Watching from a distance, and without being able to hear them, it struck me that there was a lot of disagreement and plenty of pressure on their decision-making processes. When the leadership group lacks co-hesion, that filters down to the team. So I thought 'right, let's get stuck into them before they've settled down.'

Vaughan had always come across as very clinical, very precise and always very calm, like nothing was ever wrong and he was always in control of the situation. This was the first time I'd seen him emotional.

Another sign of unhappiness and discord came 45 minutes be-fore the start, when England had picked their team but before the toss. Mickey was standing in the tunnel area between the change rooms and Paul Collingwood, who'd been left out of the XI, walked past him and said: 'You give everything for this team and then they just leave you out.' He is a great team man and that wasn't in character for him, but the fact that he didn't care about disguising his disappointment was another sign that we needed to strike while they were weak.

We had struggled to take early wickets in the warm-up matches, and Lord's was even worse in that regard, so I was slightly nervous as we walked out to start the Test. But what happiness! Steyntjie and Morne both took four wickets and we bowled them out for 203. I was absolutely over the moon, not just for the team but for the pair of them, who had been so disappointed with themselves after Lord's and were so determined to put it right. It was hard not to get too carried away with that first innings, even though we all know how long a Test match lasts and how many twists and turns there can be over five days.

There had only been one sour moment. AB grabbed a catch at

third slip off Vaughan, and thinking it had carried, we started celebrating. But AB was genuinely unsure. He thought it had 'stuck', but came straight to me and said: 'Smithy, I'm not sure if it carried, or what happened ... can you please just ask them to check with the third umpire.' The replay showed that it had dropped out of his hands as he was diving forward with his head turned the other way. He'd then grabbed again and the ball was back in his hands. He couldn't have known. Everything was handled professionally out in the middle and Vaughan was given not out.

Unfortunately the dining area and the players' viewing areas are very close together – with the media right next door – so there is a lot of bumping in to each other. Vaughan made a couple of really acerbic comments to AB about the incident, trying to put him under extra pressure and raise the heat on a young but very important player in our team. Luckily I happened to be standing there at that moment and just pointed out to the England captain that AB had never tried to get away with anything, the situation had been dealt with properly and that he should consider keeping his mouth shut and getting on with the game. AB handled himself really well throughout.

It surprised me. Vaughan had always been so assured. He's a clever guy, and is good at playing a few 'mind games', but there was no control over this. He seemed the one under pressure. It was too heated and emotional to be planned. I saw it as a big positive for our team, and told AB that.

I made 40-odd that evening and felt really good again. It's always horrible to get out in the 40s after doing so much hard work, but it was a good delivery from Fred (he saves them up for me!) and we finished the day really well placed so I wasn't about to start moaning.

There was more than a touch of irony during our innings when Vaughan claimed a low catch at mid-off when Hashim was batting. England went mad celebrating. Hash, being Hash, started to walk. But he eventually realised that all was not as it seemed and he stayed at the crease. It was referred and then given not out when the replay looked like it had bounced. I wasn't the only one who thought that Michael was getting a bit of comeuppance for the way he had treated AB.

It was a fantastic moment in the changing room. I was briefly concerned that the amount of emotion we displayed was the complete opposite of the attitude and approach we had tried to adopt during Test matches. Calm, controlled and unemotional had been our mantra. But then I thought – sod it, the guys need to let off some steam, and it was bringing us even closer together. I'm afraid there was quite a bit of swearing about the England captain that evening. He didn't deserve it, but at the time it felt OK.

The next day was crucial. Warm-ups went well and the team chat was very positive – all about the three bloody Ps again! We reminded ourselves that they had been in the field for several days and that if we could build a couple of substantial partnerships we could put them under serious physical and emotional pressure. The partnership between Ashwell and AB was an incredible effort, so precise, clinical and disciplined. The shot-making was one thing, but the way they left the good balls was equally important, as always. It was great to watch.

I was sitting outside in the tiny viewing area, which is always freezing cold, watching the Western terrace go berserk. People were dressed as everything from donkeys to pink panthers and nuns, going crazy and swilling beer. The security guys told us that sixty people were thrown out of that stand on that afternoon. I'm sure they drank more and more and became less and less interested in the cricket the more we dominated the game. It was a good sign for us. Ash and AB, having played so sensibly, then attacked Panesar with great effect. A total of 522 put us in complete control of the game. England were wilting, noticeably. We couldn't have been in a better place that evening going back to the hotel. It was all buzz.

I had dinner with my folks that night and we chatted about how shocked they were with the crowds and the people in Leeds, how partisan the atmosphere really was. I couldn't help but smile. It's all part and parcel of touring England, and touring the world really, you get to interact in different cultures and different atmospheres. It's a bit of an odd feeling that you're more worldly-wise than your own folks. Of course, you're not! It's only in the very specific and small capacity of international cricket that you might know a bit more than them.

In bed that night I started planning the next day. Good, long, uninterrupted nights of sleep have been very rare in my career. Even when I've had a perfect day, I lie awake wondering or worrying about the next day. I was obviously hoping for a cloudy day so the ball would swing around, but when we got up in the morning it was clear. Fresh and sunny. Funnily enough, that might have been a good thing. Overcast, murky conditions might have relaxed the bowlers into thinking it would 'just happen' for them. As it was, they knew they were going to have to work their backsides off.

And they did. The bowlers put in some seriously hard yards, everyone played their role and we worked hard for our wickets. The really big one for me was Vaughan's. We had managed to add to the pressure he was obviously already feeling – now was the time to hammer another nail in. Steyntjie had already knocked him over with a beauty in the first innings and we had really good game plans for him. We honestly felt we'd worked him out – for the moment. You never, ever get complacent with cricketers as good as him. He came in with an obviously different attitude, to be more positive. He made a good start, too, but then Makhaya nicked him off. I had played more than enough Test cricket to know that there was still a long way to go, but he was a crucial wicket. I admit that I thought we were a significant step closer to victory.

Michael had walked over to Mickey when they were looking at the wicket on the third morning, basically seeking some reassurance around the AB catch and his own. It was probably the result of the previous evening's press conference at which we'd asked Mickey to express our 'surprise' at how strongly Michael had reacted in the dining room. It was genuinely motivated but, at the same time, we were also aware that it might create a bit more pressure on Michael. It was something a bit new for us. For too long we had all just innocently answered questions at press conferences rather than considered what the ramifications might be, or what impression we could create. It wasn't remotely cynical, not at all. Just calm and assured. It was just a small step in moving away from feeling like helpless victims in the media, a chance to actually say something.

When he was talking to Mickey in an attempt to 'clear the air', I knew for certain he was feeling the pressure. I happened to walk to the wicket at the back-end of their chat and I joined in. We exchanged views and nobody backed down. It was a firm but cordial conversation but it was obvious to me that it wasn't the same Michael Vaughan I had been accustomed to dealing with. He was obviously under pressure and not happy.

Obviously his own game wasn't in great shape, but I could see, as a captain, that a lot of off-field stuff was getting to him and weighing him down. Michael had been a brilliant captain and, much as I don't like to remember them, he'd had a couple of great moments against me. He'd been calm and assured. Now he wasn't. It was the first time I'd ever seen a difference in him, having started our captaincy careers at the same time. It used to bug me that he was one step ahead of the game. I respected him for that.

Alistair Cook batted for a long time and we had to come with some new game plans to him. Jakes bowled really well to him. We used more 'grippers' and adapted to the wicket; we were thinking on our feet. We finally had him caught at short cover.

There was a big and frustrating partnership at the end of the innings in which Stuart Broard really flourished. He's a very technically accomplished batsmen at number nine and we bowled poorly to him. We were so close to winning and simply became desperate to finish the game. We lost control of the game plan and he belted a very good 67. But Dale and Morne were both in the thick of the action, as always, and we were left with a victory 'target' of 10 to win.

It took quite a while to sink in. We were one-nil up in the series and we'd won at Headingley, one of the most hostile environments I've experienced in international cricket. It was a great achievement.

The cramped, cold and terrible changing room was still there to greet us afterwards, but strangely, it didn't feel quite so terrible after the game. Suddenly it felt a lot warmer. We were so, so happy.

We had a little 'fines meeting' that evening, as we often do when there is a meaningful break before the next international match. We sing a few songs and have a few beers and cool drinks, and the guys 'fine' each other for all the hilarious, odd, weird or embarrassing moments they have witnessed each other having over the preceding couple of weeks. It's very much a 'team thing', but has changed for the better over the years with more of an emphasis on all of the cultures in the team, whereas the point used to be on 'downing' a few beers.

Everybody's instinct was to carry on the celebration a little longer after we left the ground, but things conspired, happily, to keep us all in check. I had dinner with my folks and, being a Monday night, the bachelor boys drew a blank in their search for a 'happening' bar. They ended up having a meal at Nandos and going to bed. There wasn't a hangover in sight the next morning, which was brilliant because everybody woke up to the fact that we could create history by winning the next Test match – and the series – if we could win at Edgbaston, Birmingham.

The Birmingham Test

Cricket must be the only sport in the world in which you go on tour for so long you sometimes need two haircuts! That was my mission in Worcester, to get a good haircut. I used not to care much about my appearance, but it gradually dawned on me that I needed to look presentable and smart. So I've become a bit more finicky about my hair!

A quick break for a game against Bangladesh 'A' had given J-P and Robbie P the chance to actually play some cricket on tour. We always like to keep as many people as possible in their usual place in the batting order so, with Neil Mac having a rest, J-P opened with me. Ashwell was also having a well-deserved rest after scoring hundreds in both Test matches. His wife and baby son, Joshua, had just arrived, too, so he was given proper time away from the team to be with them.

Dale had taken a knock on his left hand while fielding off his own bowling at Headingley, so he was going to rest, too. We had no idea how serious it was; we all thought it was a bruise. But he went for an x-ray and it showed that it was fractured. Still, at least it was his left hand. Mickey and I assumed we could just strap it up. We didn't need his left hand, it was the other one we wanted. And I didn't care if he couldn't bat.

I'll never forget the discussion in the back of the physio room at New Road, Worcester, between me, Mickey, Shane Jabaar, Dale and team manager Doc Moosajee. The realisation that we were going to have to play at Edgbaston without him was sinking in very slowly for me and Mickey. We kept starting sentences with: 'But what about...' and 'But surely...' We were only thinking about it from a cricket perspective, not a medical one. Dale was, too. He would have let us cut his hand off if that's what it took.

The medical staff had their job to do, however, and they decided it wasn't worth risking him. He would be fit for the one-dayers but if he took another blow on it before then he would require surgery and could be out for months. I didn't like what they had to say but I respected it, grudgingly. So Mickey and I were outvoted. It was difficult to know who was more disappointed, between me, Dale and Mickey. It was such a crucial Test match, it could shape our entire careers if we won. Dale had just taken seven wickets at Headingley and I wanted him to play again, desperately. Eventually we accepted our fate.

There seemed to be a lot of indecision in the England camp. I was staggered that nobody was accepting any responsibility for 'Pattinsongate' and the media were having a field day. Both Vaughan and Geoff Miller seemed to imply that it was the other man's decision to play him in the XI. I heard Jonathan Agnew going berserk on BBC radio that England should play an Aussie! Pattinson hadn't bowled badly, but he wasn't much of a threat, to be honest. We played him well. I must say we shared the media's view on the subject, although we kept quiet. The selectors pluck a 30-year-old Australian out of nowhere when experienced campaigners like Matthew Hoggard and Steve Harmison were kicking their heels in county cricket! It made us laugh – we followed the saga in the papers quite closely. It was like a soap opera.

At one point I think they had a 'crisis' meeting at which Vaughan, Moores and Hugh Morris tried to clear the air. I'm not sure that it was very successful, if my sources were accurate. We were obviously very interested in their selection for Edgbaston, but it was difficult to know what was true, what was rumour and what was pure media speculation. In Worcester, meanwhile, we almost had two consecutive hours of sunshine. It was a cause for celebration.

It had been a horrible summer so far and the guys were all desperately missing feeling the sun on their backs.

The wicket bounced no more than knee high and the bowlers were mostly schoolboy pace, so batting was pretty hard work. I was staggered to see about 500 spectators. I hope they didn't pay too much for their tickets. J-P made a big hundred and Jakes was back in the runs, thank goodness.

It can be difficult managing a large squad with several guys who aren't playing much at all, but we were really fortunate with guys like Monde Zondeki, JP and Robbie P. Nella was set to take Dale's place at Edgbaston, which was good for the team, because he's not such a good tourist when he's not playing!

I made 90 on the first day, but it wasn't much to get excited about. Good to feel the ball in the middle of the bat, though. I watched the rest of the day, sitting on the most uncomfortable chairs I've ever experienced in a changing room. Little, cramped, wooden bench-type things. Anyway, I had a bit of a stiff back by the close of play, when I was asked to do a media interview for the Sunday newspapers. They wanted to chat about the Champions Trophy scheduled for Pakistan and how I felt about security. There were a few other contentious issues around, including 'Pattinsongate', which they were desperate to drag me into. I thought the best way to add fuel to the fire and keep the argument raging was simply to say that I was 'surprised' by the way it had been handled.

After two hours sitting on the torturous bench, and then standing for the press conference, I joined the boys for a game of soccer on the outfield without stretching properly, which was pretty naughty and irresponsible of me. I stretched for a pass and ended up twingeing something in my back. It was a bit stiff that night but I didn't take much notice. When I woke up the next morning I knew something was very wrong. I've never been the greatest 'mover', but now it felt as though I was disabled. I spent hours on the physio's bench, but it refused to ease up and I fielded that day in constant pain. Shane's hard work eventually started to pay off and I could move without pain, but only slowly. It was better by the time we moved to Birmingham after the third day, but the injury was to make an unexpected return.

Five years earlier we'd stayed right in the middle of the city, but this time we were at the Radisson Hotel, which wasn't quite in the centre. There are pros and cons to both – depending on your age and status. We had three days to prepare for the Test and my back was feeling much better. Then, during a fielding drill after stretching and warm-ups I picked the ball up and threw it at full power to the 'keeper, in the process twisting my back. I felt the same spasm as in Worcester – but possibly worse.

The remaining 48 hours of my preparation for the Test was pretty much spent in hospital or on the physio's couch. I went for some scans which were inconclusive, but the theory was that I'd hurt a ligament on a disc, or something like that. I didn't care what it was, I just wanted the incredible pain to go away. I couldn't move properly, couldn't bend down to pick anything up, I couldn't even go to the toilet properly. But that's probably enough detail! I was hobbling around trying to move as little as possible and hoping it would ease and get better in the two days before the Test match. There was talk of an injection in the back to take away the pain before I went out to bat. I wasn't keen on that, but I didn't want to think about it until closer to the time.

I didn't train the day before, just the traditional media conference. Again, there were many questions concerning the England team. Would Harmison play? Where should Flintoff bat? Everyone still seemed to be reeling after the Pattinson incident. There was even more uneasiness in their leadership group between Vaughan and Moores, and that was coming through in the media. But they had at least made one good move in recalling Harmison. We thought it was a good move, anyway. There's no substitute for genuine firepower in the bowling attack.

For me, though, it was a race against time. As I sat there talking to the media, I honestly didn't know whether I'd be fit enough to play. I did as much stretching as it was possible to do in two days, just hoping it would work.

We discussed the crowd at the team meeting, amongst other issues. They can be hostile but not as hostile as Headingley, but there are more carrots, vicars, Robin Hoods and pink panthers than you've ever seen in your life before, so we needed to prepare a strategy to stop ourselves laughing! It was critical that we started well. I believed very strongly that if we could get our noses in front early in the game and make them chase us for the first two or three days, they would become desperate and make mistakes. But I went to bed that night just desperately hoping I'd be able to play.

It was still very sore the next day. I went down to the ground with Shane and Mickey before the rest of the team and had a fitness test which I passed, sort of. I wasn't good. I'm not sure that they would have given a 'pass' to many of the other guys. But they knew I had experience of 'managing' injuries and they were happy for me to play through the discomfort. I barely did anything during the warm-ups, it was an effort just to bend! It must have looked very strange. But it was just such an important game and I felt I had to be a part of it, even if I was only at 75 or even 70 per cent.

England won the toss and decided to bat, as we would have done. It looked like a good wicket which would simply deteriorate in the normal way over the course of five days. The media had gone to town a bit on Nella in the build-up, with all the old stories of his split personality, his alter ego – 'Gunther' – and his 'white line fever'. I was hoping he wouldn't be too hyper when he actually came on to bowl.

We bowled really, really well, and England were gone for just 231. Nella was great with 3-47 (although he became completely distracted by the crowd, contrary to the team plan!). Jakes was equally good value for his 3-31 and, for the first time in the series, we found a bit of swing. Once again we struggled for the first wicket, but then we were able to put the middle order under pressure. Vaughan went cheaply once again, which was a key moment of the innings – maybe of the match. There'd been plenty of media talk about his lack of runs and poor form, and we needed to keep it that way. When the opposing captain is down, you need to keep your foot on him.

We batted that evening and Flintoff (!) had me caught behind for seven. He really can be unplayable at times, especially to left-handers. Way too good for me on the day. But I still went to bed feeling extremely good about the day and looking forward to a big lead.

Mac batted really well for his 72, Jakes made 64 and Bouch 40.

It wasn't a bad performance by any means, but it might have been even better had it not been for a brilliant spell in gloomy light from Fred. We were in control and looking to impose a big lead, but he ran in at full speed using both the yorker and the short ball with great control and to great effect. It was during that spell that we first noticed the problem with the sightscreen at the pavilion end.

There were two glass sliding doors just above the sightscreen in the president's suite which were dark. Flintoff's release point from around the wicket was in the glass and it became impossible to see the release, especially the yorker. Jacques and Mackie both completely lost a couple of deliveries and Fred took a couple of wickets which set us back a lot. Still, it was a great spell – sight-screen problem or not.

The next morning we addressed it with the match referee and suggested that, at the end of the innings, once both sides had batted, we could put a white board on cloth on the bottom of the glass door. But Vaughan said 'no'. Both captains have to agree to anything which amounts to a change in playing conditions, and obviously it was far more in England's favour than ours. I think Morne's delivery point was too high and all the other bowlers were too short to take advantage of that 'blind spot'!

Fred was threatening to bowl them right back into the match until Bouch came to the rescue. As with so many times in his career, the scorecard just reflects '40' and not the full extent of its worth. He marshalled the tail with massive skill and eased us up to a lead of 80. We would have preferred 180, of course, but I still believed it would be significant. It was satisfying to see the tail show some guts and character. They'd all worked hard on their batting and they were there for the team when we needed them.

Now we needed to bowl as well as we had done in the first innings, and we'd be close to the series win we'd all dreamt about. The weather was good, the pitch was good and there wasn't a lot on offer for the seamers. We spoke long and hard about being patient and precise, and about controlling our emotions. It was a packed house, and the Barmy Army seemed to have called in its reserves. There would be an awful lot of beer drunk. We could not, under any circumstances, allow ourselves to become caught up in the emotions of the crowd. Methodical and clinical would be our watchwords.

I decided to give Nella the new ball purely because we'd really struggled to break the left-handed opening partnership and he was usually very good against them. Neither Cook nor Strauss ever took a big stride on the front foot, so if we could get Nella thundering in from around the wicket and attacking off stump with a full length, I thought he'd have a chance of knocking one of them over. Then we'd go back to using Makhaya.

And it worked! Cook was stone-dead, lbw to his second ball! 'Not out,' said the umpire. We couldn't believe it. It was absolutely stone-dead. Having spoken so much about controlling our emotions, here was a bloody stiff test for all of us two minutes into the innings.

We all did very well, except for Nella, who started getting involved in egging on the crowd and rising to their bating. He is an emotional personality and cricketer, so you have to allow him some expression, but there is a time and a place, and, having just spoken about how important it was to stay calm, it was very disappointing. The crowd turned on him and then on the whole team. I know it affected our focus and took attention away from what was important. It was very frustrating.

I made the change quickly and went back to Makhaya and Morne but, to be honest, we never bowled well all day. We were actually fortunate to have England in trouble as we did at 104-4, basically 21-4. Cook and Bell both gave us their wickets by pulling the ball straight up in the air.

Collingwood was under enormous media pressure. He was going through a horrible loss of form and hadn't scored double figures for about two months. When he came out to join Pietersen there was an unmistakeable feeling that his career was on the line. It was make or break time – and, good man though he is, it was our intention to break him.

But we never, ever got the ball in the right area to him, and leaked boundaries all over the place bowling both sides of the wicket, trying too hard and being impatient. Suddenly it felt like we'd systematically done the opposite of everything we'd discussed before the Test match and during the course of the first two and a half days!

I brought Harry back into the attack and thank goodness he provided some consistency and balance. It was obvious Pietersen wanted to attack him, but by tea we were seriously on the ropes. The lead had been stretched to about 130 and I was honestly at a loss as to how I was going to regain control of the game, let alone take another six wickets and start the run chase. Apart from Harry, I had no one to turn to. Perhaps that's why Pietersen wanted to attack him – but it definitely had a lot to do with his ego, too.

He gifted us his wicket and let us right back into the game when he was on the verge of taking it away from us. We made a change in the field by moving short leg to a 'tempting' mid-on, probably half way back to the boundary, just enough to make a batsman think about taking the shot on. On 94, he went for the big shot but didn't catch it cleanly and AB took a good catch. A lot was said about it afterwards, but I kept quiet at the time. It should have been obvious enough to everyone that it wasn't in the team's interests to play a shot like that. I was very grateful, however.

We had an animated talk in the huddle after the wicket, about building pressure and bowling the ball in the right area, simple stuff. We'd lost our spring in the field and nobody was bowling well. To be fair to everyone, there wasn't a dissenting voice. Everyone knew we were messing it up. Two balls later, we got Flintoff. Jeez. If ever there was a short period of Test cricket to illustrate how quickly the game changes, there it was. Harry had him caught at short leg, bat-pad. It was massive. Absolutely massive. Fred has several 'weak' points, but on his day he can take a Test match away from anybody. This was an opportunity for him to do that. A 50 or 60 then may have buried us.

We didn't take another wicket on the third evening and we finished the day emotionally drained and very tired. I was still struggling with my back, but my tennis elbow was even worse. I can cope with pain, I'm no different to most professional cricketers in that regard, but this was something I hadn't experienced before. It was getting worse and worse. I felt under a lot of pressure that night, but hoped that nobody else had noticed.

I struggled to get to sleep. We had been in complete control of the game, but we had now conceded that control. They were 200 ahead overnight and only six wickets down. I was feeling the pressure of having let things slip. It doesn't matter if batsmen bat badly or bowlers bowl poorly, you still feel the responsibility as captain. It was driving me mad. I wanted the series win so much. I was feeling pretty drained. I had room service, watched some arbitrary movie and tried to chill out as much as possible and get some rest.

I always wake up very early on 'big' days, and this was nothing unusual: 5.12 am, I think. My head was pumping with thoughts. I usually get out of bed an hour before the bus leaves for the ground, giving myself half an hour to get showered and dressed and another half hour to get some breakfast. Half an hour for food is especially important if it's a batting day: if I bat for most of the day I won't eat anything else. I tend to live on meal replacements, energy bars or the energy gel sachets which you suck to keep you going throughout the day.

This morning, however, I didn't make breakfast as I got out of bed late. I felt exhausted and wasn't looking forward to the day. There was so much at stake and so much to play for. We had played so poorly the day before that I was still wincing from the memory. We were now under pressure on a deteriorating wicket offering more and more to the spinners. It was all weighing heavily on my shoulders. I was very aware, however, that the exterior looked extremely solid, sound and composed. I could actually see people taking their lead from my body language. I obviously came across as bullet-proof. But my insides were eating themselves alive.

Unusually, I plugged my i-pod into my ears on the way to the ground. I needed to chill out – and, in retrospect, it probably helped the guys to see me with a smile on my face. I love modern rock – Green Day, Prime Circle or Red Hot Chilli Peppers, anything like that. When we arrived I asked Bouchie to play his i-pod in the changing room because he enjoys similar music and I was keen for the team to share my good mood. There was a good mood that morning. Even I had managed to put my worries to one side …

The second new ball was available and we had to make it count. Morne bowled Tim Ambrose with an absolute beauty – it pitched on off stump and held its line and Ambrose played inside it – he never really had great foot movement, he always played from the crease looking for a cut or back foot punch. We had bowled well at him the whole series.

There was more frustration with Sidebottom and Collingwood, however, and another partnership which took the lead to 250 or 260. There was another catch off Jakes's bowling which AB and I both felt had carried but, given the acrimony of the last Test, we felt we had better refer it. TV showed there was probably a bit of grass involved but, as so often, you just couldn't be sure.

Eventually it ended when James Anderson chopped on for a single and Collingwood, in the company of Panesar, nicked Morne behind. He'd played brilliantly for his century. Another half hour and we might have been dead and buried. As it was, a target of 281 was going to be difficult enough.

We had a couple of overs to bat before lunch, the sort of ten-minute period I hate. You have so much eating away at you, so much still going on in your head. I find it very hard to take my captain's hat off in such a short period of time and switch into batting mode. One day I'm going to get all the world's opening batsmen to form a union and campaign for the break between innings to be extended from 10 to 15 minutes! Anyway, by the time I'd padded up and prepared as best I could, I was walking out with Mac: 281 felt like a very long way off.

I was absolutely nowhere in that little spell. I played and missed at just about everything that Anderson bowled at me, apart from the one which I nicked through first slip and nobody laid a hand on it. I was well and truly on the ropes, I just couldn't find my lines, didn't know what to play at and what to leave. I was just desperate to get to lunch.

I was able to settle down during the break and compose myself. I never went to the dining room, I needed some time to myself to be calm and reflect on things. The pitch was still good, the sun was shining, there wasn't much swing. Things were good. We still had a great chance to win the series. But the new ball was the key. I had to get through it, I had to survive the new ball. After that, as the bowlers tired, life would get easier. I had an energy sachet and half a glass of meal replacement drink.

I felt a lot more settled straight away after lunch. My balance was better, my feet were moving well, I was seeing the ball a lot better and I was starting to find the 'play-leave' rhythm. Once I'd survived Anderson's spell I just started to play. Neil Mac and I were cruising and had 65 on the board when Flintoff came into the at-tack for a spell from the pavilion end with the dodgy sightscreen. It was a deliberate ploy, although I was confident that Mac was playing well enough to survive. As Fred was running in to bowl I was thinking: 'If we can get to 100, we're going to be really well placed to win the series ...'

That delivery was a yorker which Neil, just like Jacques, never saw at any stage. He turned away, as you do, and was plumb lbw. It was very much 'game on' once again.

Hashim looked good, briefly, but Panesar trapped him lbw, al-though from the non-striker's end it looked like it was missing leg stump: 78-2.

Jakes came out at number four with Flintoff in the middle of a fearsome spell. Another attempted yorker – it was actually a low full toss – and Jakes was gone, lbw for five. Once again, he never saw the ball: 83-3.

I was feeling very little emotion, strangely enough. I was con-centrating hard on staying calm and focused, thinking about my batting and what I needed to do. I was very aware that there was nothing I could do for the team about the sightscreen, or from the non-striker's end for that matter. I needed to bat.

Flintoff has a unique relationship with the English crowds and when he celebrates a wicket, 20 000 people celebrate with him. The reaction of Jacques towards the sightscreen, and Flintoff's cel-ebration, sent the crowd into a frenzy. The Members' stand to the right of the changing rooms went completely berserk. I was wait-ing quietly for the 12th man to come on with a drink and watch-ing the crowd go unbelievably mad, singing and chanting. I was blown away by the atmosphere, it was a cauldron of pressure I'd rarely experienced before and I was thrilled and honoured to be in the middle of it. I felt so lucky to be there, to have the chance to measure myself in this situation.

I had my drink of water and just wanted to get back to work. I was having a real battle with Panesar, who was getting turn and bounce out of the rough which suddenly seemed to be getting worse by the minute, or perhaps I was imagining that. It was obvi-ous that he was my biggest threat. My game plan, again, was to bat on off stump and get myself slightly outside the line off stump so I couldn't be out lbw if one turned sharply or shot along the ground. I took one mode of dismissal out of play. As in the first innings, the key was to work with the spin, get on top of the bounce, tuck it off my legs – and then run like hell for the other end! It was in the best interests of the team that Panesar didn't get to bowl an extended spell to me. Sooner or later something was going to happen and he was far less effective against the right-handers. I wasn't backing away from the challenge, just trying to be sensible.

Anderson was brought back into the attack straight after Flintoff's brilliant spell, and looked inspired and pumped up. When he removed Ashwell with a good away swinger almost immediately, we were in trouble. Half an hour after I'd been thinking about a hundred partnership with Neil Mac, we were 93-4 and AB was walking to the wicket.

I was very calm with AB, and I never, ever thought about the outcome at any stage. I never contemplated the facts – that we needed another 180 with only Bouch and the tail to come. I just focused on my batting, my innings. All I knew was that the team needed me to be there until the end. All I was thinking about was being positive and building towards tea. I wanted to work 10 runs at a time towards tea and, hopefully, get AB to build a partnership with me. Even if it was just 50 or 60, I thought it would be enough to put us back in control. Or at least back in the game. [Editor's note: De Villiers said afterwards: 'He smiled at me when I walked out to bat at 93-4, he just smiled and said: "I just need someone to stay with me, AB: I'll score half of them but I need you to stay with me – just bat and enjoy it!']

Staying calm was very important for me. It obviously wasn't a very 'calm' environment, but it was a simple case of logic. If I wasn't calm, we lost the Test match. I needed to be calm, therefore I was. The bloody sightscreen was still a problem and Fred was now trying to bowl every ball out of the 'blind spot'. He'd obviously worked out where he had to be on the crease at the point of delivery to bowl the 'blind' delivery and he was getting it right more and more. He bowled one perfectly to AB straight after tea which he didn't see at all – he barely flinched. Fortunately it just missed leg stump. We had another piece of luck just before tea when AB and I made a mess of a single and I should have been run out. Fortunately, England made an even bigger mess of it with Bell and Ambrose both fumbling the ball to give me a life.

Mickey came up to me at the tea break looking very nervous. I told him that I was feeling pretty good but that, as coach, he needed to get someone to stay with me! All that time I'd spent going on and on about partnerships, the three bloody 'P's, now I wanted one more than ever before. I knew we could still get home as long as I stayed there. By now it was obvious that I needed to bat through the innings. But I needed partners.

First or second ball after tea Anderson dragged it down short to me and I instinctively pulled it for four, right out of the middle. I was back in the zone straight away. I knew I could do it, bat through the innings. AB was looking calm and we were slowly building our way towards the target, 10 runs at a time. Then Panesar turned one just enough to catch the edge of AB's bat and he was caught at slip. Good delivery, fair enough. We'd added 78 and, as I'd hoped, we were back in the game.

We still needed 110 when Bouch strode out to the crease. I couldn't think of a better man to have alongside me in that situation. He looked bullish and confident, too. But I suppose he always looks like that. We both knew we had to get a large chunk of the runs between us. Morne had been in trouble against Panesar every time he'd faced him so far ... and then it was the tail. I didn't want to be chasing down a fourth innings target in the company of nine, ten and 11.

Vaughan brought Flintoff back straight away to bowl at Bouch – from the 'sightscreen end'. Bouch hung in there, gutsed it out. The first 30 or 40 minutes of his innings were very tense, very very tense, as much tension as I have ever experienced. The series was on the line, right then and there. I was living and breathing every ball with Mark. Flintoff couldn't go on for ever; this was probably the last roll of the dice. We needed Bouch to survive this spell and then concentrate on just playing himself in and settling down.

For a while every ball survived felt like an achievement. Then, slowly but surely, we started to build the partnership. The longer we stayed, the more desperate England became. There was less noise, less encouragement, their faces became sterner.

The bowlers started bowling straighter, attacking the stumps and looking to bowl more and more wicket-taking deliveries, but the result was more balls to hit, more 'four-balls'. Panesar was particularly frustrated at not being able to get rid of me, considering how much the rough was helping him, and he started to lose his cool and then his rhythm.

A tired Anderson came back for yet another spell late in the afternoon and we cut and drove him twice to the boundary and took 10 off the over. I was still rigidly working in 10 run 'sections' – sometimes it felt like it had taken an hour to put one together – now suddenly we had one in a single over. Then, when I started cover driving Flintoff really well, it was a sure sign that I was in control and the tide had turned in our direction.

I was still desperate not to get too far ahead of myself, however. Even when we only needed 40 or 50, I refused to contemplate winning. We've all seen enough batting collapses to know what can happen, particularly under pressure. I could hear Snapper's (Jeremy Snape's) voice in my head: 'Focus on the process, not the goal.' My process was to score the next 10 runs. And then I realised that my process had put me within sight of a hundred.

It came with a nudge past point off Panesar, which gave me two. They may have been the only two runs I scored off him through the off-side all day! Great moment, especially at Edgbaston, with all the memories from five years earlier when I really kick-started my career with the double hundred and the SA record. Over the years I'd often thought about that game and what direction the series would have taken if England hadn't been saved by the rain and we'd won it. There's nothing you can do about the weather, so you'll never find a cricketer who's bitter or angry about rain, but it was certainly a pity from our perspective that we were denied a win. Still, here I was at the same venue with another hundred and a chance to win not only a Test match, but a series.

If someone had said five years ago that, one day, I would play an innings better than that 277 I would have found it hard to imagine. But here it was. Chasing a large fourth innings target under pressure on a deteriorating wicket made it better already, but I was sharply aware that it would be forgotten very quickly if it wasn't a match-winning century. I was determined that it wouldn't become a 'good but not good enough' innings.

So we worked ten runs at a time and started to score quicker and quicker and the game started to develop. As time went on runs were starting to flow, myself and Bouch were starting to get going and the score was starting to get closer and closer. I looked up at the boys and saw Morne padded up, I saw Mickey on the big screen stand up and want to move and the boys pulled him back down in his chair. The boys are quite superstitious with those sorts of things and don't like to move much when things are starting to go well.

They bought Flintoff back for what would obviously be his final spell – this really was the last roll of the dice. He was clearly the main strike bowler and he'd troubled all the right-handers with the dodgy sightscreen behind him. I asked Bouch if he wanted me to take most of the strike to try and see off Flintoff. I was very pleased and grateful when he said 'no'. Actually, I think Bouch was reading the game the same way as me – that Flintoff had been bowling virtually all day, was tired and desperate for wickets and would most likely serve up a few 'freebies' and four-balls!

Even when we just needed 30, I was thinking: 'That's three more sections of 10.' One wicket could change everything. I looked at the stand which had exploded with emotion three hours earlier, and it was flat. I saw men sitting with empty plastic beer cups and I thought: 'Well, if they've stopped drinking then things must be very serious.' But one wicket could still change things.

The first time I even thought about the target was when we got to 120. By then I was so sure I would stay until the end and score between half and 60 per cent of the runs that I started halving the total we needed. So at 120 I thought: 'If I can't back the tail for 50 runs between them then I'm doing them a disservice!'

But I was fortunate to have Bouch with me – he has always handled pressure well – and, in my opinion, hasn't always received the recognition he deserves. He's inconspicuous behind the stumps and he's brilliant with fielding angles, he always notices if someone is too fine or too square. And he knows the bowlers and their actions so well – as well as they do, probably. He's a superb on-field communicator and always has an idea or suggestion when a captain is looking for a bit of help.

Needless to say, batting with the tail often means scoring 40,

50 or 60, rarely headline-grabbing stuff, but almost always vital to the team. He's prepared to do the dirty work and has probably become used to not being appreciated outside the team as much as he might be. I was especially grateful to have his experience at a time like that.

The last big decision we had to make was whether we would claim the extra half hour or come back to finish it on the fifth morning. There was a new ball round the corner: if one of us was out, Morne would be up against it. The light was deteriorating, too, so we decided to think about it for a couple of overs.

Just two balls before the close of play I told Aleem Dar that we would like to take the extra half an hour. It was definitely the right thing to do – their bowlers had worked so hard during what had been an extended session anyway. The last thing they would have wanted was to keep going for another seven or eight overs.

Vaughan brought Pietersen on to bowl, which was a clever move, not just because the quick bowlers were tired. He has a funny habit of taking wickets, and not always with good deliveries. But he started off with a couple of loose deliveries and we picked up two cheap boundaries. Suddenly we were there – almost. One boundary needed.

Pietersen dropped another delivery too short and I pulled it through midwicket for four and my whole body suddenly went cold. My eyes, which had focused so well, were suddenly blurry (not from tears, not yet anyway) and the satisfaction hit me like a wave.

Having batted through the whole day was a great achievement, I can't deny that, and there had been periods of pressure which I had not experienced before, which made it even better. But while it was great to look up at the scoreboard and see that I'd made 154, it wasn't about my innings and that won't be my abiding memory of the day. To have hit the winning runs to win a series in England and then see the boys trying to charge on to the field with dignity and dive all over me to celebrate, that is what I'll never forget. The shared feeling of success that you experience when you achieve something rare or very special as a team is hard to survive. No, it's not a matter of life and death, it's a game. But it's a physically and mentally demanding game and the results mean an awful lot to many, many people.

I was physically tired and emotionally drained but delirious with happiness, too. I'm sure it wasn't just the tiredness making me feel delirious. This was a moment in history that we could all be proud of, and we were aware of the significance. For guys like Makhaya, Jacques and Bouch, it was something they'd been waiting ten years to achieve after the controversial ending to the 1998 tour. For me, it was a beautiful way to banish the frustrations of the 2003 tour, when we led 2-1 but lost the final Test to square the series.

Jeez it was a really special feeling.

After all the media commitments we had a team photo in the dressing room, which is massive at Edgbaston, more like a small town hall! Then a huge celebration could really begin. It was probably around 7:30 or even 8:00 by the time the fines meeting began and there were plenty of empty beer bottles around. Many people have asked me over the years whether it's awkward having quite a few non-drinkers in the squad, and the answer is an emphatic 'no'. We had become so used to each others' space and company that, as long as we could see each other happy and celebrating, it didn't matter what the preferred method of celebration entailed.

Neil Mac headed up the fines meeting with Bouch, and it was one of the funniest things I have ever been a part of. We felt more than just a close team, we were like family. We'd been through an awful lot together and we'd been getting on so well. Even the 'family arguments' we had from time to time ended up with a laugh.

Mac and Bouch made Jakes down a beer directly in front of a high-powered fan as punishment for his moaning about being made to bowl into the wind all match, and they made me down a beer or two in a compromised position for having *die groot balles* to bat through to the end. We had all sacrificed a lot to get to this point and the warmth we experienced towards each other that evening was something we'll never forget.

We climbed on board the team bus singing, and we were still singing when we walked into the hotel where so many people had been waiting for us – the South African media, the fans and many of our family and friends were all in the hotel bar. After a quick shower we were all downstairs again to share 'the moment' (albeit a long-lasting one) with everyone.

I had a beer with the media guys and it was great to see how much it meant to them, too. We partied till the early hours of the morning in the bar. It was a wonderful feeling, and a great evening, and something that I will keep close to me for a very long time.

At about 11 pm I was struck with the reality that I had eaten nothing since breakfast. A meal replacement drink at lunch was all I'd had. So, careful not to ruin the party, I slipped out of the hotel to find some food. There was a Lebanese shwarma café just a few hundred metres away and within minutes I was sitting alone with a plastic knife and fork and a paper plate and reflecting on what had happened. There were a few happy people drifting past the café window, one of whom stopped briefly and looked at me with that unmistakable 'he looks a bit like Graeme Smith' expression, but for the first time all day I was alone. It was the first chance I'd had to think about what had happened and it was most certainly the first time any of it sank in. I knew then that I would need to have my thoughts together for the next morning's media enquir-ies.

It was probably the best knock I have ever played. I am a very lucky man already to have some special innings to choose from, but to have played like that with so much at stake ... I obviously hoped I would play a few more important innings in my career, but that evening, if somebody had said 'that was it – the highlight of your career' – I don't think I could have had much to complain about. To have been so calm and controlled under pressure, to have been in that 'zone' for so long – it was amazing. It was so rewarding.

The next morning we were woken by the hotel fire alarm drill-ing straight through our heads. It was probably only 7:30 am, but it felt like we'd only been in bed for half an hour. We had to walk down the stairs from the 10th or 12th floor feeling pretty hung-over and sore from the celebrations and the emotions of the last four days. I bumped into several of the boys looking suitably rag-ged as I made my way down the stairs. J-P was downstairs on the pavement in his boxer shorts, which was hysterical. A few of the others were looking very rough. We were out on the street for 45 minutes while they checked the fire alarm and the fire engines came and went. It was all extremely funny. Odd how these things are made even funnier when you're all feeling dreadful.

Winning on the fourth day meant we had a full day off to recover and we ended up going for an excellent lunch at a little restaurant next to a canal. People often say that, wherever you are in the world, you'll find someone from India. I think the same can be said about South Africans! There were certainly a lot in the centre of Birmingham that afternoon! But it was also very noticeable and much appreciated how many Englishmen came up to us and congratulated us.

I had tried not to think about my elbow during the Test but I knew it was serious. I'd taken a pile of pain-killers for both the elbow and my back, which I hadn't enjoyed doing at all. I've always tried to keep medication down to a minimum and the thought of all those pills and injections had made me feel queasy. A day after the Test, however, the back was well on its way to recovery but the elbow was becoming a disaster.

The following morning we were travelling to London. I checked my phone messages on the way down to breakfast and there were five or six that didn't make much sense: journalists and radio stations wanting comment on the England captaincy. Weird. As I walked into breakfast an English journalist approached me and was quickly joined by a couple more. They said Vaughan was going to resign. I was completely taken by surprise. It had never occurred to me, so I didn't have a comment. I hadn't ever thought about it.

I did, however, while I was eating. I was still surprised. He had been a really great captain and was always ahead of the game; he had always had a calm and assured demeanour and always had the respect of his team. There had been stages during the series where we'd managed to exert a lot of pressure on him, and I'd seen a different side to his captaincy personality, but I had always assumed he would weather the storm and bounce back fighting.

I honestly felt genuinely sad. The things he had said, and the obvious emotions he was going through, resonated strongly with me. We'd been captains for the same period of time and the pressures which he spoke about, the responsibilities, how they can wear you down was all stuff that I recognised and had been through, and am still going through. I guess all captains do.

When Nasser resigned at Edgbaston on the last tour five years earlier, I was just 22 years old with a naïve, balls-to-the-wall approach to the job, trying to make my way in the world and make an impression. I had absolutely no idea why Nasser would want to give it up. Nothing he said at the time made any sense to me.

Now, watching Vaughan, I realised how far I'd come and I felt deeply for him. I sent him an sms wishing him all the best in the future. He's a great cricketer and a great ambassador for the game and nobody would be happier than me to see him be successful again in the future. Hopefully never against us though! A man in his position is required to give so much of himself and his time to the game and England should always be proud of him and the job he did. The England captain has a big influence in the game and, with a powerful and wealthy board, it's vital for the world game that he has vision beyond his own team and is passionate about the long-term success of the sport. In my experience, he had all those things and did his job extremely well.

There was plenty of talk about Michael's decision on the bus to London. Some of it was a bit unflattering from the younger guys and it made me smile. I might have been the same five years earlier. Wait until their next tour to England, they'll be thinking differently then.

By now the card games on the bus were becoming extremely competitive. We watched a very good DVD and stopped at a highway service station to pick up some lunch. Funny how novel and pleasant it still felt to be driving in a bus with the ability to watch a movie, have a cup of coffee, eat a meal at a table and go for a pee whenever you need to.

When we arrived at the hotel my phone was going berserk. My message inbox was full for days. So many messages of congratulation from all over the world, most from home, obviously, with many tales of how happy people were and many stories about where people had been when they watched the final few overs.

There were many, many interview requests, too: from *You* magazine to SuperSport. I was still feeling really tired and drained, so I found it very difficult to relive the innings, the match or the series. I wasn't the best interviewee at that stage. I could have gone straight to bed when we arrived and slept until the following morning, but that wasn't an option, unfortunately. It's a part of my life I've gradually become more and more used to and better at handling. The most important point is to understand that nobody is trying to make your life difficult. Not only are they doing their job, but people are interested in how the captain and the team are feeling. I haven't always balanced the requirements well, and there have been times when my game has suffered as a result, but I think I managed reasonably this time.

The Oval Test

The most important discussion before the final Test revolved around selection. Did we give the 'squad' players a Test, or stick to the '1st XI'? Training sessions for a couple of days had been a bit off. We were like a balloon that had popped. The series victory was a huge weight off everybody's mind: we were emotionally and mentally drained. An England tour is heavy duty, the media and the public are always there, on your mind or in your space. Or both! I was aware of the problem but I didn't want to admit it. I'm not sure I knew what to do about it, how to turn things around. I guess I just adopted the 'it'll be all right on the night' approach.

Kevin Pietersen's appointment as Michael Vaughan's successor had been another significant distraction; with the rich history between us I'd faced a thousand questions about his ability to do the job. My views were simple and I stayed strictly to what I believed and never became entangled in another media conflict. He's a wonderful batsman and it will be interesting to see how his approach to his own game, his free-flowing nature and his 'I do it my way' attitude – which had been so successful as an individual – could succeed for him as a captain.

I said repeatedly before the Test that only a fool would judge KP on what happened at The Oval, and that he deserved at least six months in the job before people started forming an opinion of his captaincy. I didn't really have an opinion on whether he would be successful, to be honest. I could see a few reasons why he might struggle, but he had a history of proving people wrong and there's undoubtedly a touch of genius about him, so I wasn't committing either way – publicly or privately. I guess the only doubt I had was about his ability to swallow enough pride and make enough sacrifices with his own game to succeed. But I was prepared to be surprised.

We decided to go with the same team. We felt that it was the right thing to do: the guys deserved to play the final game. We spoke endlessly about our desire to finish on a high, and we talked a good talk, too! The keys to our success had been our patience, our discipline, our focus and our ability to outperform England at the key moments. But our patience, despite faltering on a couple of occasions, had won the series. We had left the ball brilliantly, we had bowled with control at key moments but, generally, we had batted better than we had bowled throughout the first three Tests.

The top six had adopted the 'never satisfied' approach with great success and that had been the greatest difference between the sides. We'd been ruthless and we were determined to keep that hardness. As I said, we talked the talk very well. But walking the walk was easier said than done.

AB played brilliantly for his hundred but generally our skills and discipline lacked the edge we'd had previously. We had a few moments of success but never sustained them. We dropped catches, which we hadn't done previously, and Pietersen played tremendously well to score a hundred in his first game as captain. We dropped him twice and that obviously contributed to us losing.

Harmison's recall was also significant – with bat as well as ball, oddly enough. He bowled really well after a period out of the team and then belted 49 at the back of the innings, which did a lot to transform a good total into a winning one.

Later, we realised we had learned a few painful but important lessons, both as individuals and as a team. None of us had been through anything similar to the emotional 'flatness' that we experienced before and during that Test match, but we systematically tried to learn from it. It was a disappointing way to end the series, and we all felt we could and would do things differently if we ever encountered a similar situation again.

Perhaps we should have made one or two changes to the XI and given some fresh faces an opportunity to try and share in the success of the tour. But who? Nobody was putting their hand up and saying 'rest me'. You wouldn't expect them to. At the same time, nobody was really beating themselves up about losing the Test either. Jeez, we'd won the series for goodness sake – and that was still reason to celebrate.

Holding the trophy in the changing room and sipping a quiet beer (as opposed to the noisy ones we had at Edgbaston) was, once again, quite emotional. Very emotional, in fact. Suddenly everything that I'd kept bottled up inside for two months came pouring out of me. Not noisily or embarrassingly, but I certainly shed a silent tear or two. I really believe in the theory that emotions are best set free rather than trapped inside you, but as a captain and leader you have to compromise on that theory for the good of the team. You're not acting in the best interests of the rest of the squad by wearing your heart on your sleeve all the time.

I'm not a regular shedder of tears, but I had a few in my eyes that evening. Bloody hell, it wasn't only that last two or three months we'd been preparing for and talking about this tour, it had been a couple of years. Five years in my case … and ten years for others. We were all quite emotional.

We had a good night out in London afterwards, with much clinking of glasses to celebrate the first post-isolation win in England. In between the beers and celebration it struck me often that losing is a part of winning, that here we were celebrating victory having just lost a game. You have to be able to celebrate both victory and defeat, because you are never going to win everything. There was much back-slapping and hugging that night, guys telling each other how much they had appreciated each other's performances at various times. Funny how much more animated we all become after the event and how much more honest we are when it's all done and dusted.

I was already thinking about the one-day series. Test specialists were about to leave and new faces about to arrive. It wasn't a new scenario but still needed a careful balancing act, with energetic new guys bouncing around the place and others who were focusing mainly on trying to rest and stay below the parapet. The new guys are always keen to train and have nets while the majority of us are keen to rest in between focusing on our one-day skills.

The one-day series
Leeds 22 August 2008
Nottingham 26 August 2008
The Oval 29 August 2008
Lord's 31 August 2008
Cardiff 3 September 2008

The itinerary was actually kind to us, with a fun and light-hearted game against an England 'veteran XI' at John-Paul Getty's ground in the beautiful English countryside. It was far more of a social event than a serious cricket event and the intention was to raise funds for the PCA, which works closely with our own SACA, so we all bought into the occasion and thoroughly enjoyed the day.

Then we moved on to Leicester to play the England Lions (A-team). We rested our senior players and gave an opportunity to those who hadn't played much cricket on the Test tour, as well as the new guys who hadn't played much cricket for months because it was winter back home. We won, but that wasn't the main objective.

Jeremy Snape organised an afternoon braai before our next game. Some old friends of his, Tim and Annie Haywood, owned a beautiful house in the Derbyshire countryside and we enjoyed a special day cooking our own meat and doing some very English things like playing croquet. It was cold and grey again, unfortunately, but it was a bloody good day anyway, an antidote to the inevitable hotel cabin fever that sets in on a long tour.

Derby was the venue for our second warm-up game. We pretty well played our first XI. My elbow was dreadful at this but I was in a state of denial. I couldn't pick up a glass of water without pain, let alone a bat. It was cold, it was grey, and it was miserable. It was dreadful all round. And we lost, heavily. Embarrassing, but not the end of the world.

Then it was Durham for a Twenty20. By now we were all flat. The weather had been awful for 10 days and we were wearing beanies and rain jackets the whole time. We hadn't had a proper training session outdoors for weeks, and after two days' training indoors at Durham, they announced 24 hours early that the game was abandoned due to a waterlogged outfield. We weren't having much fun!

The one-day 'specialists' hadn't played much cricket before they arrived and now they were spending more time dodging rain showers than playing cricket. It wasn't ideal. In fact, we were so desperate for some time on grass that we went to Headingley an hour and a half early before the day/night match just to use the nets.

We started all right with the ball but then bowled really poorly at the death, which Pietersen and Flintoff loved. They carved the bowling up and what should have been a total of 240 or 250 suddenly became 275 with KP making 90 in no time.

It was a very different looking line-up at Headingley. Herschelle was back, Vernon Philander played, J-P was back in the team at number five and Johan Botha was there, too. Despite having two members of the top six who had about 25 minutes' batting between them in the last three months, we actually chased quite well and had a genuine chance of getting there but for a big wobble in the middle overs. Jakes played especially well and enjoyed a good partnership with AB, but we lost our way and faded to 255.

Trent Bridge was the venue for the second ODI, and naturally the talk was about the need to improve. But we were becoming a bit sick and tired of talking: we wanted – and needed – to walk the walk now. Rarely can so much determination have resulted in so little! We were thoroughly embarrassed, bowled out for just 83. It was supposed to be another day-nighter, but they didn't even get to turn the floodlights on. Stuart Broad bowled exceptionally well with the new ball, but we had no excuse. It was one of the first times in my career when I'd experienced genuine booing – not in fun or jest, but anger. It was horrible.

To have made the journey from uninhibited joy and celebration to humiliation in three weeks was very, very frustrating. We weren't only bowled out for 83 – we then lost by 10 wickets in a dozen or so overs. We didn't just let ourselves down, we let down hundreds of thousands of South Africans at home and several thousand at the ground. No wonder they were angry. ODI tickets in the UK are extremely expensive and they'd just been short-changed on about four hours' entertainment.

The press conferences and interviews are terrible after days like that. You want nothing more than to go and hide and sulk in the changing room with your team mates. It is a part of captaincy that I have never enjoyed, having to take the responsibility for the team's performance. It is a lesson I learned quite early on and one which still brings a smile to my face. When the team wins, it is the team which takes the credit and celebrates. When the team gets hammered, it is the captain who has lost! But that's the way it is – I've made my peace with it.

The great irony for me is that I was about five minutes away from withdrawing from the team on the eve of the match. I hadn't been able to bat at all in the nets leading up to the game and the pain was incessant. I don't know why I played. It could have been Jacques up there facing the media!

There was absolutely no point in dissecting the performance afterwards. I'm not afraid to speak the hard words which are sometimes necessary to bring the best out of players, but this was a time for everyone to take personal responsibility for how poor we had each been. Every one of us had to find a way to come to terms with what happened, as individuals, before we could address anything as a team. All I said was that there can be no excuses for a performance like that, and that I hoped everyone remembered that we were a much better team than was indicated by a performance like that!

In the few days' gap between the Trent Bridge game and the third match at the Oval, I went to see a surgeon in London about my elbow. Nothing of much significance showed up on a scan but the pain had been increasing daily. The medical staff, Shane and Doc Moosajee, had decided that I needed a significant break before the season started again in a couple of months' time with games against Kenya and Bangladesh. But it was the tour to Australia at the end of the year which was on all of our minds, obviously.

The decision was taken to give me a cortisone injection and send me home for a second opinion and then to start a course of rehab. So that was it – in my last game on what had been a fantastic tour, we were bowled out for 83. I often smiled about it in the months which passed afterwards, but it wasn't very funny leaving the tour in those circumstances at the time. It wasn't very funny leaving the tour early at all, in fact.

Unfortunately, the guys never turned the corner after my

departure and lost at both the Oval and Lord's before the fifth game was washed out in Cardiff. I watched on TV and felt very helpless and uncomfortable. Jakes took over the captaincy because of his experience and the way he handles himself off the field as much as on it. When things aren't going well in England you don't want a 23-year-old captain fronting up to the media on a regular basis – he'll be cooked.

If there was any consolation, it was in the lessons we learned. We cannot have guys arriving in England after two months off. On future tours to England we have three options: travel with an extensive squad and keep them busy, try and place 'reserve' players with English clubs and call them up if and when you need them – or, and this may be the most practical option – keep a small reserve squad in training at a facility in South Africa such as the High Performance Centre at RAU.

We spoke about the need to become more emotionally robust in the future, too. We couldn't afford to burst like a punctured balloon every time we achieved something special, no matter how fantastic it was. There's nothing wrong with having massive peaks on your emotional chart – we like them! But we needed to learn how to avoid having deep troughs afterwards.

7.

Honing our skills

Kenya and Bangladesh: October – November 2008

LIMITED OVERS VS KENYA
Bloemfontein 31 October 2008
Kimberley 2 November 2008

LIMITED OVERS VS BANGLADESH
Potchefstroom 7 November 2008
Benoni 9 November 2008
East London 12 November 2008

TWENTY20 VS BANGLADESH
Johannesburg 5 November 2008

TESTS VS BANGLADESH
Bloemfontein 19–22 November 2008
Centurion 26–28 November 2008

I had some more scans soon after arriving back. The cortisone injection in England hadn't really worked, so I saw Mike Solomons
in Cape Town and he prescribed a second injection followed by
four weeks of doing absolutely nothing – with my arm, that is!
It was an aggressive cortisone treatment with plenty of needling
(literally) in order to create bleeding in and around the tendon
in order to encourage and speed up the healing process. I don't
have any experience of childbirth, obviously, but I'd be interested
to know from any mothers who have also had this treatment for
tennis elbow how the two procedures compare for pain! I thought
I was going to pass out.

I did a little gym work, a bit of cardio training, but nothing with the upper body. I wasn't allowed to pick anything up, let alone a cricket bat. No upper body work at all, really. After four weeks the cortisone wore off and I started rehab once again. But after a single session of 'shadow batting' (think air-guitar!) I could feel pain. After a second session the pain felt the same as it had a month earlier. Mike immediately diagnosed a repeat dose of cortisone and 'needling', which made me briefly consider retirement ...

The cortisone gave me welcome relief, but if it didn't work long-term we were facing a very difficult situation looking forward to Australia. It felt like the biggest tour of my life – as England had been – and I was desperate to be a part of it. I would have considered just about anything to find a way of getting through it, even with my dislike of medication. All our planning and focus had been towards Australia from the moment we arrived back from England. To be honest, we'd been thinking about Australia for two years.

The series against Kenya

I didn't take any part in the two ODIs against Kenya. We had a training camp before them in Kimberley at which everyone worked hard at fitness. Just about everybody was ahead of schedule and the test results were great. We could all see the amount of work that had been done after the England tour.

We also invited some new players to the camp to give them a taste of life in the national squad and to see what they were about. We had heard some good things about some players at domestic level, so we were really focusing on that. Lonwabo Tsotsobe impressed everyone, as did Wayne Parnell. Actually, all the new guys made a good impression.

Johan Botha – 'Botes' – had officially been appointed vice-captain of the ODI team, so he took charge against Kenya. He has a fantastic work ethic and set a good example. We had an excellent understanding from very early on and I knew he was going to be a valuable ally. With respect to Kenya, we won both games easily, although we were all impressed by their determination and willingness to compete. The influence of two of the four Kirsten brothers, Andrew and Peter, on the coaching staff was obvious.

Throughout this period I had been diligent about my rehab. I was with the squad all the time but doing my own thing because I couldn't bat or do fielding drills. Shadow batting with a stump and carrying a hammer around in my left hand for most of the day are memories I won't forget. But it felt like there were about 300 exercises I was assigned to do – all of which I did. Sometimes through gritted teeth.

The series against Bangladesh

I was feeling pretty good when I came back to play against Bangladesh in Benoni. Shane and the Doc are trained to err on the side of caution, and I respect that very much, so I understood their caution about me coming back when I did. They might have preferred another week or two, but I knew my body and believed I was ready.

I had missed the action more than I had admitted, even to myself. I was straight back into it, and felt good. I made 60-odd in that game and had no alarms as we won the series comfortably. I had ice-packs on the elbow from time to time, which interested the more observant members of the media, but it was precautionary more than anything.

The two Test matches against Bangladesh were far more important, however. We spoke for hours about the importance of honing our Test skills before Australia. We were very, very aware of not being disrespectful to Bangladesh, but at the same time, we felt it was important to be honest about our priorities and where our focus was. We wanted to spend as much time in the middle as possible and then bowl quality overs. We felt it would be dishonest and, frankly, disrespectful to Bangladesh to pretend that all our focus and energy was on beating them. We wanted as much tough and hard competition as they could give us, but it was Australia who were commanding our attention. And Mickey conveyed that message to the media in as diplomatic a way as possible.

A huge distraction was the inaugural Champions League due to be staged in India in the week before the tour. Having carefully organised a 10-day preparation period in Perth before the first Test, the reality was that eight or nine of us were only going to be joining the rest of the squad four days before the Test. But that was the way cricket was working at the moment.

We made 441-9 in the first Test in Bloem and I made 150, which was awesome for me because I'd done so little for so long before. It wasn't the core that mattered, it was the time I was at the crease. Every half hour I would think 'will the pain come back?' But it didn't, at least nothing like it had been.

Hashim played beautifully and his hundred cemented the belief that he was the 'finished article' for Test cricket and was as ready as you can ever be for Australia.

Bangladesh followed on and we beat them by 129 runs. Everyone was looking in good shape, although it was obvious that we had a little bit of work to do with Morne – he was all over the place, brilliant and erratic at the same time. But I always felt he would come right as time went on, gaining confidence and being encouraged to keep things simple. When you are struggling you get a million pieces of advice, all very well-meaning, but to a young guy who is still learning about the game and learning about his action, they can be problematic. He obviously has enormous potential, everyone knows that, and he sometimes suffers as a result of trying to live up to it. I just wanted him to develop naturally and kept telling him to relax – the more he plays the better he will become.

The second Test, at Centurion, was interesting for a moment. We crashed to 134-5 in our first innings, still over a hundred behind, before Ashwell and Bouch scored hundreds in a sixth wicket stand of 170-odd. It wasn't an easy wicket to bat on but we won comfortably in the end by an innings and 48 runs. We won both Tests by an innings but, encouragingly, there was an acceptance within the team that our skills would have to improve significantly if we were to make the dream of winning in Australia come true.

Goolam Raja had been on a recce to Australia during this time to try and sort out a couple of issues that had adversely affected us last time. There had been moments of racism and a couple of security issues when leaving grounds that had made us all feel uncomfortable. Not life-threatening, but very uncomfortable. Although, who knows what is life-threatening and what isn't any more?

The negative emotions we had experienced three years earlier were something we were keen to avoid, so Goolam's brief was to take care of some very simple – but vital – details. We could do without screaming, abusive fans being able to run towards us as we boarded the bus after a day's play.

Apart from that, we would prefer to pay for net bowlers who weren't from the local under-15 'B' team or 39-year-olds in need of a bit of extra cash. OK, that's probably harsh, but we certainly felt that some extra investment in our net bowlers would be worthwhile.

We started talking in earnest about Australia during the second Test. It was very honest and open, about how we wouldn't allow any squad or team member to become 'isolated', and how we would stand together. We had already talked about the importance of respecting the media, and we believed that, but at the time a player can become a 'target' unless his team mates stick up for him.

We spoke about our natural instincts and what characterised us as cricketers and people – showing guts and determination when things were tough, when our backs were against the wall.

We also discussed talking on the field in different languages so the Aussies couldn't work out what we were doing and where we were heading. All South African teams have done it, but it was still important to chat again – especially with guys like Dale, who barely speak Afrikaans. Mine's not that hot either.

We spoke about discipline, pride and removing emotion from our decision-making processes. Another important point was the removal of the phrase 'best team in the world' from our discussions. South African teams had been using that term for over a decade, as a mark of respect, but 'Snapper' was quick to point out how psychologically counterproductive it actually was.

They are a very, very good team, but so are we. We needed to be better mentally prepared this time. We all realised how brainwashed we had become. Years and years of hearing about 'Australia, the best team in the world'. Yes, they had been, but that was no frame of mind to have entering a series against them. You're at least 1-0 down before you've bowled or faced a ball.

During the Centurion Test the terrible news of the bombings in Mumbai reached us and the immediate consequence was that the Champions League tournament wasn't going to be taking place. It meant a massive loss of income for many players and Boards, but the wider implications were even more scary.

We had all stayed in those hotels, and would presumably be staying in them again. We would have been staying in them during the Champions League, in fact. It was yet another reality check about the world we live in and the importance of security. India is such an incredible place to play cricket in, and to tour, and I was deeply saddened that criminals might have jeopardised that.

The tournament was postponed to a later date: the only bonus to us, albeit a pretty shallow one, was that we could all get together in Australia earlier and prepare properly as a team.

8.

Deep, deep satisfaction Down Under

Australia: December 2009 – January 2009

TEST MATCHES
Perth 17–21 December 2008
Melbourne 26–30 December 2008
Sydney 3–7 January 2009

TWENTY20
Melbourne 11 January 2009
Brisbane 13 January 2009

LIMITED OVERS
Melbourne 16 January 2009
Hobart 18 January 2009
Sydney 23 January 2009
Adelaide 26 January 2009
Perth 30 January 2009

We arrived around midday and immediately started the task of overcoming the jetlag. Although we were going to be there for ten days before the Test started, in order to make the best use of the preparation time we wanted to get our body clocks onto local time as quickly as possible.

Goolam had arranged a boat trip on the magnificent Swan River that afternoon with a fridge full of cool drinks and a few healthy snacks. Its main purpose was to keep everyone awake in order to have a really good sleep that night, but it was thoroughly enjoyed by everyone. We relaxed and enjoyed the sunshine and the views. Perth is a very attractive city to look at, especially from the river.

The next morning we had a little run around at the ground, no actual nets, and then went to the beach in the afternoon with a couple of cooler boxes of water and energy drinks and snacks. We played a whole bunch of different beach games, frisbee, racquet ball, touch rugby ... and we swam, too, of course! The objective once again, apart from having fun and doing a bit more 'bonding', was to keep everyone moving and stop them from going back to their hotel rooms and sleeping!

It worked perfectly for the players but for poor Goolam the whole thing backfired spectacularly when he sat down for a 'little rest' in the shade of a large rock and fell fast asleep. That would have been fine if a couple of seagulls hadn't woken him up by dropping several large bombs all over him and his clothes. He didn't think it was very funny but I'm afraid he was in a minority of one.

On the third day we started work on our cricket skills – although, once again, I was sidelined because I'd had yet another cortisone injection in my elbow after the Centurion Test match and was still under strict orders to keep it stable. I wasn't going to be taking part in the first warm-up, a one-day game against a Western Australia XI that became quite a contentious issue.

Over the last couple of years we had learnt exactly what we needed to do as preparation and how to maximise our practice opportunities. This time, instead of playing a one-day game as a limited overs match, which would have been of limited use if not actually set us back a bit in terms of Test preparation, we wanted to treat it as if it was the first 50 overs of a Test innings.

We didn't want to be under pressure to play one-day cricket and, frankly, the result wasn't important to us. It was about the 'feel' of spending time in the middle and honing our skills. The WA players, understandably, wanted a contest of some sort so they played it as a one-day game and the Aussie media claimed victory afterwards and slammed Jakes for batting too slowly! It was hilarious, to be honest, and the senior players were unaffected by the kerfuffle. So were the younger guys, once they realised that we weren't affected by what the media said.

We achieved our objectives – the top order spent quality time at the crease, most of the bowlers had a good workout ('Lopsy' Tsotsobe impressed all of us again) and we all spent time being knocked about by the 'Fremantle Doctor', a prevailing wind as relentless as the Cape Doctor.

The first four or five days of the tour had been smooth and calm and the first few press conferences had been relaxed and issue-free. We'd got our message across without being accused of arrogance and we hadn't stirred the pot in any way. We were always amenable towards the media, which was made a bit easier this time because economic realities meant there were only four or five journalists around during the preparation time, so it was easier to form a relationship.

There were no big statements from us or about us – and no big statements about Australia, either. We just wanted people to see us for what we were – happy, hard-working and very determined.

We had chatted about the occasional problem on previous tours when players' comments had been deliberately twisted in a tabloid manner to imply something different, but now there was no sign of that at all. I wasn't sure whether it was because we were better prepared, or whether there had been a shift away from that sort of newspaper writing in Australia.

We spent a lot of time doing video analysis, having changed the way we went about it. We now had a core 'analysis group' comprising me, Bouch, Fletch, Mickey, Snapey and Vinnie, and we'd come up with a few theories and tactics before getting the relevant people involved. Then all the batsmen would get together to watch their bowlers and discuss them – likewise the bowlers with their batsmen.

One of the key tactics for us may have been obvious, but it was worth talking about often so that it became ingrained. Without Shane Warne in their ranks we believed that substantial partnerships at the top of our order, both in runs and in time, would have a double effect. We felt that Ricky would consequently push his fast bowlers harder than he should, bringing them back earlier and bowling them for longer. With no Warne to throw the ball to for an hour and a half, he would struggle if we could dig in and bat for a long time, with the result that Brett Lee and the others would risk injury and exhaustion. It was a good plan in theory!

I had lengthy one-on-one chats with each of our own bowlers and gave them a 'battle plan' for each batsman. It had a picture of the batsman and then the intended plan for the first 20 balls, followed by the tactics if he 'got in' and was starting to settle. It wasn't rocket science, it was simple – which is exactly how we wanted to keep it, as much as possible. Simple, but (hopefully) effective. It's amazing how much difference it can make having something written down, and with a graphic. It's simply the equivalent of taking minutes at an important meeting.

I believed we had some really good game plans against the Australian top six, but they were reliant on the bowlers absorbing the information, reading their check-lists first thing in the morning and last thing at night, and then implementing them in the nets for three or four days before the Test. They all knew what was expected of them – and how much they had to improve as a unit if we were to succeed against Australia.

As always, however, the main theme was around discipline and creating pressure as much as possible. We had plans for specific batsmen, based around their strengths and weaknesses, but they did revolve around bowling 'miracle' balls to them. For the most part, as with all top international batsmen, the emphasis was on just bowling the majority of deliveries in the right place to prevent them from scoring.

From a practical point of view, a couple of guys were going to have to work their backsides off into the wind. Jacques and Harry were going to be our main men for that job. I volunteered them (with the promise that Jakes, at least, would get the occasional spell downwind).

Our batting plans were also based on simplicity – be really strong for the first 20 balls: they always attack you hardest during that period. Patience was critical – we had to leave the good balls consistently and be mentally strong enough to absorb periods of pressure when we weren't scoring. But absolute commitment to every shot was critical: whether it was the best forward defence ever played or a full-blooded cover drive, we said absolutely no 50/50 shots.

We discussed at length the role of their spinner and being able to use him as an opportunity to put the rest of the bowling attack under pressure. That wasn't taking anything for granted, far from it. But, whoever the spinner was going to be, he wasn't Warne – and filling those shoes would make anybody feel the strain. He was going to be nervous – and we needed to be ruthless.

Finally, good, confident body language was going to be important. The effect it has, from both junior and senior players, is often under-estimated.

Matthew Hayden has always had the body language – and he was a key figure. He was still a fantastic batsman, world-class, even though it was the autumn of his career. His only weakness, if you could call it that, was that he fell into the 'ego' type category. Perhaps we hadn't recognised that before, or been able to capitalise on it. Nothing made him happier than when he was able to power his way through a bowling line, using his physical size to intimidate bowlers. Our answer was going to be to try and manipulate that ego and then cut off his favourite angles to stop him scoring. We decided not to have a cover point for him, which looked unusual, but we would probably have a short mid-off in a catching position to distract his eye, and then a deeper mid-off behind him. If we could drive him onto the back foot by bowling back of a length on off stump, or just outside off stump, then perhaps we could nick him off to the slips. But first the plan was for Dale to swing it back into him at pace and trap him lbw.

Makhaya was going to bowl around the wicket at about 'fourth stump' and look to get him driving at wide-ish deliveries. Morne's plan was similar, but with his pace and bounce, he might pose added problems if he could hit a consistent line and length. His only special job was to hit him hard with a really good bouncer early on, in the first eight balls or so, but then not bounce him again for a while as we tried to play with his ego.

We had similarly detailed plans for every Australian player. In some cases we put in hours of work and came up with the same conclusions that people had reached years ago, and in some cases we came up with a new strategy. But in all cases, we put in hours and hours of work.

It was the final training day before the Test. I was feeling good – calm but reasonably confident. Anticipation had built steadily through the nine days – a little too steadily, I thought at times – but tension and excitement was exactly where I hoped and wanted it to be. The team was settled. Or so I thought.

Makhaya bowled a jaffer to Ashwell in the final nets session which rose up off a good length and broke his thumb. Ashwell had been an integral part of the batting line-up and had handled so many pressure situations so well. It was the last thing we needed on the eve of such an important Test, but the consolation was the amount of respect and trust we had in the ability of J-P, who had been travelling with the team for so long. As much as Ashwell didn't deserve to miss out in such a fashion, J-P had done everything – and more – to justify a chance.

He had worked particularly hard on the mental side of his game with Snapey, who had prepared J-P in exactly the same way he would have done if he was going to make his debut. He did not have a premonition that this would happen, apparently, but we were all very grateful, relieved and impressed at how calm and assured J-P was on the morning of the Test. He seemed extremely self-assured, which I took as positive sign. Normally your expectations of a young batsman on debut would be modest, but mine of J-P were not.

By the evening before the Test there weren't any doubts at all about how big the series was. It had been relatively quiet in Perth for the first week, but now there wasn't a single dissenting voice around the world – at least not that we heard: it was being hailed as the world championship of Test cricket, and even Ricky Ponting had said: 'Yep, fair enough – if they beat us here then they deserve to be called champions.' That was something no Australian captain had said about any team for a decade and a half.

Snapey seized on that quote immediately and cut it out of the newspaper the following morning. He had a photograph of Ricky on a small poster and drew bubble thoughts around his head containing the various worries and distractions he was experiencing. One of them of course was that he might become the first captain for 16 years to lose a series on home soil, and the first one to lose number one status since the rankings were introduced.

There was a calm confidence around the squad, although there were a few nerves. Just about the right balance, I thought.

The team dinner that evening was excellent. We did our usual toasts before and after dinner and then drifted off towards our rooms for an early night. I thought there might be a few guys struggling to get to sleep as I saw them leave – and a few early risers, too!

The Perth test

I woke somewhere between 4:30 and 5:00, as I usually do. My brain switches on very early and there isn't much I can do about it. I can't go back to sleep but I do try and stop focusing on the cricket too much by watching TV or reading. In years gone by I've been mentally exhausted by the start of a Test match, so I've learned my lesson. But as hard as I try to distract myself, it's difficult to focus on the weather report or an analysis of the financial markets when your brain is screaming 'Test match!' It's like telling someone: 'Think of anything you like, but don't think about blue elephants.'

On the way to the ground Makkie spotted a sign on the wall outside a nursery school with three little ducks on it – he wasn't too happy about that so he told the bus driver that we were going to have to take a different route to the ground for the rest of the Test match because he didn't want to drive past three ducks during the Test match. Someone did point out that they were Australian ducks, so maybe it was a good omen, but no – Makkie had decided that it was a bad sign. It made everyone laugh.

I don't know whether it's simply our imagination, or whether there's any truth in it, but on the morning of every really big match there is a distinctive buzz of expectation in the air. We normally arrive two hours before the start of play so there's no more than a couple of thousand people in the ground, but the sense of excitement and expectation is something you can really feel.

The ground started to fill quickly and we had a brilliant warm-up, very intense. The only worry was whether it was a bit too intense! A few of the team noticed the Channel Nine commentators arriving in their smart suits and ties – you couldn't miss them, there were about 20! All the big names, Richie Benaud, Tony Greig, Mark Taylor, Ian Healy ... definitely the 'A' team.

Ricky won the toss and decided to bat. We had just a few minutes left now and I looked at everyone's faces to gauge the mood. Nobody was too tense; nobody had turned pale! Actually, the vibe was good. Like sprinters on the blocks, the bowlers just wanted to get started.

There was just time to reiterate the basic points of the bowling plan and to stress the need for a strong, emphatic first hour and then the need for patience. We were expecting Hayden to start strongly – we knew how he thought: punch us hard in the first hour and we might stay down for the rest of the Test, maybe even the series. He tried.

Hayden hit two powerful fours in the opening couple of overs. The wicket looked good and there was no swing. I thought: 'We're going to have to be strong today'. Wickets would have to be worked for and earned, but the first one would be key for the bowlers to keep their faith. You need to be rewarded for hard work.

Makhaya bowled a beautiful opening spell, especially to Hayden. Ball after ball was in the right area and eventually he pushed at one that was a bit too wide and nicked it to me at first slip. Everything fell into place there!

Sometimes teams make a plan to use verbal intimidation against particular opponents, and to defend themselves against opponents who are known to make regular use of their mouths! Hayden was the king of sledgers, but we didn't have a 'plan' as such. We were just aware of it and nobody was in the mood to back down.

Dale's first delivery was very wide and Hayden said something like: 'Nervous, hey? Well, get used to it, because you're gonna feel like that all day.'

Quick as a flash, Dale replied: 'I'm not the nervous one, that must be you! I'm not the one who has to sit in the middle of the pitch the day before the match trying to picture where I'm going to score my first run.'

Ponting's wicket was even better. Makkie put the ball in the perfect spot, exactly the area we spoken about endlessly. Ricky is vulnerable early on (most of us are, to be honest!) and he nicked it to second slip. When Mike Hussey also nicked it to second slip Australia were 15-3 and we had made a dream, dream start. There was no need to remind anyone of the quality still left and the hard work still required, but at the same time we all knew that we had just potentially got rid of three or four hundred runs for almost nothing.

But Katich was still at the crease, with Clarke and Symonds to come, and we had spoken a lot about the strength of their tail, with the likes of Mitchell Johnson and Jason Krejza well capable of scoring fifties. And we were absolutely right about all that, too, because Australia ended up with 375!

We had been hoping for closer to 300, but I wasn't too perturbed. It was an even better batting wicket than we'd first thought, and their bowlers were going to have to work as hard as ours had. Makhaya's 4-72 was an outstanding effort, but Harry had been just as important. He'd slowed the innings down and controlled things beautifully, just when I'd really needed it, and had taken a couple of key wickets, too. It was a huge confidence booster for him and also a massive boost for me. He was fit, mentally strong and very much up for a fight. I knew all of that anyway, but it was good to have it reinforced. He was going to be an important part of the series.

I made a good start in our reply, but you can be very hard on yourself as a top order batsman when you make a score like 48. It doesn't help the team and you can feel like you've wasted a great deal of effort. I chopped a ball from Johnson onto my stumps. He has an unusual action and bowls a 'heavy ball' at genuine pace. It was the first time I had faced him in a Test match (I had in one-dayers, but it's never the same thing). Bowlers become different animals when they can bowl however they like to you, all day.

I knew I had to act, and act fast. Sitting in the dressing room gave me the time I needed to formulate different game plans against him for the second innings. We were cruising and doing well at 230-3, heading towards the second evening with about 10 overs to go. I was as chuffed as I could be – 10 overs away from an unbelievable day which involved more good, resilient bowling and some fine batting. Another 25 runs before the close, a good morning session on day three and we'd hit the lead around lunchtime, perhaps just after. I'd done the sums. Things were looking good.

Mitchell came back on to try and rescue something from the day for Australia and produced one of the more remarkable spells I've ever seen. Suddenly – and it really did feel very sudden – we were eight wickets down in the space of five overs. It felt as though someone had sucked the life out of me. I was literally short of breath. We went from 234-3 to 241-8 after working so hard to get into that position. But, even at the time, I had to admire the way he had bowled, running in as hard as he did at the end of the day and making every delivery count. That's what makes Test cricket unique: you are constantly tested and have to be on top of your game in every session.

That evening we left it for a while, didn't talk about what had just happened. The Test match started so late each day that we had dinner at the ground after play, and that's what we did that evening. Because of the two-hour time difference between Perth and the big viewership cities of Sydney and Melbourne, we started at 11:30 and it was 8:00 pm before we ate. Then we'd go back to the hotel and pretty much just shower and go to bed.

On the other nights I went straight back to my room and chilled out, making sure I had enough time to recover mentally and emotionally for the next day's play. Before we left the ground that evening, however, I sat the players down and in a very calm way spoke about the fact that there was nothing we could do about what had happened in the last half hour of the game, that Johnson had bowled well and that tomorrow's play was the most crucial of the Test match. I told them that they could give up now, if that's what they felt like, or they could have a good night's sleep, dig deeper than ever before, and arrive back at the ground with the right attitude and a lot of heart to give us the best chance of bouncing back.

We were well behind in the game, but if we could squeeze out a few more runs, get a bit closer to Australia's total, cut the lead down and then bowl really, really well ... who knows? I talked a bit more about the discipline we needed to exert the next day, but my main focus was on arriving with the right attitude. I was adamant in my own mind that I'd rather use a 12th man than have a team mate on the field who didn't think we could win. It wasn't a serious thought, but probably just an angry reaction to how dramatically the game had changed course.

To be fair to everyone, we didn't spend any time moaning and groaning about what had just happened. I was upbeat and positive and, however they may have felt privately, the team responded.

That night, however, when I closed my bedroom door, I lay down feeling pretty crap and fed up. I'd done my job – got through the day, handled adversity and tried to lead from the front. Now it was my time. I lay in my room for a while, watched some TV and fell asleep surprisingly early. But as drained as I was when I fell asleep, I was fresh and buzzing when I woke up the next day. Sometimes that happens for no apparent reason, but I was really up for the third day.

Bouch scrambled a few runs the next morning and we reduced the deficit to below 100, which felt like quite an achievement. If we'd really thought about a deficit of 94 we might have been a bit negative, but we didn't. History tells you a lot about the game, but it doesn't tell you everything. History also tells you what you have to do to make history.

We were back in the field shortly before lunch and Steyntjie bowled beautifully to Matty Hayden, probably had him dead lbw second ball, but it wasn't given. Fortunately fate played its part and he got him caught and bowled shortly after, although replays suggested he hadn't hit it. Steyntjie really deserved that wicket: he ran in hard, slightly into the breeze, and found a little bit of swing, the first sign of it in the whole game.

After that, we settled into the rhythm of our work. Despite what the numbers were telling us on the scoreboard, we actually felt like we were ahead of the game. We squeezed them hard, we bowled in good areas, Harry was bowling superbly well and kept them under pressure, never allowing the scoring rate to increase. Harry was immense that day. He virtually dominated his end, allowing the seamers to stay fresh throughout the day.

They never got away from us until the end of the day, when Haddin played a tremendous counter-attacking innings, which most people thought had finally taken the game away from us. The lead was 413. As strange as it may sound, we never focused on a 'target' of 414. It was simply the 'process' and preparation of batting which occupied our thoughts.

Haddin apart, we'd had an excellent day and exercised good control over all the other batsmen. Our game plans had worked and the team had committed body and soul to each other. There could be no doubt that everybody had arrived with the right attitude in the morning. I was very proud as a captain. We had gained a lot of confidence from the first three days and it was only one outstanding individual performance from Johnson that had put us this far behind the game.

I felt that we'd all settled well and found our feet. I was completely comfortable that, whatever happened in the last innings, we had progressed. Many of the team were starting to believe that we were capable of beating Australia in Australia. I could see that, literally. A sense of quiet confidence was coming through. Could we win?

It wasn't a question that ever came up; it was just never mentioned. If any of the batsmen had been asked whether they could bat for five sessions on that wicket there would have been a loud chorus of 'Yes, of course we can!' – and with total belief and conviction. And yet, there was so much time left in the game that we could all work out for ourselves that, if we did bat out five sessions, we would win. Perhaps, subconsciously, we were wary of saying anything which could be turned against us. 'We can chase 414 – Smith.' We weren't interested in headlines like that.

But the atmosphere in the changing room was awesome. In many ways it probably stemmed from the fact that we had taken 20 wickets on a pitch which was getting better and better to bat on with each session. It had been an astonishing effort, easily appreciated as much by the batsmen as the bowlers. We almost felt as though we had something to celebrate before the fourth innings even began. Subconsciously we had probably been expecting to chase 1000.

Mac and I walked out calmly. He smiled a sort of 'Mona Lisa' smile which could have meant 'we're dead' or 'we'll have this won in about 12 hours' time'. It made me smile, too, whatever it meant. I didn't ask. Australia bowled really, really well and there was nothing on offer, not a ball to hit for over after over. Lee and Johnson bowled as tight as can be. Siddle came on and continued the good work and after what felt like hours the scoring rate was 1.2 per over. But it was crucial to soak up this initial period of attack – we were both experienced enough to know that scoring opportunities would eventually arrive if we could survive.

Unfortunately for Mac – maybe fortunately for me – he soaked up a lot of the pressure but only scored 10. In walked Hashim. I had a drink and thought: 'We are going to have to work really, really hard to get through this.' I knew things would become slightly easier as the ball got older, and that's what happened. Hashim and

I started to flow together in a partnership and we started to score more freely. When Hashim flicks one off his pads to the square leg boundary it is so fluid, so easy on the eye – it quickly makes the bowlers start to have doubts. Gradually the pressure started to transfer, even though we were chasing a monster.

We played Krejza really well. He was going for over four an over and I had the very distinct impression that Ricky didn't know how to use him at this stage of the game. It was putting him under immense pressure and, just as we had hoped, he kept going back to his seamers before they were ready for another spell. An unseasonal rain shower meant that the day was going to finish close to 8:00 pm. We knew that from early in the day and it was an important part of our thinking. A tired bowling attack for the last hour and a half of a day can be very vulnerable.

Near the final hour of the day, I was approaching my first hundred against Australia. The 'process rather than result' coaching with Snapey was paying off. I was only thinking about the next ball. Mitchell came back and I was unperturbed. I went through the nineties quickly with a couple of boundaries – and there it was, a hundred in Australia. I was absolutely over the moon – what a moment! I was asked in the media conference afterwards about my subdued celebration. It didn't have anything to do with the match situation; it was simply the result of a new desire to be a lot calmer out in the middle.

Yes, of course it also had a lot to do with the fact that we still had another 230 or 240 runs to chase down, and that was my priority, but I was also aware that I didn't want to portray a hundred in Australia as the greatest achievement of my life if we went on to lose the game. I was also aware that I wanted to be seen as a man who had prepared himself thoroughly, who believed in himself, and who knew he was always capable of doing this. I wanted people to see that this was not a 'once in a blue moon' thing ... that there would be more. I wanted to dance about and scream and shout and hug everybody and celebrate, but there were more important things to consider!

As it was, Mitchell beat me with a short, slower ball which gripped a bit and hit me on the pads, out lbw. I was desperate not to lose a wicket shortly before the close of play, but Hash and

I were both dismissed with an hour or so to go. Hash played superbly for his 53, but it still left Jakes and AB to cope with the last hour.

Australia were going to throw everything at them. Just one more wicket and they would have felt home and dry. They attacked Jakes with a heap of short balls and tested every aspect of AB's game, mentally and physically. But again, they just soaked up the pressure, as we had discussed.

The bowlers were tiring visibly – we could smell our supper cooking below us! – and they faded particularly badly in the last 40 minutes when we picked up over 30 runs in three overs. Krejza and Siddons were absolutely belted by Jakes, who showed incredible strength of character in launching such an assault so late in the day, and with so much at stake. If he'd got himself out he would never have forgiven himself, but instead he took 34 runs off three overs and utterly transformed the fifth day target. Instead of being 200 and plenty, it was 187 with seven wickets in hand.

It was set up for a fantastic Test match. We had fought our way back into the game from being seemingly dead and buried. From the chat at the end of day two, we had done everything we said we would do. We'd won every session, and shown a huge amount of skill, character and self-belief along the way.

At the press conference that night I played down the chances of victory. I spoke only about how much we had gained as individuals, and as a team, since the Johnson spell. I made it very clear how proud I was of the team and that there would be no rift or disappointment if we didn't win. And I meant it.

I know there's an old media cliché about the 'first hour will be important', but this time it really did ring true. If we could get through the first hour, we could win. If they took two or three wickets, they probably would.

I had one of my worst nights' sleep of the tour that night. If I'd still been batting I would probably have got a solid six hours in, but being helpless for the last day kept me awake for most of the night. Good old Australian 24-hour TV. It's terrible!

One of the most important lessons you have to learn as a captain is to trust your players. Often, as a leader, you feel pressure to try and do everything for everybody, bowl every ball and bat every ball. You can't. But I had learned gradually, over the years, that the captain can play a part – even when he can't get onto the field.

I reiterated many of the obvious points: process rather than result, commit to everything you do and no 50/50 errors. But most importantly, I asked them to enjoy it!

We pretty much controlled the whole of that last day's play. Jakes and AB got us off to a solid start and the second new ball was an awkward 15 overs away for Ricky, which made things tricky with how long to keep his frontline seamers in the attack.

The second new ball did account for Jakes, but he and AB had solidified the morning for us. In walked J-P on his debut. I was desperately nervous for him and wanted him to do well as much as everyone else. He had had a terribly rough decision in the first innings, caught off his helmet, and knowing Australia they were going to be merciless and ruthless towards him in the second innings. They were going to come as hard at him as any batsman had ever experienced.

My insides were eating me alive. As he walked out there, no one would have known how much I was hurting – although I was sitting very still. J-P and AB managed to get through to lunch. I saw them both at lunch and AB was in a great zone and knew what he wanted to achieve out of the afternoon session.

Surviving until lunch had given J-P a huge boost, although the tension of the occasion led to him being physically sick fairly soon after getting back to the changing room. Doc Moosajee assured him that it was perfectly normal behaviour for a young man in his situation ...!

I sat outside, watching the afternoon in complete awe. Two young guys who had played so much cricket with and against each other as school kids, now out there together in the process of winning a Test match against Australia, in Australia. The only thing that made the hair stand up on the back of my neck more than my own emotions was the thought of the emotions of so many people back at home. We were all acutely aware of how they had lived and breathed every ball with us in the early hours of the morning.

As the final session progressed, I went to the toilet at one stage and found Mickey doing laps in the toilet area through nerves. Jakes was sitting with his little teddy bear that his girl friend had given him before the series and which had now suddenly become a good luck charm. I shared a joke with Mickey about him walking around in the dressing room. I sat outside again and watched AB and J-P play incredibly well and handle the situation with such aura, confidence and skill.

Eventually the runs started to flow as Australia's desperate seamers tired and made mistakes. AB posted the best hundred of his career, certainly in terms of the pressure and the match situation. He played incredibly well, and it was another big step in his career. He never lacked confidence and always believed in himself, but from that day on and for the rest of his career, he will always believe in the impossible.

It was equally special watching J-P hit the winning runs and getting to an unbeaten 50. He'd waited so long and so patiently, never complaining. And now, on debut, he was experiencing a win so big, so sweet that some cricketers play 100 Tests and don't experience something like that.

The page in my batting diary for the last day is blank. I didn't have any words to describe how I felt or what it meant to the team, and I still struggle to do it justice when I'm asked about the win. I find it easier to explain a heavy defeat than I do this victory. It was just such a wonderful achievement. The dressing room was so, so happy. Any teenager who ever felt like that would never experiment with drugs again! To come back and chase 414 from the position we were in at the end of day two, it defied logic.

The magnitude of going 1-0 up in the series was slow to sink in. There was so much warmth and happiness in the dressing room – everyone you looked at had a permanent grin on their face and it was impossible to stop hugging people for quite a while. We had become such a close knit unit after so long together, and the sense of pride we had in ourselves, and in each other, was exactly like that of a family. We could not have been more proud of our brothers and sisters than we were of each other that day.

Our phones were going berserk with messages from home, and the number of interviews we all did afterwards was hilarious. But nobody was about to refuse to talk about it. Any one of us would have taken a call from Burgersdorp FM and chatted to them for half an hour. We were in the mood for sharing! We knew we had achieved something very special, but even so, I was a little surprised by how many messages of congratulation we received from all over the world.

I simply couldn't answer every call I received – I was just too busy! But I vowed to listen to all the messages and eventually call everyone back. The trouble with that was that my message box was full after about 15 minutes! Some of the messages I did listen to were from friends I never even knew I had! But it was all good.

One call I would never miss, however, was a call from my Mum. She was very emotional, telling me how the match was on every television channel and how people had been watching, or listening on radio, the closer we got to victory. Meetings were cancelled or postponed as victory approached and office workers were all gathering in the boardroom to watch the television. Other guys had heard similar stories from their friends and families. It made us all feel very proud and humbled that we could be such a happy disruption to so many peoples' lives!

When things had settled down a bit and we'd done all our immediate media commitments (well over three hours after the end of the match), the families that were on tour at that stage joined us in the players' dining room for a meal and a glass of wine and then went back to the hotel.

We then went back to the change room to start packing up, but before we did so, we sat down for the final time to absorb as much as possible of the atmosphere, the emotions and the memories. We had another chat about what we had achieved and, just as importantly, how we had achieved it. We had a couple more drinks together and shared the glory of the moment. None of us wanted it to end.

Celebrating success in the right way, giving it the appropriate time, had become quite an important part of the team's ethos. We treated every Test match victory with the respect it deserved and took nothing for granted. We all knew how hard we had worked for those victories – but especially this one.

The team and I had had so many highs since Pakistan, but none was higher than victory in Perth. My first hundred against Australia was a hugely important milestone in my career, but as pleased as I was to score it, nothing brings a bigger smile to my face than when I remember the team chasing 414. Yes, four hundred and fourteen runs to win a Test match in Australia…

I woke up the next morning feeling as satisfied as I ever have in my life. Then I left before the rest of the squad to fly to Melbourne and see a surgeon about my elbow, which had flared up painfully once again at various times during the Test.

Back to real life!

I flew with Shane Jabaar early on the morning after the Perth Test to see a specialist surgeon. My priority was getting through the series but I was also desperate for some long-term answers. The euphoria of victory had dulled the pain but it wasn't going away and I was getting fed up with it.

The short-term solution was to have another cortisone injection, but making use of an ultrasound scanner so he could see exactly where the cortisone was going. It is an extremely precise science – a matter of just millimetres to get to the most badly damaged area of the tendon. It was very short-term – just enough, hopefully, to get me through the Melbourne Test.

By the time I caught up with the boys again that evening it felt like I'd been on the go for 24 hours. It had been an early start, a three and a half hour flight and then what felt like endless hours in doctors' waiting rooms. But I knew I was jumping the queue and they were doing us a favour by squeezing me in, so I was very happy to wait.

The guys, meanwhile, had enjoyed a leisurely lie-in and didn't arrive until well into the evening. I caught up with a couple of them for dinner and to chat informally about preparations for the Boxing Day Test at the MCG – and to do a little more celebrating after Perth.

It's always an interesting time of year for us with families, wives and girlfriends forming a sort of 'super squad.' There were also as many single guys as I can ever remember in Australia, so while it was a bit sad for us that we couldn't find a girlfriend, at least we had plenty of mates to spend time with and weren't lonely!

It's a tradition before the Christmas lunch that we buy each other a small present. If you are single you just buy a 'boy' present – if you have a wife or partner on tour then you have to buy 'his and hers' presents and have then wrap them up for after lunch on Christmas Day. There's usually a financial 'ceiling' placed on the value of the gifts – you have to use a bit of imagination that way rather than just grabbing an arbitrary bottle of aftershave.

I've played a few times at the MCG now but the novelty hasn't worn off one bit. It is still the most jaw-dropping stadium in the world – at least that I have been to. It's amazing just walking in to the place. The dressing rooms are in the basement underneath the stadium and they are enormous; I reckon you could have a full net inside them.

Your first experience of walking out at the MCG stays with you for ever; at least, it has with me. The vastness of the stands and the fact that they stretch all the way around at the same height without relenting. Everyone I have played with says the same thing – that you can imagine what the gladiators would have felt like in the middle of a Roman Coliseum. Other cricket grounds also have a unique atmosphere, even when they are empty – Lord's, Newlands and the Wanderers certainly do – but for its sheer enormity and ability to feel a little intimidating without a person in sight, the MCG stands alone. It also has a proud sense of history about it, with huge bronze statues all the way around the perimeter depicting heroes of both cricket and Aussie Rules (which is actually played there far, far more than cricket.)

Any sense of warmth and affection you may feel for the place before the match is fairly quickly snuffed out when you remember how much abuse you can receive from the crowd!

We had two pretty good training sessions building up to the Test match – at full throttle on Christmas eve and pretty much the same on Christmas day, although for a shorter length of time. They were the only practices we had before the Test, so it was vital to hit top gear and maximum intensity, even for just a short time each. Bouch took charge of the tail and worked with each of them in the nets with the bowling machine, bouncer after bouncer. We all felt their ability to stick around could be key. Ever since we first decided to go with four out-and-out bowlers, with no Polly, we'd been concerned about the length of the tail – but now we had a feeling it was crunch time.

The squad was brimming with confidence. You could see J-P

growing in stature by the day, almost by the hour. He seemed so assured during training and ready to start again. Everybody had as much desire and determination as they had before Perth, but now there was the added ingredient of confidence. We chatted often about what a wonderful opportunity we now had to be successful at what was such an important and iconic ground for Australia. If we could win the series here it would hurt Australians more than we could probably understand. The MCG – heartbreak for so many teams over the decades. Now we had the chance to break theirs.

The Australian media had taken their focus off us for the first time on tour and turned the heat on the Australian team, which was fun to watch. We were almost flying under the radar while they were taking a lot of criticism. Hayden was inadvertently commanding headline after headline with his age, whether he deserved to be there and suggestions that retirement was the best option. The media were virtually jumping on the bandwagon to have a go at the Australian team who were one-nil down for the first time in over a decade in a home series.

We were constantly congratulated by people we met in public, from airports to hotels and restaurants, even in the gym. There were plenty of people who told us they were happy that we had won in Perth because the Australian team had become 'arrogant' – but, for the most part, we simply had the impression that the majority of Australians loved seeing good, hard, competitive sport and could appreciate a great performance, even when it came from the opposition. But the majority still wanted Australia to win!

The build-up went absolutely according to plan and confidence was high. I wouldn't have been surprised if I had detected a little bit too much hype and determination as the Test approached – the thought of winning the series was a pretty all-consuming one – but there was none of that. Self-belief was shining through brightly in everything we did. The bowlers might still have been a little nervous, but the top six were settled.

Christmas lunch was a lot of fun. Goolam organised a Santa Claus for the families and kids and the presents were fun, containing the usual silly pairs of underpants and other odd but amusing gifts. The lunch itself was extremely relaxed. Even though some of the squad were at the beginning of their careers, everyone had played enough cricket to know how to relax between games. Even before a game as big as this.

We finished around mid-afternoon and everyone drifted off to relax in their rooms or went for a walk along the South Bank of the river Yarra until the team meeting at 6:00 pm. You will be aware by now of what happens at the captain's meeting ... the three Ps – partnerships, patience and pressure – and committing to our decisions. Once again, we had to put a peg in the ground on day one, mark our territory and make a statement. We were not going to be overawed or intimidated.

We spoke at length about the massive crowd and the noise – we needed to remember 'the three-second chill'. The theme had mostly served us well previously on big occasions. We had to be able to make good, sensible decisions under pressure, no matter what the Aussie team or the crowd were saying or doing – to see through the 'red mist' which can sometimes descend. I finished the meeting with a simple quote: 'Determined people, working together, can do anything.' I think it resonated because it summed up all the success we had already enjoyed.

I woke up early, as usual, on the morning of the Test match. There were quite a few supporters and sponsors staying in the hotel, media too, and I said a cheerful good morning to all of them at breakfast. Couldn't help feeling they were up early! There was such a vibe wherever you looked. The MCG Boxing Day Test is a sporting institution which stretches way beyond the world of cricket. It is one of 'the' great sporting events in a city renowned for its love of all sports.

The drive to the ground was quiet but very calm; it wasn't the uneasy atmosphere you can experience when people are nervous. Individuals were doing their own thing, preparing in their own way. Several iPods were in action.

Within a kilometre of the MCG it becomes obvious that a big day is about to start. Even two hours before the start, there are thousands of people walking the pavements from the train station, the taxi stops and the trams. Public transport is brilliant in all Australian cities, but especially in Melbourne. You can get anywhere easily, but especially to the major sports venues.

Then the bus pulls into the basement parking area and you lose track of the real world for a while. You can barely even hear the crowd before emerging again half an hour later for warm ups. It was filling up very nicely.

The Melbourne Test

I lost the toss, again, and Australia chose to bat. Just time for a few more words in the dressing room. Jeez, the boys must have been tiring of hearing about the three Ps ...

The wicket was very slow and there was virtually no swing at all. We hadn't experienced much swing at any stage of the tour. Our patience and discipline were going to be tested again.

Hayden was clearly a man under pressure. He tried to impose himself on us, as he had done so many times before, but drove at a wide one and was caught at point. Katich and Ponting got away from us a bit before lunch, but we didn't bowl well to them. Makkie dropped Ricky just before lunch, so we went in to the break feeling a bit down.

I took a deep breath and called a stern chat before play began after lunch. I spoke about raising our standards, taking responsibility, creating pressure and doing the basics right. A lot more bloody right than we'd managed in the morning session!

Steyntjie, the soldier that he is, bowled beautifully after the break. He knocked over Katich and we controlled much of the rest of the day – barring Ponting. He played really, really well. Magnificent. When he's at his best, he scores quickly; he takes the game to you and makes it extremely hard to stay ahead of the game. It was really a great moment when he reached his century; it was one of the loudest cheers I have ever experienced at a stadium: 70 000 or 80 000 people stood up and cheered for him. It doesn't matter, just for a second, that you are on the receiving end. It was a wonderful sporting moment.

But then Harry had him caught bat pad just before tea and everything turned sharply back into focus. It was an enormously important wicket because we managed to squeeze a couple more out just before the end of the day. I was keen to emphasise that we were slightly ahead at the end of the first day, but most people thought honours were just about even. It had been a hard and tiring day, but already my thoughts were focused on the next morning: the second new ball held the key to who would take first innings honours.

I had a quiet night with room service and rested. I also had a quiet coffee with Harry. He had a few personal issues going on back home and it was healthy for both of us to chat for a while. They weren't my issues, obviously, but it helps both a player and a captain to know a bit of background. Harry was busting a gut for the team, he was doing everything he possibly could, but if things went wrong he was not in the right place to receive a gobful from me. It took maturity and courage for him to talk to me and I hope I responded in the same way.

As a captain you must have an open door at all times. You have to know when to put your arm around someone and when to be hard on them. Having an understanding of emotional intelligence, and knowing your players from the inside as well as the outside, is the key to being a good captain. Many people can move third man a bit squarer, but understanding where he is as a cricketer and a person is a little harder. I'm still learning. And I'm quite certain I will still be learning at the end of my career. And after that.

A captain needs to do everything possible to get the best out of his players, and if that means giving some of them special licence or special treatment, then so be it. But it also makes it far easier if you have enough trust in your relationship for the players to talk to you. Harry is older than me and has consequently seen a bit more of life. But he also knew that I'd seen a few things in my time, too, and having the respect to talk to me added to the mutual respect and affection we had for each other.

I spent breakfast the next day worrying about the fact that Michael Clarke was still there with the tail. I've never enjoyed that scenario; it can be a nightmare for the fielding captain. In many ways they are 'pressure-free' and unburdened by expectation. The bowlers, however, have taken six wickets and have the number eight in. They are expected to end things quickly.

Clarke was excellent for his 88, as it turned out, with some very good support from his 'tail'. The tail-enders were actually very accomplished with the bat. But they were also really positive. There were no signs of nerves or tentativeness; they committed to everything, in attack and defence. I couldn't help smiling because it was the core of my approach, too.

The total of 394 was at least 60 too many. We'd been hoping for just over 300. But that was what we had to deal with, and I made that perfectly clear to everyone. What is done is done. Look forward. We needed to score more than that.

I padded up in the usual way – it's not superstition, it just helps me switch on. I always bat in Adidas socks, tights and always start with the box followed by the front pad, back pad then thigh pads and the arm guard. I always have two pieces of chewing gum before I walk out to bat – it helps me control my thoughts and control my nerves. And I always do a similar preparation in the changing room, grooving a few shots to get my feet moving.

It's so important to make a quantum shift from captaincy to opening the batting, to make conscious and even subconscious changes from captaining and batting. It helps me to have a different and specific routine as a batsman before I walk out. I also always have a couple of key thoughts in my head about my batting, whether it is about my balance, watching the ball, or just having my game plans ready for the bowlers that I am going to face. A quick glance at the batting diary always helps.

Peter Siddle and Brett Lee took the new ball and they both gave it everything in the opening overs. It was clear to both Neil Mac and me that they wanted to kill us, which is only right. Lee pinned me on my arm with a short ball, which hurt. He ran in so hard that I could clearly feel the intensity of how much this meant to Australia. Being one-nil down, they needed to make this count. It was intense competition, but I managed to stay calm. I was able to shut out the exterior distractions and stay in my zone, focused on my game plans and managing to keep emotion out of the equation. I was intensely focused on surviving the new ball and cashing in when the ball was older and the bowlers tiring.

The wicket was slow. You always have to work unusually hard for your runs at the MCG, because the outfield is never fast and can be very slow, a legacy of the fact that it is primarily a 'footie' venue. It makes batting harder physical work then normal because you have to run! There are probably more threes run at the MCG than any other ground, and all-run fours are not uncommon. I'm pretty sure we had a couple of run fives, as well.

I survived the initial onslaught but Mac, unfortunately, didn't. Hashim once again started superbly and I was excited by our potential partnership until he smashed one to gulley where Symonds held a cracking catch. Jakes and I reached about 100-2 just before tea when he made a mess of a sweep shot against Hauritz, a horrible way to get out – horrible for the team, too. I'd just been thinking that with a really good session to finish the day we could lay an excellent platform to challenge the Australian total on day three.

But after tea we lost our way completely and before we knew it we were in desperate trouble, closing the day at 198-7. From 100-2 to 198-7, that hurt. They had bowled well, particularly Siddle on his home ground. Ricky had set better fields than in Perth, slightly more defensive – more 'patient' field placings. But once again we were behind. Actually, much further behind than we had ever been in Perth.

We didn't speak much at all that night. Mickey tried hard to be positive in the press conference at the end of the day but even Mickey, the world's most optimistic man, was struggling. Almost 200 runs behind with three wickets left. Amongst many lessons I have learned over the years, one of the more relevant applied now: Don't hold a team meeting when you're fed up or miserable!

The following morning my job was to give everyone focus so that we didn't just drift through the rest of the Test match allowing nature to take its course. Fortunately, Perth was still fresh in our minds so the guys were able to use their imagination a bit better than if we hadn't just won an 'impossible' victory.

The first goal was to bat for the whole of the morning session. We pointed out to Harry, Dale and Makhaya that it was now time for all the hard work they had put in on their batting to pay dividends. This plan was built on the assumption, of course, that there was absolutely no way that J-P would be dismissed.

The second part of the plan was to score between two and a half and three runs per over. That would give us 90 runs in the session and reduce the deficit to around a hundred. If we could somehow squeeze it down to 80 or 90-odd, that would be what we had faced in Perth so, mentally, we could cope with that. Harry and Steyntjie had worked so hard at facing the short ball and, while it was asking a lot of them – and of J-P in just his second Test – at least it was a plan. And not a bad one, actually, in the circumstances!

Harry was typically bullish. He loved the plan and was cheerfully talking about the half century he was going to score. Dale adopted a philosophical 'wait-and-see' approach, but one thing I could be absolutely certain about was that neither of them would be lacking in guts and determination.

J-P had played so comfortably and fluently the night before that it was no surprise we took him for granted. He seemed completely unfazed by our expectations. He was obviously in a very good space, or perhaps he wasn't in any space at all – uncluttered by thoughts and analysis.

I couldn't sit in the underground changing room, obviously, so I started the climb to the players' viewing area as they walked out to bat. It's a long way up there – 55 stairs, to be precise. I counted them often on that third day. Most of the guys preferred to stay in the comfort and privacy of the change room and watch proceedings on TV, but I was restless and needed to be outside.

They started solidly – no early scares. Harry and J-P built a partnership, slowly but surely, and after what felt like hours of sitting very still, I suddenly realised that things were going quite a lot better than we had dared to hope. J-P showed a lot of fluency and discipline while Harry showed a lot of guts with his ... er ... technique. He doesn't look the best but he commits himself to whatever he needs to do and has never been afraid of taking a few in the ribs for the sake of the team. This wasn't the first time he'd showed courage during a vital partnership. He hasn't always scored many runs during those stands but he has worked damn hard. Having said that, he has a pretty decent slog in his armoury and can clear the ropes as well as most.

In many ways I've always thought you can gauge the mood and well-being of a team by the way its tail-enders bat. If they are committed and prepared to fight, and don't give their wickets away lightly or cheaply, it provides such a lift to the rest of the team. It gives a huge boost to the specialist batsmen who then redouble their efforts the next time they bat. Fighting, spirited tail-enders, in my experience, are one of the first signs of a healthy and united team.

Just when I started thinking that he might have been right about scoring a half century, it transpired that he was having the same dream ... only in his dream he moved from 44 to 50 with one shot. He tried it against part-timer Mike Hussey and holed out to long on. 'Harry, they brought a part-timer into the attack because they were desperate – it meant you had won the battle for the time being. What the hell did you do that for...?' I was disappointed but happy at the same time. He'd set a very good example – but could have done even more.

Just before lunch I moved down to the dressing room. At the break J-P was 78 not out, with Dale on 25. I was over the moon with the way the session had gone. We'd scored 106 runs for the loss of a single wicket and trailed by 'just' 90. I had a small lunch and a brief chat to J-P about his thoughts and reiterated that he was to keep trusting the tail, don't complicate things by trying to steal the strike and turn down runs. This was a team game and they needed to play their part.

But I also smiled and made sure that he was relaxed and knew how proud we all were of him already. He'd basically brought us back into the game ... although I did say that a few more runs would be even better. Dale had been working hard on his batting, and J-P had just batted a whole session without any difficulty, but not a single one of us, in our wildest dreams, could have imagined what happened next – that they would still be there at tea and end up batting for most of the day until we had a lead of 65!

It was an incredible thing to experience and hardly a day went by for months afterwards when I didn't feel a little shiver down my spine when I thought about it. For many of us it was our best-ever day's Test cricket. We sat in our chairs and didn't move for hours as J-P piled on the runs with Steyntjie. It was as though we were hypnotised.

It may be forgotten over time but it must be mentioned that Australia were a bowler short with Brett Lee injured and unable to bowl all day. Strangely enough, I was actually happy for us to take a little credit for that. By doing what we had done in Perth, Lee had been asked by Ricky to bowl an awful lot of overs without sufficient rest. Once we'd survived the morning session the remaining frontline bowlers were already tired and it became harder and harder to keep coming back for yet another spell.

Having said that, the boys batted beautifully. When J-P was approaching his hundred we all left the changing room and stood in the players tunnel, right on the boundary's edge. This was a moment everybody wanted to be a part of. Nobody would have forgiven themselves if they hadn't been there. Seeing the look of disbelief and excitement on his face brought a lump to my throat and a tear to the eyes of a lot of those standing with me. It wasn't just the fact that he'd scored a century, it was the class of the innings and the match situation which made it, in the view of many experts and cricket historians, one of the finest debut hundreds ever.

It is still difficult to find the right words to describe and do justice to that day. For once, just the numbers do justice to the achievement and the enormity of the comeback. At the start of the day we were 198-7, trailing by 196. By the time J-P was out for 166, seven hours and 28 minutes after he'd gone in at 126-4, we had a total of 459 and a lead of 65. Perhaps it is tempting fate, but I doubt I will ever be a part of a day to better that. If I do I hope my heart and nerves can take it.

Actually, I wasn't a part of it – most of us weren't! I went out onto the ground shortly after the day's play precisely so that I could be a part of it and to feel the atmosphere and share the sense of dazed bewilderment on one side and disbelieving joy on the other.

As much as J-P deserved the headlines, I don't rate Dale's career-best of 76 any less highly. Neither would have been possible without the other, but whereas J-P had undoubtedly gone well above and beyond the call of duty, scoring runs was still his job. Not only had Dale also gone above and beyond, it wasn't even in his field of expertise. He stuck to his game plan, by and large, and enjoyed the benefit of a couple of dropped catches. And yes, I do believe you can help to make your own luck!

When the two of them had walked out to bat after lunch they were very serious – relaxed too, but serious. When they both walked back again at tea time there was a little moment of silence before the two just started giggling. They couldn't quite believe what they had done. But I'm afraid it all became too much for Steyntjie when he walked out yet again after tea and looked up at the scoreboard which read: Duminy 120, Steyn 70. He lasted another 14 overs, though.

The tide had turned dramatically – we had won the pivotal third day on which so many Tests are decided. But I wasn't convinced that it was an irreversible shift. We still had to really make it count with the ball.

I had spoken so many times about 'intensity' and 'discipline', but this was really, really the time to combine the two. Perth was Perth, a magnificent Test match victory. This time, I said, it was worth double, or triple, because there was a series victory in Australia at stake. This was our opportunity, a chance that we had created through a miracle fight-back. It would be a pity not to make use of it, I said, although not quite in those words.

A wicket on the third evening would have been nice, but we only bowled three overs in Australia's second innings and I wasn't about to get greedy.

The fourth morning was going to be vital for me as captain and it was something I was well aware of as I lay awake at night and then again early in the morning. If we didn't take at least a couple of early wickets before the lead had been wiped out then it would very much be game on again. I know what it feels like losing wickets when you are still in arrears and we had to give Australia that feeling.

As we drove to the ground I knew the wicket I wanted most was that of Hayden. Although we had done well against him so far, there remained the feeling that he could bounce back at any stage and score quickly enough to change the game and transfer the pressure back to us. But he was also a man under pressure and it was vital that we maintained that pressure on him.

We had another very good warm-up with plenty of catching practice. Then I had one-on-one chats with all the bowlers about game plans, discipline, patience and prudent use of the short ball.

I couldn't have been happier when Hayden emerged in an aggressive, counter-attacking mood. It gives you something to work with when a key opponent lets you know how he is going to play. I changed the field slightly by taking a slip out of the cordon and putting him in to short cover, dropped point a bit deeper to allow the bowler some freedom to attack off stump and just outside, 'fourth stump'. It worked perfectly; a ball or two later Hayden drove it straight to cover, which made me look very clever. I felt pretty clever, too! It's great for the captain when things like that work out and it feels very satisfying. But for every move that pays dividends, there are 20 that give you nothing.

Just about everything went according to plan after that, although we were lucky with Katich, who played a loose shot to a wide one from Steyntjie and was caught behind. But Morne bowled an absolute ripper of a bouncer at Hussey and had him caught off the helmet at square leg. It was an absolutely beautiful bumper which had been our tactic throughout the series to him, and it had paid off.

Australia were in serious trouble – three wickets down and still 16 behind. But Ricky had played magnificently in the first innings and picked up exactly where he left off, scoring freely all around the wicket and looking as good as he has ever done. He takes the game away from you quickly when he's in that form and I felt threatened.

He added 96 with Michael Clarke and it was testament to how well they played because we bowled as well to them during that stand as at any time during the series. The ball beat the bat any number of times, but the luck, for a while, had left us.

A little while after lunch Dale had another go and bowled his first bad ball of the day, or that's the way it felt. A long hop outside off stump which Clarke belted straight to cover. The ball wasn't worth a wicket, but we were! We'd worked exceptionally hard for it.

Immediately afterwards Symonds nicked Dale just short of second slip and I thought 'Jeez, either it's going to be our day or not.' But within a couple of deliveries he nicked another one straight to Jakes and we were right back in control – five down and just 80 ahead. Ricky was still there and I was worried about Haddin until he flashed at a wide one from Makhaya, giving Jakes another catch. With his dismissal came the first, slight but unmistakeable sniff of victory.

I had a little tingle of excitement but knew how critical it was to remain composed, not to over-attack, but attack enough to make sure we kept moving forward. We had catchers in front of the wicket, as much to keep the runs down as for wickets – I had to be aware of the lead and keeping it down.

Ricky was still the big threat to us – he was batting with 'Bing' Lee, who was perfectly capable of making 50 and sharing in a match-changing stand of 120-plus. On days like that, with so much at stake, you feel the pressure of captaincy every single minute. One wrong move can cost you that day's play. You've got to keep the bowlers fresh enough to ensure they can always give you an attacking spell when you really need it, even in the last half hour of the day.

This was a key day in my development as a leader and I was aware of it all the time. Could I orchestrate the final rites in a Test match to become the first team to win in Australia for 16 years?

The ball was old just before tea and had started to reverse swing. There aren't many better men in the world than Jakes to take advantage of that, so I asked him to take another spell. And what a beauty! A late inswinger to Lee, which bowled him and rounded off another fabulous session for us. Australia were 180-7 at tea, a lead of 115.

I knew that if I was excited, the rest of the guys would be, too. So at tea we spoke about focusing and controlling the small things, the next delivery, without ever looking ahead to the finish line. We all knew what trouble you could cause for yourself by taking things for granted. And we knew how much this Australian tail could wag.

Ricky was still batting after tea and quickly moved from 87 to 99. He was a man on a mission, because he was now batting with the tail. Bouch was keen for us to set a very straight field to try and persuade him to play across his pads in search of the leg-side boundary. He thought we had a chance of trapping him lbw. I chatted with Morne and he wanted to bowl wide rather than straight so, as is often the case, I allowed the bowler to have the final say. It was obvious that he wasn't going to graft for the century, he wanted it as soon as possible. So we were going to make him 'chase' it, feel outside off stump. The theory was that he might chip one in the air. So once again we moved a slip to short cover. I put myself in that position and, for the second time in the innings, a move worked magnificently. Morne got the delivery spot on and he spooned it straight to me at short cover. You could feel the disappointment around the ground, the collective groan of 30 000 people can produce an extraordinary sound. For us, however, the groan was quickly drowned by the sound of our own cheering. Ricky was gone.

Just the two tail-enders left. I was on a captaincy 'high' and I knew I'd had a good day, both tactically and from a personal leadership point of view.

Jakes bowled Hauritz with another reverse inswinger and Steyntjie wrapped up a 'tenfor'. It was a huge achievement for him. He had done so well through the whole year and then had to cope with the disappointment of Lord's and the injury. The hype persisted on arrival in Australia, so to produce a performance like this was probably the final 'arrival' stamp on his career passport. His development as a cricketer had been outstanding. His development as a person had, perhaps, been even more remarkable – largely because he hadn't really 'developed' at all.

Dale remained as faithful and as true to his humble roots as any cricketer I have ever met. He had changed inside, naturally, but you would struggle to see it unless you were very close. When people approached him for a chat or an autograph, he was as amenable and as chatty as he had been five years earlier when he was a teenager just starting out. Sometimes I'd look at him chatting to supporters, signing autographs and just being the 'kid from Phalaborwa' while we were waiting to leave on the bus – and vow to remember how true he was to himself.

The target was 183 and we had six overs to bat on the fourth evening. I was more nervous than at any other stage of the tour. Padding up even became clumsy. Perhaps it was the cumulative result of the stresses and strains of the day's captaincy, but I felt the nerves as much as ever before. I hate the ten-minute turnaround between innings. Why so short?

Anyway, my brain was burning with the importance of surviving unscathed and still having ten wickets intact to chase down the target on the fifth morning. Fortunately, I was feeling as good about my batting as I could remember, my feet were moving well and I had solid and coherent plans against all of the bowlers.

I started well by driving the first ball straight down the ground for four! I made a flying start, no stray thoughts cluttering my mind. Just me, the bowler and the ball. No matter how many overs, nothing. Just one ball, on merit, at a time. I was 25 not out overnight. Mac was a bit more nervous, desperately looking for a start but not really settling. He was bowled by Lee on two – off a no ball. We finished the day on 30 without loss to cap yet another of the best days' Test cricket I have experienced.

It was difficult to get to sleep that night and equally difficult to get back to sleep when I woke up after about four or five hours the next morning. My head couldn't decide whether I was more pleased about day four, or more nervous about day five. We needed another 153. At least I could have a say in the matter. It was far worse in Perth when I had no say in what happened on the final day. That morning I said to myself, yet again, 'You'd make a terrible coach. You can't handle this.'

I went to breakfast early – even before the other players and certainly before the majority of fans and other people involved in the game. There were a couple of Chinese businessmen trying to conclude a deal with some Australian businessmen just behind me, but their lines of communication weren't great. It was fun listening while I contemplated my yoghurt and muesli. But it was just a minor distraction from the business of the day: 153 runs.

We were just one good partnership away from making history. We needed to be calm and methodical. If they managed to put us under pressure with a couple of quick wickets, we needed to absorb that pressure without panicking. There was much to ponder, although I refused to allow myself to think of how we could cock it up. Just 30 or 40 overs, that's all we needed.

A good morning session and the game was done and dusted. We played a game of 'foot tennis' in the indoor nets, hit a few balls and then made our way to the dressing room. I had a bottle of water, put some sun-cream on my face and went through the rest of my routine. I dressed slowly and calmly and tried not to be emotional. Two pieces of chewing gum are the last thing before I go out to bat. I put them next to my seat ready for when I walk out.

A number of people have told me that they don't like seeing me chewing gum on TV and I've thought a lot about it, but it has been such an important part of my ritual for so long that I'm not sure I can change it now. It helps me to control my nerves and emotions – it helps me to think like a batsman! I'm not conscious of chewing while I'm doing it but I'm very, very conscious of when I haven't got my gum. Perhaps it's the rhythm of the chewing which helps me focus. So everything goes on, and in, in a particular order and when the five-minute bell goes I'm ready.

Mac and I made our way up the tunnel and into the coliseum of the MCG. There were 'only' about 30 000 people there on the final day, but the South African contingent in the crowd made themselves very vocal and easily seen waving their flags and cheering madly for us. I felt good. Really, really good. I soaked in the noise and the atmosphere and absorbed as much as I could about the occasion.

I was a bit nervous to start with but quickly found my rhythm and whipped a couple of early boundaries away which felt almost like they were worth a bit more than four each, given the situation. Mac also looked more settled and we started to build momentum; we communicated well and we scored freely. My game felt good and the late cut was working particularly well. It had never been a particularly strong point of my game before, but the elbow had been sore for so many months that I'd adapted to not being able to square cut properly, it was too painful. It may have been the one and only positive to come out of the injury.

I was lbw to Nathan Haurtiz for 75 just before lunch. I was disappointed but not furious. Mac and I had set up the win and we were just 60 away with nine wickets left. The thought had crossed my mind about how good it would have been to be there at the end, but as long as we won I didn't mind who finished the job. At lunch we needed another 51. I had a bite to eat and began to savour the moment. We were inches away now. I was eating chicken pasta, I think, but I was beginning to taste victory!

I climbed back up the 55 stairs to the viewing area after lunch and everyone else resumed the positions they had been in during the morning's play. You don't move around much when your team is batting well, especially during a run chase – it's an old cricket superstition which has been around for donkey's years. I sat upstairs and watched Hashim and Mac go about their work and slowly edge us towards the 183 we needed. Every run brought another sigh of relief. I was pretty certain we'd win, but I really didn't want a sudden flurry of wickets to complicate things.

Just over an hour after lunch the electronic scoreboard flashed up a giant South African flag with the words 'South Africa need three runs to win the series'. I felt my face slowly break into a huge smile. I'd been pretty stoical up to then, but it was almost as if the scoreboard operators were waving the white flag by doing that. We were just about to win a Test series in Australia. It was an incredible feeling. I was numb – although that might have been the result of sitting on the edge of my seat for so long.

A lot of South African supporters had made their way over to the viewing area and most of the players had made their way up once they'd accepted the inevitable. When Hashim scored the winning runs there was no flood of emotions, no screaming and running around like headless chickens. Just a deep, deep feeling of satisfaction. Once again, as at Perth, the most prominent emotion was pride, both in each other and in ourselves. The family – the band of brothers who had been through so much together and already enjoyed so much success – was now even closer.

I was also proud of the way we celebrated, because it said much about who we were as people and our values. On the field, led by two of the finest men I know in Hash and Neil Mac, there was humility in victory and respect for our opponent. But inside me I already had the New Year's Eve Sydney Harbour fireworks going off and my heart was doing cartwheels. It was the most rewarding feeling I've yet experienced in sport – and I didn't think I'd be saying that just five months after Edgbaston and just a week after Perth!

We did all our media duties after the game, which takes a lot longer than most people might realise. At least two television interviews, two radio interviews, various other 'one-off' interviews and then the press conference for the newspaper and agency journalists. I know some players are more comfortable than others with doing media work, but I defy anyone to tell me they would have resented doing interviews in that situation.

While I was doing the press conference I think just about

everybody else was still being interviewed on the outfield. I know SABC radio interviewed eight or nine of the guys. And judging by how many interview requests kept pouring in direct from radio stations back home for the next 48 hours, people just couldn't get enough of the success.

There's usually a decent discussion in the changing room about who deserves to keep the souvenir stumps after a memorable game and the 'stump referee', Vinnie Barnes, has had some difficult calls to make over the years. But there was no doubt in anybody's minds that Dale was getting one after his staggering, man-of-the-match performance. He was brilliant in the press conference. Very honest, funny and humble. Very Steyntjie.

Finally we got back to the dressing room. Brett Lee and Shane Watson came and had a beer with us and several families were on tour by now too, so the atmosphere was about as relaxed and special as I have ever felt. The wives and girlfriends were clinking glasses of wine together and a few kids were running around ... the 'cricket family' had suddenly turned into a real family! I couldn't help noticing cases and cases of beer and champagne being delivered. Were they gifts? How long were we going to stay here? It was obviously going to be one of our biggest and longest celebrations ever.

After another hour or so the 'real families' decided to return to the hotel and leave the boys to be boys for a little longer. A cricket fines meeting is no place for ladies or children. So we sang our team song, sang some more favourite songs and drank our beer. The fines meeting was hilarious as always, led by Neil Mac and Bouch.

Once that was over everyone suddenly needed a bit of fresh air, so it was back up the tunnel for a last visit to the middle. The security guards weren't too impressed – it was over four hours since the match ended – and then Harry got into trouble for lighting a celebratory cigar. The MCG is a smoke-free venue, like all the grounds. So there he was, having a puff in a gigantic stadium without a single one of the 100 000 seats occupied. But we all know that 'rules are rules', especially in Australia.

I ran around chasing seagulls for about five minutes, I don't know why, apart from a couple of beers! Then we did our team song one last time, standing on the pitch. Beer always enhances emotions, but I am pretty sure it would have been one of the proudest moments of my life if I'd been celebrating with rooibos tea.

As the sun was setting I noticed a room high up in the stand with its lights still on. It was a large room ... oh dear. It was the media room, and even from that distance I could see it was still pretty full. And we'd just given them quite a show! It was mentioned in most newspapers the next day, but thankfully with plenty of good humour and understanding. They knew how proud we were – and no harm was done.

I spent quite a bit of time with Jakes after that, he was understandably emotional after the win. It meant so much to him. He began his career against Australia and had been on the receiving end of some disappointing results and tours. But now he could finally put a tick in the box that meant the most to him. Some of the squad had barely started high school when Jakes went on his first tour to Australia, but this was his fourth tour and he'd taken enough beatings. He'd seen coaches lose their jobs and players lose their careers. A lot of that emotion was set free now.

The celebration continued back in the hotel with friends, family, commentators and a couple of SA journalists. It was a very, very happy and proud time to be a South African cricketer.

The next day we made our way through to Sydney. We'd been looking forward to the fireworks display on the Harbour Bridge for the whole tour – but now, having won the series, we were like a big bunch of kids waiting to go on a favourite school outing.

Circular Quay is a breathtaking place with the bridge on the left and Opera House on the right. Over a million people from all over the world come to celebrate the New Year so it's an enormous event. Fortunately, KFC had become an official supplier to CSA and they had hired a boat for the night so we could watch the display on the water with a few drinks and snacks.

Mickey had promised on arrival in Australia that he would swim in Sydney Harbour on New Year's Eve if we had won the series by then. And he was as good as his word! The boys cheered like mad when he whipped his shirt off and dived off the boat into the ocean. He was happy to do it, of course. He had put so much work into the squad and had never, ever complained about the relentless demands on his time and how much work he did behind the scenes. He is a selfless man, happy for the players to take the glory and credit when we win.

Once he was back onboard and dried off, we settled down to watch the display, which as usual was spectacular; it is an amazing place to experience New Year. Many people think touring is a holiday, but it is not. It was very different in times gone by, but the modern tour is an endless procession of hotels, practice grounds, nets, stadiums and airports – with very little time to buy a new razor blade, let alone go shopping or sightseeing. But this was different – this was most definitely a perk and a brilliant one, too. Everyone thoroughly enjoyed this evening.

Then it was about preparing for the Test match and reassessing where the squad was. I had thought about taking a rest. We discussed it, but decided instead that I would make one last push against the pain barrier and then leave the tour immediately after the Test match and go home to rest and recuperate and prepare myself for the home series.

At the same time we had decided to opt for a course of blood injections into my elbow in an attempt to speed up the natural healing process. Blood was to be taken out of my right arm and injected directly into the tear in the ligament in my left elbow. I would have the treatment as soon as I returned to Joburg. I was just going to battle through Sydney with pain-killers.

To say the 48-hours before the Test were frenetic would be an understatement. Chaotic would be more accurate. I don't think there was a single member of the squad who didn't do at least half a dozen radio and TV interviews. If I had been physically able to speak to all the people who asked for an interview, I would have done over 50. Michael Owen-Smith counted the requests.

It was becoming obvious that our lives had changed for ever as a result of the series win, and that was an interesting realisation – a little bit intimidating for some of the younger guys.

The Sydney Test
Much of our conversation on the evening before the Test, and on

the morning, concentrated on the fact that we were two-nil up. We thought a lot about what had happened to us against England at the Oval when we had already won the series – but this time, fortunately, it was obvious to me that nobody was suffering any sense of emotional anticlimax. The build-up to this Test match was very different and everybody was determined to prove beyond doubt that we were the better team.

There were many obvious distractions; the Australian media were all over their team like a rash – while, at the opposite end of the scale, J-P's mother had been flown out from Cape Town by a generous benefactor to watch her 'overnight sensation' son. I smile every time I hear that expression in sport because I know that behind every one there are usually years of hard, unrewarded work. The gesture was something we all felt very special about and hoped that he would be able to rise to the challenge of impressing the most important person in his life.

We went through another exercise with Snapey which he had introduced us to almost a month earlier in Perth. We stood in a circle and discussed 'what is important now?' We kept all the things that were important in the circle – partnerships, pressure, disciplines, and so on, and discarded all the things we didn't want in 'our circle'. Things like crowd intimidation, media distraction, and anything else which any of the squad felt distracted by.

Driving to the SCG three years earlier was an interesting experience because of the carnage on the streets of the city the day after the biggest New Year's party anywhere in the world. This year it was a day later because the Test match was starting on the 3rd rather than the 2nd but, nonetheless, even after an extra 24 hours to clean up there were still piles of rubbish and discarded bottles on every street corner. Australians are justifiably proud of their ability to maintain law and order and keep their streets looking clean and tidy at all times, so it brought a smile to our faces to see that even they took a little time to clean up after a party for a million and a half people.

The SCG has a very special and 'traditional' feel about it. When you arrive you are aware that you are going to become a part of history for the next five days. It is much the same as Lord's in that regard.

An unfortunate down-side of this wonderful stadium, which has refreshed and refurbished itself superbly over the years, is that the changing rooms remain tiny and compartmentalised: it's impossible for a large, modern squad to sit together. It must be a throwback to the days when there were only 12 or 13 people who used the changing rooms. These days there are 15 players and 10 members of the management team, but at times it was difficult to find each other in the pokey little rooms which comprised the players' area.

Australia had brought Andrew McDonald and Doug Bollinger into their Xl, which was a challenge for our research and analysis team. We had a little bit of information on them, but not a lot. We hoped that the occasion would be too much for either of them and we vowed to be aware, at all times, of any opportunity to put them under pressure. Bollinger had told a media conference two days before the Test that he would be 'giving 150 000 per cent' during the Test, a phrase I repeated in my captain's press conference on the day before the match, producing a lot of laughter amongst the Aussie media. It wasn't a deliberate attempt to score any sort of media points, but his comment had made me smile when I first heard it and it was worth repeating.

The wicket was very dry and likely to become very difficult to bat on as the game progressed. Having lost the first two tosses this was one I really wanted to win. I didn't – and Ricky took slightly less than a microsecond to announce that Australia would be batting first.

We bowled poorly in the first hour, with Katich and Hayden making a useful start. Jakes broke the partnership just before the drinks break when he had Katich caught at second slip, and Morne then had Ponting caught behind for a first-baller.

Hayden was going through a form of torture, however. He just wasn't himself. He wanted to dominate, he wanted to impose himself and he wanted to be the Hayden of old, but it just wasn't happening for him. I understood what he was going through, although the difference was that he was at the end of his career and I wasn't. He was tense and scared of getting out; he looked like he was suffering from the fear of failure that affects all of us at some time or another. At lunch he was just 22 not out.

After lunch he smashed his first ball 'on the up' through cover and it was clear that he wanted to be positive and hit his way back into form. I changed the field and removed the cover point, offering the chance to hit square of the wicket on a pitch which was too slow to do that with any confidence. Perhaps it was just luck, but perhaps the plan worked yet again, because he dragged a delivery onto his stumps from Dale trying to hit it square.

I am proud of the way I have learned to read the game and to read the way individual batsmen play according to the conditions, but I wouldn't have learned as many lessons as I have without the input of so many experienced and senior players around me. It might have been a really good day had Hashim held on to a catch off Clarke at square leg just before the close of play when he had made 69, but on the second morning he went on to 138 and added 142 with Mitchell Johnson, who made 64.

The day didn't start particularly well when the local doctor on duty declined my request for a local anaesthetic in my elbow. I was disappointed and didn't really understand the reason why, but Doc Moosajee understood and I had to accept it. Apparently he was concerned about creating further damage to the tendon because my naturally defensive reaction to pain would be compromised. So I took some painkillers and asked Doc 'Moose' to put a local anaesthetic patch on the elbow. Given how uncomfortable I felt, I made a good start and was confident that I could make a decent score when I reached tea on 16 not out. Soon afterwards, however, a ball from Johnson hit a crack and time stood still as I saw it lift sharply towards my hands. It was agony from the moment it struck. Shane came out and did all he could, but when I couldn't put the glove back on I knew it was serious and eventually accepted my fate.

I got changed and went to the hospital for x-rays, which revealed an 'angular fracture'. The doctor said that another blow in that area would probably result in surgery. He put a huge cast on the hand, which I wasn't particularly happy with. I returned to the ground to watch the rest of the day, not yet having absorbed or accepted the fact that my tour was over. I was just 'dealing with the moment' and watching the cricket, which actually finished well for us on 125-1 with Hash and Jacques looking well set.

That evening Doc and Mickey suggested that I went to Melbourne the following day to get a second opinion from a hand specialist, but also to get the first of the blood injections into my elbow, which would speed up the process of recovery by a week and improve my chances of being ready for the home series.

I wasn't keen on the idea at all. Basically I was feeling completely miserable and didn't want to leave the team at a very important time. Eventually they persuaded me and I couldn't deny that it made sense.

I visited the hand specialist first, Dr Greg Hoye. He is an eccentric man but clearly brilliant at what he does. He understood immediately my desire to have a more manageable cast on the hand and even asked me whether I wanted him to build something which might allow me to bat again. I knew he was joking and replied with an emphatic NO!

As we walked out of his surgery and climbed into his secretary's car to go to the next appointment, there were three or four photographers waiting to take pictures of me. It was absolutely bizarre and I simply could not understand it. The Test match was happening in Sydney and yet there was a group of photographers in Melbourne just to get a picture of a broken finger. How did they even know I was in Melbourne? We have very little experience of paparazzi in South Africa, so I was unprepared for this. I found it all very strange. I just couldn't see how my finger was 'a story'. Or my elbow, for that matter.

We drove to the second appointment with Doctor Frank Burt, who was an expert in elbows. He drew blood from my left arm in order to inject it into the tear in my right elbow and I left the surgery with a bruised and swollen lump the size of a golf ball. It looked awful and I felt the same way. As a parting gesture I was asked whether I would like a gadget which clipped onto my belt to help me carry things, given that I was banned from using my right arm to pick anything up and my left hand was broken. I laughed initially, thinking it was a joke, but then declined very seriously when I realised they were serious. I was not disabled: I would make a plan and cope. The image of somebody walking around with a couple of shopping bags clipped onto their belt still makes me chuckle. Australia is the kind of country you could be arrested in for doing something like that.

On the way back to Melbourne airport Doc and I listened to the radio commentary in the taxi and were pleased to hear that Morne and Bouch were mounting a fight-back after a clatter of wickets in the middle order. But by the time we landed we had been bowled out for 327.

On the fourth morning I was feeling very, very lost, once the realisation had set in that I was out of the Test. Mickey and I decided that Neil Mac would take over the on-field captaincy, but I had a few one-on-one chats with the players. Australia batted exceptionally well and set us an unlikely target of 376 in the best part of four sessions.

I was in more discomfort than ever before, after five and a half months of dealing with the pain of the tennis elbow. It's difficult to describe how debilitating and depressing the pain can be, because you don't realise how often you use your elbow during the course of the day. Just pinching your fingers uses the elbow ... everything I did, every movement I made was painful. I couldn't spray sunscreen without a nagging wince, and I certainly couldn't reach the back of my neck; I couldn't clean my teeth properly, sometimes I couldn't even pick up a glass of water. I used to order things from room service based on how easy it would be to eat. The less cutting, the better. I just lay on the bed trying not to move much. I tried to pick a TV channel and then stick to it so I didn't have to use the remote too much! It was bloody miserable. I was glad that we had at least started the process of long-term recovery.

They declared after lunch and we faced the decision about who would open in my place. Did we keep numbers three, four, five, six and seven in place? Or move Hashim up to open with everyone else moving up another place too? Mickey and I weighed up the pros and cons and decided that promoting Morne from number 8 to open was worth the gamble. Morne's excitement at the prospect of doing the job certainly played a part in our decision. It back-fired when he was out to the second ball, but we were happy with the decision. Hash and Mac finished the day strongly and we were reasonably well placed at 62-1 by the close, but there was an awful lot of work still to be done.

It was the final day of what had been a magnificent Test series and we needed to bat out the day to ensure a draw and keep a clean sheet. When I woke up it never, ever occurred to me that I might play a part in the day. Even later in the morning, when I started to imagine a scenario with 10 balls to go and nine wickets down, I shook my head and immediately dismissed the idea. The surgeon had told me that one more blow to the same area could result in surgery and metal pins, three months out of the game, so I'd easily come to terms with the fact that I wasn't going to be able to play.

I didn't even take any whites to the ground. At warm-ups I did some captaincy stuff – it was all I was good for! I chatted to the batsmen about a few little technical things, but then backed away and allowed them to do their own thing. You have to trust your players – there was nothing I could do for them.

The wicket was too dry on day one and had dried out even more since then. Batting for a whole day was going to be very difficult. We would need some luck.

We lost wickets fairly consistently throughout the day. We had little partnerships along the way, but each time we threatened to frustrate the home side, something would happen. Bouch got an absolutely shocking decision just before tea, which put us under a lot of pressure. He'd batted extremely well with AB and the two · of them were our last realistic hope. It was a full toss missing leg stump by a lot.

Even at that stage, going in to tea, not a single thought had entered my head about batting. There were thunder clouds hovering and talk of bad weather. But I was still hopeful that AB could bat with the tail and somehow get us through the last session to safety.

With about 25 overs to go in the day's play I was sitting on the bench outside the changing room when I looked across at Makhaya, who was padded up, waiting. Our last line of defence. For once he was quiet and seemed very serious. Suddenly he seemed all alone – and that was when I first thought about trying to contribute something myself.

I felt tired and sore, but a big part of me didn't want to let Makkie down. And another big part of me was terrified about what could happen if I was hit again. The surgeon had really put the wind up me by using the phrase 'career-threatening'. I didn't really have any arms, to be honest. My elbow was swollen, which meant I couldn't grip the bat properly with the top hand; and I had a broken knuckle on the bottom hand, which also wasn't ideal for gripping a cricket bat.

How would I go about batting, practically? For about five minutes I sat in my own little world contemplating the possibilities and the possible consequences. Eventually I walked to the back of the changing room to try and have a very quiet word with Doc Moosajee, the voice of reason.

But Mickey and Snapey obviously knew what was on my mind and they jumped in like a flash to suggest that we tried to see if we could get my hand into a glove before we made any further decisions. We used the scalpel from Doc's bag to cut open the wedding and pinkie fingers of my glove and then gently slid my hand in. I couldn't bend or split my fingers so kept them buddy-strapped and slipped them into the glove together. Then they started building some plastic around the glove to seal it back together and Shane melted some more plastic onto the outside of the glove to provide a solid 'casing' for a bit more protection. Finally it was done and everyone backed off to admire their handiwork. There were a few nervous smiles from everyone but I got the distinct impression that, having worked so hard just to see whether they could get my hand into a glove, they weren't about to start undoing it. So clearly there was no turning back now!

The next challenge was to get dressed with my broken hand already in a glove. I had some pants in my coffin, which I'd used to wrap my spare bats in for the journey home. Jakes lent me a shirt and Morne helped to dress me and put my shoes on and tie the laces. He was pretty hopeless at putting my pads on – somehow they just didn't feel comfortable.

I was dressed and ready to go. Sort of. How long could I try and survive? By now there were about 20 overs left. Should I wait for the last 10, or the last five? In my own mind I needed to make a decision, I had to have a point of focus. I chatted to Mick and Snapey, and Jeremy said quite clearly that I should start preparing to bat immediately.

Snapey lobbed me a few under-arm balls so I could try and figure out how I could hold the bat and, in particular, how I was going to play the short ball because that was worrying me. Instinctively I would play a pull or a cut shot but, without arms or hands to speak of, that would be impossible. I decided that I was just going to have to fight a lifetime of batting instinct and take it on the body.

So they brought me Morne's chest pad and tried to strap that around me, but I told them to throw it away because it was the most uncomfortable thing I had ever worn, in or outside a cricket match. I put on Harry's jersey as another layer of protection. It was only once I'd started batting that I saw it had a massive lunch stain on it. It looked like he had eaten his hamburger off the bottom left side of his pullover.

I was very nervous in my stomach but quite calm in my own head, if that makes sense. I knew what I would be trying to do – I had a plan, at least – the question was whether I could pull it off.

By now Makhaya and Dale were batting really well, showing enormous determination and courage. I was watching the overs dwindle down. I was watching from the back of the change room because I didn't want either the batsmen or the fielding side to know that I would be coming out.

Ricky was bowling his main seamers into the ground and I could see them tiring by the minute. If they weren't at top speed against me, all the better. I needed all the help I could get.

Dale was lbw with a little over eight overs remaining. The Australians were standing and staring at the pavilion, trying to see what was happening. They didn't know whether to celebrate a Test win or not.

The changing room doors opened for me to walk out and I heard a couple of shouts of goodwill and good luck from the Members as I walked through the doors. I put my head down and just walked. I was desperately going through the new batting checklist in my head, trying to focus on what I needed to do. I was going to stand very still and watch each delivery more closely than ever before. Then, if they were straight, I was going to get something in the way of them, if not the bat, then me.

While all this was rushing through my head I realised that the whole of the Members' stand was on its feet, cheering and clapping. I got goose bumps. When I realised that it wasn't just the

Members, but most of the stadium, I had a bit of a battle with my emotions. But in amongst those emotions was a little bit of fear, so that soon beat the other emotions into place.

I walked straight up to Makhaya and said: 'Well done, you are doing a great job, buddy, just keep going.' He replied that he had been quite calm up until then but that I was making him nervous now! He hadn't known that I was coming out. When he saw me walk out and experienced the standing ovation, I think the sense of occasion suddenly dawned on him. He'd just been good old Makhaya, taking it one ball at a time until then. Now I think he suddenly realised that we could actually do something extraordinary and save the game.

I tried to relax him again and assured him that, no matter what happened, we could only give it our best shot and play it one ball at a time. I grinned at him and he grinned back. I'm not sure which of us was more nervous.

MacDonald bowled the first two deliveries I faced and I focused on keeping my backlift low and all other movements to a minimum. They both hit the bat and trickled away, so I was on my way.

Makkie faced Bollinger in the next over and promptly nicked it straight to Hayden at slip – who dropped it. The let-off seemed to relax Makkie and he managed to climb back into the zone he'd been in for an hour before I got there.

Ricky brought Mitchell Johnson on for the next over, which didn't surprise me in the slightest. This was it – the challenge that I had been thinking about for the last hour or so. I expected no mercy – quite the opposite, in fact. He had the pace to shake me up, intimidate me in this state, and I expected him to use it.

I focused on small movements, watching the ball, trying to keep it out no matter what ... Oddly enough, I'd had very little experience of just blocking. For as far back as I can remember, I'd always still hit the ball even when I was in a defensive position.

Fortunately he didn't bowl many straight deliveries in that over and I could leave four of them. One delivery was wide and tempting and I instinctively moved to cut it. My elbow and hand screamed at me simultaneously and I cringed with pain and pulled away. So much for fighting my instincts.

The funny thing was that, ever since I played with Makhaya all those years ago, we have always had 'option A' and 'option B' for him. Option B is when he is allowed to play with freedom and smash a few deliveries – usually when we have a lead of 400 or something similar. But for most of the time, much to his frustration, we issue him with Option A instructions.

So when I tried to cut the ball, Makkie scurried down the wicket and said: 'Biff, Biff – just remember option A!' It was hilarious hearing that from him. But even funnier was the fact that he was absolutely right. He was the senior batsman, he'd batted for over an hour and I was doing his job, just hanging around and trying to stay with him!

We hung around and hung around, somehow. We could sense the Aussies' desperation and frustration but they never really resorted to bouncing me. I had expected more short balls.

Then Johnson switched ends to where the cracks were at their worst. It was the end from which he'd broken my hand. With 11 balls of the match to go, I blocked one to mid-on and we could have taken a single. I don't know why we didn't. Probably the same instincts that led me to try and hit the ball early on. We weren't trying to take any risky singles, but I should have taken that one. The next ball was a cracking delivery which pitched in the same crack and deviated to hit the top of my off stump. It would probably have got me out if I'd been fully fit.

I walked up to Makhaya and we gave each other a hug. He could be incredibly proud of the way he had gutsed it out. It would have been amazing if we had lasted another ten balls – a genuine fairytale end to the series. I shook hands with the Australians. Ricky said it was one of the bravest things he had ever seen on a cricket field. It was the beginning of a series of messages I received along similar lines. So many people told me how moved and inspired they had been by seeing me trying to bat, I was astounded.

It took ages to hit home, to sink in. It wasn't a reaction I had ever considered, that people might be affected like that. When I arrived home there were hordes of people at the airport just to see me, all wanting to talk about the tour, the series win and my injured batting.

The 'Captain Courageous' stuff seemed to have taken hold

amongst the supporters of the team, and even amongst people who didn't follow the game particularly closely. I remained completely blown away by how much people seemed to have been affected by the moment. I had just done what seemed natural.

One guy wrote me a long and quite moving letter saying that we don't have politicians who can make speeches like Barack Obama, but I had provided a moment of pride which could sustain and motivate people for a long time to come. He said I had made many people feel proud about themselves and their country. I was deeply moved but, at the same time, I did have a feeling of 'bloody hell, what have I done...?'

The e-mail:

'What a day of contrasts. The early hours saw one previously unpopular South African; walking down the stairs of the SCG, to a standing ovation and bringing even the hardest SA fan close to tears of pride. That's us isn't it? That's you and me, or at least visions of how we'd like to see ourselves, battered and bruised but defiant in the face of improbability.

'I have this constant debate with my wife who fails to see the point of sport. We may not have an Obama to give us a speech that invokes in us strength to keep believing in the impossible, but even my wife sat transfixed this morning as a picture of a man striding down 20 steps said, without uttering a single word, to the rest of the world: "Try tell me that I can't."

'Later in the same day headlines are made by another ex-South African who quits his role as England cricket captain after just 5 months at the helm. The odds were too tough to make it happen in South Africa, the greener grass of foreign pastures too alluring to resist. Without realising it, KP, you represent so many others like you. You are not alone, there are many like you who figure the odds are stacked too high to make it happen here in South Africa and look for the easier option. But you forget one thing; you forget that dealing with adversity in life breeds strength and character. Having the chips stacked against you, only to believe in something enough to defy the odds to come through these things again, and again, and again ... that's something another coloured passport cannot offer you.

'Thank you Graeme Smith, you gave us the Obama moment that reminded us why we love being South African this much. We are in for one hell of a tough year this year with no promise of what the end result might be. The rest of the world keeps telling us that we are just another part of the crippled body of Africa with no hope and a one-way ticket to failure. Seems like a pretty good time to go and bat then.'

After a few days back at home I knew that I had changed as a person and developed as a cricketer and as a captain.

I know I created the wrong impression when I started in the job five and a half years earlier as a very young man, and over the years I had managed to gain some peoples' respect through my performances and team results. Now, perhaps for the first time, I think I sensed a bit of affection, too.

Having tried so hard, too hard a lot of the time, to be the captain I thought I needed to be, I could now take a deep breath and just be me. For much of the last 18 months things had fallen into place with the team, me, my leadership, my personality and even my lifestyle. There had been some very lonely moments, even to the point where I asked myself why I was doing the job and for so little appreciation, but now I felt I had the answer. I am very stubborn when it comes to a challenge and I refused to give up the challenge of making a success of the Proteas' captaincy.

My hand and elbow were still a bit sore, but I would have taken ten times the pain for the reaction of so many people when I arrived home.

After the Test match many of us went across and had a beer in the Australians' changing room. By now the one-day players had arrived and I'd chatted to all of them about our hopes and expectations under the leadership of 'Botes'.

I went out for a quiet beer with the boys that evening and actually felt a little bit down. I was still amazed at what had happened in the last three weeks, but my tour was over and I felt deflated. I went back to the hotel quite early to pack, a process which required the help of a bell-boy because I couldn't lift most things!

The one-day series
Melbourne 16 January 2009
Hobart 18 January 2009
Sydney 23 January 2009
Adelaide 26 January 2009
Perth 30 January 2009

Throughout the one-day series I was in constant contact with Mickey and the rest of the management team and was also available to chat to any of the guys. I didn't call them for the sake of it, but they all knew I was available at any time. Although the time difference could make it problematic, there were a few things that I was really looking forward to watching in the series.

The squad was still a long way off the finished article and we had many pieces of the jigsaw still to fit. In some cases we weren't even sure whether we had the pieces, and in other cases, we had a couple of guys competing for the same place, so I was keen to see how they would respond.

Role definition was a key component of the squad composition and it was something Mickey and I had spoken about often. It's not an easy notion to explain to people who haven't played cricket, or even those who only play social cricket, because surely your role is either to score runs or take wickets ... or both! But it's quite a bit more complex in a national squad when you have a five-match series coming up – and, even more importantly, the prospect of two years together building towards the next World Cup.

There were going to be opportunities for guys like Hashim, who'd started his one-day career so impressively against Bangladesh, and Hersch, who was coming back from his alcohol rehab course and had played very little cricket for over a month – none, actually. It was obviously an emotional time for him, and the way he handled that would be important for everyone.

Top: A boat trip on the Swan River soon after arrival in Perth. The idea was to keep us awake and ensure a good first night's sleep to counter the effects of jetlag, but it was a lot of fun, too.

Bottom: I was so proud of the dignity we displayed in victory. It wasn't planned – it just happened. All our instincts told us to scream, shout, hug, cry and celebrate (which we did, later). But Australia deserved all of our respect first.

Top: The management 'family table' at Christmas lunch in Melbourne. The empty chair belongs to Mickey – taking the picture.

Bottom: Mickey with the four ladies in his life, wife Yvette and daughters Kristin, Brooke and Ashton.

'Once were enemies'. Warnie didn't much approve of young Smith at the start of his career, but after linking up at the Rajasthan Royals for the inaugural season of the IPL five years later, we became good mates.

I saw it on the screen and that was the moment it first sank in. Jeepers … what have we done?

Moments after the series was won. Unconfined joy was what we felt, but we confined it and behaved with respect and dignity.

Vinnie, for once, seems happy to part with one of his precious souvenir stumps. Tell me you can't feel the happiness and joy…!

Never headline-makers, seldom given the credit they deserve. Vinnie hugs Goolam, who has been on every Australian tour, home and away. Victory meant the world to Goolam.

Top left: Jacques scored his maiden Test century at the MCG 12 years earlier – it remains one of his best. In all the years between then and now, he'd never won against them. Now he'd won the series. The emotional reservoir burst its banks on the bus back to the hotel. I was having a quiet hug with Jakes, absorbing his 'karma', when J-P decided it was a good time to goof around!

Top right: Fast bowlers. A unique breed, and a rare band of brothers. Dale and Makhaya's affection and respect for each other leaps off the page.

Above: There are 'official' team photographs, and there are 'impromptu' ones. Long after the crowds had left, we decided to have another commemorative snap of the squad in the MCG. It's not every day you win a Test series in Australia.

Above: New Year, Sydney Harbour. This was the best out of 300+ shots of the fireworks. Moral of the story? Take pictures of other things and store firework displays, even ones as spectacular as this, in your head.

Left: X-ray and plaster cast. All a bit of a laugh – but inside was a swirling sea of physical and emotional pain, disappointment, confusion and anger

Above: The Test series trophy – a dream come true for Mickey and me. A picture I will cherish forever, and a partnership I will cherish, too.

Right: Morne, Mac and me: the 'new' opening partnership for the second innings. Morne is given a lesson on how the new ball looks from a batting perspective. He seems surprised.

Left: Jakes and partner, Shamone. There was a beautiful moment after the series win in Melbourne when Jacques took her out to the middle and attempted to demystify the game with terms like 'rough', 'leg stump' and 'over the wicket'. Shamone was a quick learner!

Having won the series, we were like a big bunch of kids waiting to go on a favourite school outing: Sydney was a great place to spend the New Year!

Ouch. (Gallo Images)

Nothing has really sunk in. I'm sore, we're struggling, my hand is broken (again) and I'm miserable. Craving quiet time to relax and reflect. (Gallo Images)

Running away from the celebration, for once. I know what a plaster-cast can smell like with fermenting champagne on it!

Above: The Aussie media weren't too complimentary about the series result.

Left: Makhaya gets into the spirit of 'Aussie Rules' – imitating Bob Rose, a legend of the Collingwood Club.

Right: Bouch comes to terms with a broken toe, courtesy of Shaun Tait. He was told he'd need six weeks to be ready for the first Test at home, which was six weeks away. He was ready in three. But he had a special boot constructed with a steel toecap, just in case. He wasn't going to miss anything.

Below: The team had to walk to the Adelaide Oval for the fourth one-dayer because the roads were closed for the 'Tour Down Under' featuring Lance Armstrong. Not an unpleasant walk.

Bottom: Celebrating the one-day victory.

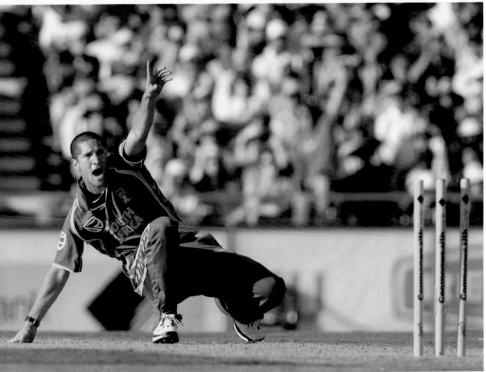

Top: 'Lopsy' Tsotsobe made a huge impression on tour with his attitude and dedication. An exciting prospect for the future. (Gallo Images)

Bottom: Wayne Parnell made incredible progress. You worry about pushing young players too fast, but sometimes they force your hand. At 19, 'Parney' looked comfortable in international cricket. (Gallo Images)

Ashwell. Seldom can South Africa have had a more driven and determined cricketer. In times of need, he's the man you need. (Getty Images)

Lahore? Ahmedabad? No – the venue is Newlands! Paul Harris revels in subcontinental conditions on the final day of the third Test. He's never had many headlines, although he's deserved some, but this was his day. Go Harry! (Getty Images)

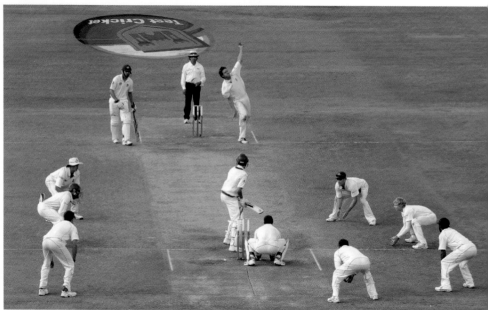

Mitchell Johnson was awesome throughout all six Tests. Fast, merciless and relentless, he made as much of an impression on the two series as anyone. Depending on how he wants his career to progress, he has the ability to become a genuine world all-rounder. (Getty Images)

On our way to victory. Drinks break at St. George's. Hashim takes water on his knees, in the customary Muslim way. I enjoy the picture – it represents who we are as a team. (Gallo Images)

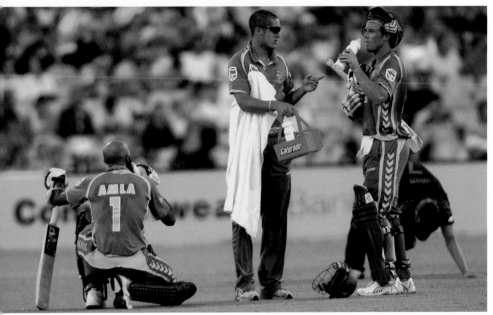

'Honours Board' recognition at Test venues means more than we can describe. Your name will be there in 100 years' time, probably more. The first names are already over 100 years old. It's a team game, but this is the pinnacle of personal pride for J-P, Makhaya, me and Dale.

The other important aspect of the squad was a culture and environment of self-responsibility and maturity in which everyone took ownership of their position. And to be honest, I was also looking forward to seeing how everyone handled themselves without me being around. I wanted to be there, obviously, but nobody is irreplaceable and I hadn't missed much cricket in six years, so it gave other people the chance to take responsibility. I wanted to see that the senior guys wouldn't just leave everything to Botes – he was going to need help and support.

It was a big effort for Botes to take over the captaincy, even though he had all the attributes. He leads naturally by example, he has a fabulous training ethic and a good energy about him. I was just hoping that he would still bowl well and that the leadership wouldn't be a distraction. As it turned out, that should have been the last of my worries. We bowled brilliantly throughout the series, and by doing so he made his job as captain so much easier. He always had someone to turn to when he needed to take control of the game – himself.

Everyone did perform their roles, especially the senior guys; they played well and it was obvious how much they were supporting the new skipper, even from 12 000 kilometres away and very early in the morning. It was fantastic to watch. It showed how far we had come in a short space of time.

I was never too worried about the two Twenty20 losses – there were mitigating circumstances and, besides, our focus was on the one-dayers. The most important thing was how we bounced back from them. The first ODI in Melbourne was stunning to watch. It gave me a lovely insight into the ups and downs, the highs and lows that fans go through watching on TV. I obviously had a little more insight than most fans, and I knew that the batting power-play would be crucial. And I knew what an explosive combination Albie and a five-over power-play could make, but it was still thrilling to see him win the game with 10 an over required. I knew instinctively what a confidence booster that would be, and how depressing it probably was for the Australians, who had played very well up until the final five overs of the match and probably thought they were in control of the game for 80 per cent of it.

The roles were reversed in the second game in Hobart, where

we probably controlled the majority of the game before losing our way towards the end of what should have been a very manageable run chase. Mickey admitted that he should probably have sent both Albie and Bouch in a bit earlier to try and catch up, but it's very well to revisit things in hindsight. There is often as good an argument to be made for sticking to the original batting line-up as changing it.

Nobody in Australia gave us the remotest chance of chasing 270 in Sydney. The Channel Nine commentators had virtually given Australia a 2:1 lead before we'd faced a ball. It was a tough challenge, to be fair. It required one of the highest run chases ever at the SCG. It's similar to Newlands, in many ways. The pitch gets slower as the match goes on and there's usually some swing under lights. I didn't think we were favourites, far from it, but I didn't write us off like everyone else seemed to.

Once again, it was magnificent to watch. Hersch came right for the first time and gave us a dynamic start with a terrific 60. I knew his confidence was a bit shaky but he knew the importance of body language and, by looking at him, you'd have thought he was in the form of his life. Jakes's experience in the middle overs helped to set up another batting power-play for Albie, who came in and smashed 40 off 22 balls. He was performing his role in the team beautifully and, as a consequence, other roles were becoming more clearly defined for different players. Albie and Botes, in particular, had taken firm ownership of their positions in the team.

I chatted to Mickey once again in the build-up to the fourth game in Adelaide. It was on 'Australia Day', which meant a lot more emotional 'baggage' for the home side. It would be wrong not to admit that it also inspired us a little more. The thought of spoiling the celebrations a little bit by winning the series on an iconic day for the country seemed to fill the guys with a mischievous determination. As Albie said, 'they would be thinking exactly the same thing if we were playing at home on South Africa Day'.

It was a great day for us. We bowled superbly and there were a couple of loose shots from the Australians, something which can happen when batsmen are under pressure. Throughout the series we had been expensive in the first 15 overs but then fought back tenaciously in the middle overs. The most exciting thing about that was how well our spinners had played – Botes and his new lieutenant, J-P, had formed a partnership that was difficult to play against. With Harry bowling so well in the Test series, it suddenly felt as though South African cricket had taken a huge leap towards a greater skill base and away from our reliance on seam bowling.

We chased down a modest total with ease, Hash finishing with 80 and AB 82. We won with ten overs to spare. Another series was won in Australia and everything we had worked for the whole season had come together. Again, I would rather have been there to celebrate, but my own fitness and health were making progress and I felt no less proud of the achievement just because I was in Cape Town.

AB said that Australia's 'revenge' had been to close the hotel bar early to prevent the guys celebrating. I'm sure it was nothing of the sort – there was probably a good reason!

The following morning I heard an interview with AB on radio in which he dedicated the win to me! It took me completely by surprise but brought a big smile to my face. I think he should probably have dedicated it to himself and Hash, or Botes, or Mickey and the management team. They were the ones doing the work. I was just driving to the physiotherapist at the time.

With only the Perth match remaining on tour, Mickey and I were both very clear that it was time to play Lonwabo and Wayne. It couldn't have worked out better. We posted a big score, 288, although I groaned out loud when Hash fell for 99, I would have loved him to have got a hundred. Everyone chipped in; J-P rounded off what had been an amazing two months for him with a 60.

Australia were dismissed for just 249 with Lonwabo picking up four wickets, key wickets, too. Everything was going so well and the team were obviously on such a high. A couple of the guys called me that evening to share the joy!

9.

Celebrating South Africa

Australia: February – April 2009

TESTS
Johannesburg 26 February–2 March 2009
Durban 6–10 March 2009
Cape Town 19–22 March 2009

TWENTY20
Johannesburg 27 March 2009
Centurion 29 March 2009

LIMITED OVERS
Durban 3 April 2009
Centurion 5 April 2009
Cape Town 9 April 2009
Port Elizabeth 13 April 2009
Johannesburg 17 April 2009

I was asked to fly to Joburg to meet the team and be a part of the 'welcome home' celebrations. Life had been very different for me in the time I had been at home, with more attention than I had ever experienced before. I couldn't really go anywhere without a lot of interaction from the public, from all walks of life, and the only guaranteed quiet time was at home. Often I was just running a normal errand – trying to go to the bank or buy some groceries. And usually I was running late or had another meeting (or physio session!) just around the corner, but it was absolutely impossible to be frustrated with anybody. The happiness and excitement that people had experienced during the Test series was a joy to be a part of. Some people just couldn't help themselves from stopping and, when the words didn't come, they said something simple like 'well done' or 'we're very proud of you'. It was a moving time.

There were thousands of people at OR Tambo airport to greet the team – it was terrific to be a part of it. I'd spent so many hours reflecting on all the hard work we'd put in over the last 18 months, and wondering how many people would ever know how many hours of hard work and planning had gone into our success in Australia. When I saw the crowds at the airport, I knew I didn't care in the slightest whether they were aware of the details; I just knew it had all been worthwhile when I saw them celebrating and had a sense of how much it meant to them. I felt very strongly that they were sharing the victory with us rather than just applauding the team, and I loved that feeling. There was a sense of celebrating South Africa rather than just the team.

Winning in Australia was something that we had never been able to do before and the public had wanted us to do it so badly every time we went. The demands on my time changed quite dramatically. As national captain I have always had a big responsibility to Cricket South Africa's sponsors, my own sponsors, responsibilities to charities, the public, the media and obviously the demands of practice and training. In the month of February I received 60 requests to speak at charity dinners and functions. I would have needed 40 hours in a day to come close to accepting the invitations.

It was hard work managing my time and making sure that I gave myself enough time to prepare for my cricket and to attend to all my other full-time responsibilities.

Fortunately I had some very good people around me to help manage my time and organise my diary. It was hard work for them, too. Every time they had to say 'sorry, but Graeme can't make that date', there was a risk that people would be disappointed and feel let down. It was a feeling I've never fully come to terms with.

I'd managed to work hard on my elbow rehab with the excellent physio, Hayley Coleman, and I'd had the last check up on my hand. I was now very close to playing again. My first game back would be for the Cobras in the semi-finals of the domestic Pro20. No option of a gentle 'easing back' into the game. It wasn't easy, straight in to the cauldron of full-on action – it wasn't international cricket, but an extremely important match none the less, with a place in the Champions League at stake.

The semi-final against the Dolphins went to a nerve-wracking third leg and was eventually decided on the 'super over', which we won before winning the final, too, at Newlands. Happy days. Both the hand and elbow were feeling good.

The national squad was gathering together in Joburg the day after the Pro20 final and it was important that J-P and I were there from the start. We flew in a private jet – which was a first for both of us – what a great experience! It looked about the size of a Citi Golf from the outside, but was actually very spacious and comfortable inside. We felt very VIP. We left at midnight and were in bed by just after 2:30 am. Even I was pinching myself when I thought about the pace of my life – J-P, however, just seemed to be taking it in his stride. The way his life had changed in the last couple of months was probably beyond comprehension.

We were up for training the following morning by 9:00 am. The national squad had originally planned to get together three days before the Test, but Mickey, quite rightly, had changed that to five days when it started to become apparent how many distractions we were all facing. Some more than others, needless to say.

Even with five days I shared Mickey's concern that it might not be enough time for everyone to get back into the groove. Despite turning down a heck of a lot of appearances, it still felt like we were doing a breakfast, lunch or evening function every day. A lot of it was for team sponsors and there wasn't a word of dissent from the players about actually doing it. There is a genuine understanding of how it all works, how much sponsors keep the wheels of the game turning; it was all stuff that needed to happen. But we also needed to find the time to do all our preparation, to make sure that we gelled together as a team. And it needed to happen really, really quickly.

Given the circumstances, I can't complain. The build-up was as good as could be expected in the circumstances, although there simply wasn't enough time to just 'be together' and regain that collective focus we had enjoyed in Australia.

Our cricket preparation actually went well: when we managed to get to the nets for the first couple of days, we put a lot of time in on our skills work. Unfortunately, rain then played a part in the last couple of days and, once again, we were frustrated.

In all truth, we went into the first Test under-cooked. But there was nothing we could have done about it. We had no desire to let down competition sponsors like Standard Bank, and with no option of playing first-class cricket, there wasn't much we could do. We considered organising a two- or three-day game against an Invitation XI, but most of our bowlers were Titans, so they wouldn't have been available because of the Pro20. We decided to concentrate on the moment and have no regrets. It was all we could do.

The Johannesburg Test

I was up early again and it felt like I'd had a long day already when 10.00 am arrived and it was time for the toss. It felt even longer when I lost, again. Four in a row. I was starting to take some flak from the guys. Plenty of comments about practising my tossing. Australia would bat. We would have done the same.

We made one of our best starts to any of the 16 days of Test cricket we'd played so far. A couple of early wickets and we were looking to take control. Just before lunch I dropped Ponting at first slip, a really straightforward catch. If anything, it came too slowly. I hadn't dropped a catch for a very, very long time and I was desperately disappointed. It was a crucial batsman at a crucial time. And so it proved.

I was so angry and down on myself about it. You should never wear your disappointment too publicly, but particularly as a captain, you cannot show your emotions. You have to put it behind you and move on to the next phase of the game. Easier said than done. It hounded me with just about every ball until he was out. He played superbly in conditions that were more difficult than he had anticipated and, with Clarke, took the game by the scruff of the neck. They were positive and scored quickly, preventing us from getting into the game until we separated them.

Marcus North batted in classic Test fashion. For a debutant, he gave us the impression he'd played 40 Tests. In the early days of my career I would have felt little beyond the frustration of a game I couldn't 'get hold of', but some time ago I tried to focus on learning in adversity as well as success. There is nothing wrong in being impressed with an opponent, and North was impressive. I admired his approach. I would have used a sledge-hammer to get him out, however, if there had been one available. Since there wasn't, I studied him and tried to learn as well as figure out a weakness. We didn't bowl the right length to him – that I knew.

Johnson relished the increasing freedom that a big total provides you with and climbed into the bowlers. He's much better than a 'hitter' and he certainly isn't a slogger. To strike boundaries as sweetly as he does, you need a good technique. He finished with 96 not out in a total of 466, which was at least 140 too many on that pitch. We were a long way behind the game already.

We only managed a modest 220 in reply, with Johnson once again at the forefront with another four wickets. He got me with an away swinger, a weapon he wasn't supposed to have in his armoury. The ball held its line perfectly. He hadn't managed to do that throughout the whole of the series in Australia – so, in terms of my preparation, he 'did' me beautifully. It was not something I had expected or made plans for. But I was bloody well going to for the second innings!

Good on him for working so hard on a certain skill and finding a delivery that none of us had expected him to have (actually, that nobody thought him capable of bowling with his round-arm action). No doubt he had been working on it for a while, but to perfect a new skill like that to Test standard in the three weeks between series was a special effort. Now we had to come up with a game plan for him.

We started badly with the ball, once again, in the Australian second innings. Too many loose deliveries; too much emotion in our bowling; not enough control. We didn't work in partnerships and had no chance of creating impatience amongst the batsmen through discipline. Instead, it was us who were impatient.

Just as the game was set to leave us for good, Jakes came on and bowled a brilliant spell, taking three quick wickets. Harry got one or two to turn and we managed to bowl them out cheaply for 207. For a brief moment it looked as though we might be able to stage an incredible comeback, but Philip Hughes, with his unorthodox and infuriating style, made 80-odd and pushed the lead beyond a realistic chase.

The truth is, we hadn't bowled well enough in the first 30 or 40 overs in either innings, and that was what had cost us.

Mac and I started solidly in the second innings and I began to believe, given our recent confidence in chasing totals, that we could produce yet another batting miracle ... provided we made a huge start at the top of the innings.

Australia bowled exceptionally well; they achieved exactly what we had been searching to achieve. They placed Mitchell Johnson at the centre of the plan and worked the other bowlers around him. Hilfenhaus thrived in a specific role and Andrew McDonald, who felt like one of the least threatening bowlers in world cricket, did a fine job by simply bowling straight on a good length for over after over. He was a fine exponent of the 'drip, drip, drip' tactic. We miss, he hits.

We just weren't 'there' as far as Test mind-set was concerned. I will defend for the rest of my life the attitude and determination of the team – there was no lack of will or effort. It was, perhaps, just the lack of intensity in our preparation which cost us. As I said, there wasn't much we could do about that.

Personally, it was a relief to collect some runs after coming back from injury. I knew I should have pushed on further from 69, but I'd rather be dismissed being positive than being tentative. I was out to a pull shot towards the end of the day off Hilfenhaus. We made 291, which wasn't bad batting last. But it was scant consolation for losing. It hurt.

After the press conference we had a very good chat amongst ourselves in the changing room. We discussed how we had let each other down and how much we needed and wanted to bounce back. It was extremely honest and powerful, one of those talks in which you show each other how much you really care about what has happened, and how much you want to put it right.

In bed that night I was distracted and worried about a few things. So many of the guys had experienced such changes in their lives since we returned from Australia. They were dealing with expectations and performing under pressures they had never experienced before: I knew it was going to take a while for them to get used to things.

With so much happening around the team I was acutely aware

of the need for some quiet time away from it all to mentally prepare – but with the first two Tests being so close together, it wasn't possible.

Could we find the time we needed to address and then work on what had gone wrong at the Wanderers? I couldn't stop thinking about it. I probably knew the answer was 'no.' That's why I was so obsessively thinking about it.

Soon enough we were on the plane to Durban. We prepared well but, again, I was subconsciously aware at all times that we had needed more time between Tests. Just 24 hours to be together and refocus.

We prepared well physically and did our best to address the other aspects that are so important. We knew what it took to come back from one-nil down and we were well aware of the advantage that Australia had being one-nil up and playing so well as a team.

The Durban Test

It started in familiar fashion, with me losing yet another toss. It was crucial. It was a very hot day and the wicket was playing perfectly. We bowled badly on the first morning again. We leaked runs everywhere and never built any pressure. Once again we never dealt with the extreme unorthodoxy of Hughes and never coped with his 'strangeness'.

He played and missed, played and missed … and then hit someone for four. It got to us. He looked dreadful, yet clearly there was something there. A lot there. I felt we never stuck to our plans, never put the ball in the right place consistently; but then again, sometimes he would hit exactly the same ball from outside off-stump through midwicket which he'd just left alone. And then he'd hit the next one in the same place through extra cover. He was a hard one to work out.

But we stuck to our guns and fought hard. If only we had been able to bowl as well at the start of the day as we had at the end. We fought with increasing determination and discipline as the day progressed and were rewarded with the wickets of Hughes and Katich. Unfortunately they'd scored 115 and 108 respectively.

There was significant rain overnight and the wicket burst into life – the ball was flying around all over the place. Kingsmead is odd like that. The wind, the humidity, the clouds ... and of course the infamous tide! They all play a part in how the match unfolds, sometimes it's no more than a myth, sometimes it's real – and other times nobody has a clue.

Morne bowled really well and Steyntjie was at his best, too. We produced the intensity we had been lacking on the first day and bowled them out for 352 – which was a superb result, given both openers had made centuries. I was feeling very positive. We all were.

About 20 minutes later I was feeling very unpositive. We all were! Mac nicked off straight away and Hashim was lbw in the same over. I was watching helplessly from the other end. There seemed to be a lot of bounce from an area of the pitch which was just back of a good length. The Australians had struggled with it earlier, too.

It wasn't tail-enders being surprised, but some of the most successful batsmen in the world over the last couple of years. Every now and then a ball which should have bounced at waist height was suddenly coming through at chest height, even throat height. Uneven bounce is a batsman's nightmare. Sideways movement is fine, but unpredictable bounce at 145 kilometres per hour makes it not only impossible to play, but impossible to avoid, too.

I was still positive, however. I was in a very determined frame of mind. Tough conditions and two-down for nothing. Backs to the wall. Not ideal, but Test cricket isn't supposed to be easy.

I got off the mark by pushing a ball from Hillfenhaus into the covers and taking a single. Now I was facing Johnson. I was methodically going through my plans against him and focusing hard on how to counter his new weapon. I was aware that we were in a bit of a crisis but I was concentrating very hard on my own game, on breathing, moving my feet well and focusing very specifically on each individual delivery. It's not only all you can do in a situation like that, but it is what you have to do for the sake of the team – you certainly don't perform any better by fretting or panicking.

I was concentrating a lot on the swing, which way he was likely to try and shape it against me, when he bowled me a beauty, just back of a length and too short to swing either way. It stood up sharply and, just as in Sydney, time stood still. Well, as still as it can when the ball is three feet away from you and travelling at nearly 150 kilometres an hour. There was nothing I could do. It crashed into my hand and deflected away somewhere. I ran through for a single with my finger throbbing.

I knew immediately it was bad, but you just hope and pray that the blood will start flowing and the pain begin to subside. Then you know you can carry on. I was trying to move it, to get the blood flowing and get some feeling back. Feeling other than pain, that is. I convinced myself that I would be OK if I could spend the rest of the over at the non-striker's end while Jakes took care of things for a while. But he tucked one to square leg two balls later – and back on strike.

By this stage nothing had changed and I knew there was something very wrong. The finger was burning with pain and when I tried to squeeze the bat handle, nothing happened. I signalled for Brandon Jackson and was still desperately hoping I could buy myself some more time before the feeling came back.

I took the glove off when he arrived and he sprayed it and ran a couple of checks. He didn't say much, but his body language wasn't hard to interpret. We couldn't get the glove back on. It was all too familiar, just like Sydney – similar pain.

I tried my best, but it was hopeless. So that was it. We were effectively 2-3.

It was a desperately disappointing start to the innings, but even in the flurry of wickets and chaos which ensued, it was obvious to all of us that Johnson was bowling an incredible spell. After me came Jakes, hit in the face by a Johnson bouncer. He needed stitches.

It was an eventful start for Brandon, who had taken over from Shane Jabaar after seven or eight years with the national team. It was odd not having Shane, but he had reached the end of the road after the Australia tour. Everyone in International cricket has a shelf life, whether you are a player, administrator, medical staff, or whatever. Eventually the relentlessness of the travelling and work gets to you: goodness knows how many times Shane spent the night waking up every two hours to ice somebody's knee or ankle and how many times he had dinner over a physiotherapist's bench while he treated someone in the evening. I first worked with Shane when I was 17, so I know how good he was – but it was time for a change.

The pitch conditions were perfect for Johnson, but credit to him for making them count. He was genuinely fast and he had a completely ruthless and merciless streak to him. And he was in the best form of his life – a tough combination to handle all at the same time. He put us under extreme pressure that day. We simply didn't cope with the new ball, just as Australia had struggled against the second new ball earlier in the day.

J-P played an extremely gutsy innings to make 70, but we were bowled out for 138 and I was on my way to hospital again – Durban this time, not Sydney.

The x-ray revealed an '80 per cent fracture' through the small finger. At least it wasn't the knuckle again. Thank heavens for small mercies. It didn't feel like much consolation. The surgeon told me that if it fractured another 10 or 15 per cent then I would need surgery to have a steel pin inserted. Maybe they always say that ...!

I needed to be very careful for the first three weeks of the injury, and I knew that. I also knew how I was supposed to be feeling and thinking – I'd heard it, and said it, so many times before. 'Concentrate on what you can control, not what you can't.' Be positive, and so on. But at the time I was pretty gutted.

I had never broken a finger in the whole of my professional career – ten years – and now I'd popped two in three games. The frustration of facing just three balls in the whole Test match was hard to digest.

I obviously couldn't be on the field for the rest of the Test, and felt more helpless than ever when we weren't playing well. Everything started going wrong, and getting worse. We weren't playing well as a team, we weren't scoring runs, we couldn't put one partnership together, never mind two or three – with bat or ball. From the sidelines it looked like everything we had been striving to achieve in the last 16 months, everything we had been doing so well, was now going wrong.

It was hard to digest the reality that we couldn't win the game. We'd bounced back so often in the past that I'd been absolutely confident that we could do it again. Like everyone else, I started thinking about saving the Test and trying to square the series in Cape Town. I couldn't even contemplate the idea of defeat. Deep down, very deep down, I knew it was likely.

They declared on 331 for 5, leaving us to chase well over 500. The pitch didn't behave too badly, oddly enough. It was probably harder on the second day than the fourth and fifth. But it was still very dry and cracked and was deteriorating quickly.

We managed to reach 370 – which, in isolation, was an incredible effort in the circumstances. But nothing exists in isolation in Test cricket, and we all knew that we'd let ourselves down in the first innings with both bat and ball – and that was why we had lost. We had shown a lot of character in playing 'catch-up' cricket in both Test matches, but there's only so far you can let your opponent get ahead before you lose him.

Although there was a deep sense of regret that we hadn't been at our best and hadn't done ourselves justice, we were also very aware of the spirit and determination the Australians had shown in bouncing back from a shattering defeat to do exactly what we had done to them – win the series with a Test to spare. During the final day I had been telling myself that it wasn't the end of the world, and had started planning ways to fight back. But worse was to come.

We lost the Test match by 175 runs. We'd lost the home series – and, including Sydney, we'd lost three Tests in a row. The selectors felt compelled to make changes – so they left out Neil Mac and Morne.

There had been mounting pressure on Neil after Australia because he'd had a pretty thin time apart from the run chase in Melbourne. But it was a very tough thing for me to deal with. Mac had become an integral part of our team and the leadership department. Our opening partnership had been extremely successful for over a year and we worked well together at whatever we did. As the 'senior pro' he was also immensely respected and equally liked by the whole squad.

He had also scored over a thousand runs in the 2008 calendar year; he'd put in some key performances at critical times – not just with the bat, but sometimes by helping to create an environment which was calm but still highly motivated. He was just as comfortable being a big brother to the younger players as he was sitting with the management team – and it was inevitably him that ended squabbles and built bridges with his understated modesty and great humour. He did more than anyone to make sure the team was happy and gelling together when I was attending to other duties – or in hospital!

So yes, you could say I was upset to say goodbye. We all were.

It was disappointing that the selectors had made that decision, but they felt he hadn't scored enough runs and that was his primary job. The selectors take responsibility for their decisions, but I wasn't very happy.

The J-P/Ashwell selection issue before the series had also been a tough one to handle. Ashwell had been an integral part of our success for well over a year and had been desperately unlucky before Perth. But then J-P had made himself undroppable in Australia, which left Ash feeling out in the cold once he returned to fitness.

There has long been a policy in the national team that players who are selected as injury replacements, and those who are injured, understand that there is a status quo to which the team will return when the injury has healed. J-P even said that several times in Australia and on return to South Africa, but nobody took him seriously because of what he had done.

So when the selectors changed that policy and tried to end the damaging speculation by announcing the squad 10 days before the first Test – with J-P and without Ashwell – they set a precedent which may become problematic in the future, although everybody could understand their reasons. Still, it made it a little harder to stay focused on what was important and immediately relevant.

Morne's omission was different to Neil's. He hadn't bowled to his enormous potential and needed, perhaps, to have a long bowl away from the pressures of Test cricket. He has all the attributes of a great fast bowler, not only physically but in his attitude and personality. Once he learns a little more about his action and what he is capable of doing, and learns how to apply the killer blow when he has a batsman on the run, I believe he will have a very, very successful career. So Morne was handed back to the Titans for the last round of SuperSport matches and, sure enough, took a bagful of wickets.

In a move reminiscent of the famous story about Mark Waugh's first Test for Australia, which came at the expense of twin brother Steve, Albie was given the nod ahead of Morne. He'd been in the squad for Durban but had never been likely to play. Now, with the series lost, it was felt that the time was right to see Albie in Test cricket, particularly with the ball. Nobody had much doubt about his batting.

Jakes is our integral all-rounder and the hub around which the team is built (and has been for a decade!) – but who knows how long Jakes is going to be able to bowl for? It's important to look ahead and stay ahead of the game. Some people say Australia didn't do enough of that during the 'golden years'. Albie was a proven success in one-day cricket and, thanks to that, was the next all-rounder in line. Imraan Khan had enjoyed a fantastic domestic season with the Dolphins, with five first-class centuries, so he certainly deserved a chance. I didn't know a great deal about him or his batting, but he'd put a lot of runs on the board, and although he looked slightly unorthodox, I'd learned not to judge any cricketer on first impressions.

With me injured and Mac dropped, the selectors decided to recall Ashwell as both captaining and opening batsman. I understood that both jobs had been communicated to Ash via telephone and that a discussion had taken place and he had agreed to take on the double responsibility before the team was announced.

So it certainly came as a surprise to me a day later when he changed his mind and declined the captaincy. There had obviously been a major miscommunication or misunderstanding between the selection convenor and Ashwell and there's no point in raking the embers of the fire, but the whole week building up to the final Test was poorly managed and unprofessional. It disappointed me hugely because we'd worked so hard, for so long, on creating good structures around the team, having processes which everybody understood and the right people in the right positions to handle situations with sensitivity.

The most important culture which Mickey, the management and I had tried to establish was one which placed the team ahead of all individuals, whether it was a player, selector or administrator. The team success came before any individual. It felt a little bit like all the structure, discipline and principle was suddenly being compromised because we'd lost the series. Yes, we hadn't played well enough in the first two Test matches, but we'd had an awful lot of success before that. The selectors wanted to make changes and that was their prerogative, but I couldn't help thinking that things could have been handled much better – by everyone.

I phoned Jakes and left a message asking him if he would be prepared to handle the captaincy for one game. I assured him that I would still deal with as many of the 'other' captaincy responsibilities as I could so he could concentrate on his game. He called back about an hour later and said he was happy to take the job for the final game. I was grateful for the stability and continuity that Jakes provided.

When the squad gathered in Cape Town we immediately had a clear-the-air chat with Ashwell to make sure we were pulling 100 per cent in the same direction. He explained his point of view and, although it wasn't exactly the same as mine, I had no doubt that the matter was not history.

Mick had asked all the guys who were carrying niggles to play in the last round of four-day games before the Test. Ashwell had opened for the Warriors and made 250! But everybody benefited from the time away from the tour and a few nights in their own beds. The first-class cricket was exactly the workout they needed.

Every now and then I would experience a real 'down' when the realisation hit me that the series was gone. I spent hours and hours agonising over what we could have done better. I know what we *should* have done, but it wouldn't have been fair on one of our major sponsors. We should have pulled out of the Pro20 and held a camp in a small town like Kimberley for a week and gone quietly about our work, playing sessions of Test cricket in the middle and gradually working ourselves back up again.

But the national players are the drawcards for domestic cricket and Standard Bank pays a lot of money and deserves the best crowds possible. But there must be a compromise solution somewhere ...

From the time we gathered in Joburg there were sponsor commitments every day, sometimes two or three engagements or commitments. We always felt a bit rushed, always a bit hassled. It was a classic case of 'conveyor belt syndrome' and it felt like there was never a chance to jump off it and calm down, to reflect.

Peoples' lives had changed, expectations had changed, guys had gone from being slightly peripheral figures to being national heroes – and that was going to take a bit of time to deal with.

On the one hand, I'm tempted to say that 2008 was a unique year and that we won't encounter similar problems in the future. But on the other hand, I hope we have many more years like 2008! Lessons were learned and they will be preserved for use in the years ahead.

I'd spoken at a Wanderers breakfast with Ricky Ponting before the first Test and there were 1 600 people, 160 tables. It had really put into perspective how cricket had changed and how excited people had been about the Proteas and what we had achieved. The expectation before the home series was enormous – and, I assure you, we were aware of it. I was equally aware that we needed some quiet time away from everything, and that we weren't going to be able to have it.

The Cape Town Test

I was still involved, even though I had a broken finger. Mick asked me to be around the squad to provide continuity of leadership and to help with some of Jacques's duties. It was important for the whole management team to be strong in the build-up to the Test match and to ensure that the players weren't distracted by any of the nonsense which had happened earlier.

During the second Test Mickey and I had sat down and started to build our plan for the next phase of development of the team and the squad. Cape Town was, in many ways, the end of ... perhaps not an era, but it was the pot of gold we'd been planning towards for over two years. Or it was supposed to be. Everything had gone pretty much according to plan, apart from the last couple of Tests.

Now it was time to start thinking about the next plan and the next period. We wanted new ways and means of ensuring that we still progressed, kept challenging the squad and developing as individuals. We addressed the areas which needed to improve if we were to remain as successful as we had been for the last 18 months, and become even better.

We felt almost as though the new era was beginning now and we wanted to mark the occasion by doing something special. So often you can look too hard for something when it's actually right in front of your nose – and this occasion was no different ... Table Mountain! We went up by cable car the evening before the Test and had our traditional pre-match dinner at the restaurant at the top. It was a spectacular success. I've lived in Cape Town for the best part of a decade now and it was probably only my third or fourth trip to the top. Sometimes you can take the most obvious things for granted. Some of the guys from up north had never been up, and a couple of them discovered a previously unknown fear of heights which provided much amusement for everybody else.

The dinner was good and as we caught the last cable car down it felt like we were the last people on the mountain. It was quiet and peaceful – although bloody cold! I knew the team were in the right frame of mind and I think Mick and I decided then and there to use the mountain as inspiration again in the future.

The Newlands Test was a great success in so many ways, not just the result. Everything we had spoken about before the series began suddenly clicked and worked as it was supposed to have done three weeks earlier. We bowled in partnerships; when Dale was firing the bowlers at the other end supported him perfectly by maintaining the pressure which he had built.

Harry has turned the role of 'unsung hero' into an art form but, finally, he had a few people singing his name on the final day, having bowled magnificently throughout the match. Yet again he was prepared to do the dirty work for the team, even when there was finally a bit of turn and bounce for him.

It was a spinner's dream to be able to produce the match-winning effort he did when conditions were favourable. In some ways it can be harder to deliver when you are expected to, because that expectation can make you try too hard and the batsmen are instinctively more careful against the spinner. But at last Harry had his headlines and his man of the match award. Bouch remained unsung and probably under-appreciated by the public yet again, but I was all too aware of how much he had contributed to the team and to the consolation victory. And I made sure he knew that I knew. South African cricket is lucky to have them and their competitive spirit and determination.

AB once again played tremendous cricket – his hundreds seem to acquire more class each time. Like most of us professional sportsmen he can be a little bit defensive when confronted with criticism and he wasn't all that pleased when Mickey and I pointed out in England that he still had a tendency to throw his wicket away when we needed him most.

He answered that criticism by making a huge century at Headingley, a famous one in Perth, another one under pressure in Joburg and then the one at Newlands. He didn't enjoy being singled out, but the result was that he started to think about his game so much more. He has the ability to destroy any bowling attack in the world and I reckon Mickey and I were amongst a few people who realised he had the talent and ability to become one of the best batsmen in the world even before he did. That's why we spoke to him. We were frustrated for him – and the team.

Ashwell also made a big hundred opening the batting, which was amazing given his initial reluctance. There were a lot of people watching him closely to see how he handled the situation and his response was positive in every way. Ashwell is one of the most determined characters I've ever played with – or against – and that shone throughout his innings.

It was just as special to see Jakes reach three figures once again. He had come close a few times, but actually hadn't scored a century for over a year and, although he never, ever displayed an ounce of doubt to his team mates or anyone else, I sometimes wondered whether there was a question or two inside him. I know I've questioned myself a few times when I've been short of runs.

It felt like a great luxury having Albie batting at number eight. The tail had done a good job at important times, but if you can find the right man, every captain would rather have someone with his ability at eight rather than a Harry or a Morne – with respect to them! Albie is naturally aggressive and strikes the ball as cleanly as anyone in the country. Or the world, for that matter.

Ultimately, however, it will be his bowling which defines his

Test career. He needs to play a significant part with the ball, in either an attacking or defensive role – or both, preferably. If he can perform consistently, he'll be a great all-rounder to have in the Test line-up.

Bowling Australia out for just 209 at tea on the first day put us in charge, but to reply with 651 exceeded all of our expectations. It was a total which set a number of records and which features prominently in Australia's 'highest totals conceded' column. There is undeniably a place for 'record chasing' in sport. Just as athletes pursue records when there aren't gold medals at stake, cricketers can consider records when it doesn't affect in any way their pursuit of victory. Having bowled Australia out so quickly, we had given ourselves so much time we could have batted for two and a half days.

Eventually we bowled them out for 422 after Mitchell Johnson had made quick amends for his near-miss at the Wanderers and smashed a maiden Test century. Nobody could possibly begrudge him. He was ruthless.

We won by an innings and 20 runs – and if anyone had any doubts about the worth of winning a 'dead' Test match, they need only have seen the reaction in our change room and, for that matter, amongst the crowd who had stayed right until the end of play on the fourth evening when the match ended. It was the only Test out of six which wasn't decided on the final day.

Three-all was probably a fair reflection of how the two teams had played throughout the summer – although, as you would expect, I felt that that we should have won both series, and I was still perturbed by how we had played in the first two Tests and the preparation we had before them.

It would have been good for South African cricket if we had been able to digest the series win in Australia for a little longer and reflect on the achievement. But back-to-back series was the way it was and, to be fair, we would have had four years to reflect on our success if we had played to potential at home and won both series.

The one-day series

TWENTY20
Johannesburg 27 March 2009
Centurion 29 March 2009

LIMITED OVERS
Durban 3 April 2009
Centurion 5 April 2009
Cape Town 9 April 2009
Port Elizabeth 13 April 2009
Johannesburg 17 April 2009

I have always believed that good victories are worth a good celebration. It reinforces the positive and happy memories. It isn't much different in any other profession. A good sale, a good contract won, a case solved – workers celebrate and congratulate each other.

A couple of the Aussie boys came into the change room and we chatted about everything that had happened over the last six Tests, which was great. The relationship between our teams has always been close and very respectful.

We had decided to travel straight from Newlands to Joburg after the Test to link up for two Twenty20 matches. Ordinarily we might have gone home for a couple of days – there was certainly time – but after what had happened before the first Test, we believed it was important to stay together as a squad and keep the momentum we had just built. There were also a lot of new faces joining and we wanted as much time as possible to gel together and to make them feel at home.

I was pleased with the policy of rewarding guys who had been successful in the domestic Pro20 – Roelof van der Merwe and Yusuf Abdulla had shown consistent form and deserved the chance. Besides, I have never enjoyed the perception that that national team is a 'closed shop' and have always been in favour of deepening the talent pool. Besides, there was the prospect of the ICC Twenty20 World Cup a couple of months after the series, so we wanted to see new players.

The two matches went really well. Australia made 166 at the Wanderers with David Hussey belting 88 not out. We didn't bowl in the right places to him and then we looked to be struggling after 12 overs in reply – we were 83-5, only half way towards the target. But Albie and Bouch were amazing in the final eight overs, scoring at over 10 an over. We all know how hard it can be to defend at the end of an innings at the Wanderers, so although we'd left ourselves with a lot to do, it wasn't too hard to imagine us winning.

In the second game at Centurion we made 156-5 after giving Roeloff an opportunity with the bat at the top of the innings. He responded with 48 off 38 balls. He has a pretty straightforward approach – swing hard, and often. This time it came off for him. He didn't do himself any harm with that and I was already thinking ahead to the next World Cup in 2011, which will be held on the subcontinent. His bowling shows a lot of promise and knocks like that can offer great value at the end of the innings.

Still, I thought we might be 15 to 20 runs short of a good total. Our spin combinations were particularly successful on the day, however, and it was a fine effort to restrict the Aussies to under 140 on a ground that can be notoriously difficult to defend on.

We joined up early again in Durban for the start of the ODIs because we were determined not to allow the season to end on a low. Although the injuries had been frustrating, the time with the squad had been well spent. But now it was my opportunity to contribute on the field once again. The finger had healed and I was ready to go. Having said that, medical people are always cautious, so I'd been hearing a lot of 'it's fine … probably' and 'it's fixed … just don't get hit on it again.'

I was nervous during the first few training sessions but fortunately everything went well and I was actually feeling very good before the game. Part of the reason I felt good was that everyone else had worked hard and I felt really positive about the whole squad. Well prepared and confident.

You wouldn't have thought so from our performance, though! Once again we bowled badly in the last 10 overs and conceded 90 on a pitch which was dry and getting slower. Australia's 286 was at least 50 runs too many. Australia still didn't seem quite sure about when to take the batting power-play and it was a surprise that they left it until the final five overs despite having lost wickets regularly in the middle overs. Even so, it's still a nightmare for the fielding captain. Getting the field placings right is critical – you need a bit of luck, too, but it's a skill that will become increasingly important as one-day cricket evolves to keep pace with the growth of Twenty20 cricket.

The run chase didn't last long. Bowled out for 145. The only positive I could possibly think of was that I'd made 52 and played as well as I'd felt. I knew I should have gone on to 80 or 100 and given us an outside chance, but time in the middle was a lot better than none.

I didn't feel any sense of panic at all. It felt more like a result to be curious about than angry about. How could a good team, well prepared and confident, lose like that? Fortunately everybody else felt the same way.

After the match, however, an angry fan sent a letter to Cricket South Africa expressing his disgust at our performance and suggesting that match fixing still existed and that we must have thrown the game. At first we laughed it off and forgot it. It was obviously too ridiculous to be given any serious thought, let alone a response, but a short time later I began to realise that the writer may not have simply been abusive. The tone of his email suggested that he may actually have believed what he was writing. It was a shock to all of us and there was a good deal of anger amongst the squad for a short time. I wouldn't say it added to our determination, but it did add to our concern about the repercussions of performing so badly, and it wasn't something we wanted to ever hear again.

With only one day between Friday's opening game and the second game, a 10:00 am start at Centurion, we made the Saturday afternoon practice session an optional one. The whole squad came to nets, but only a few of us actually trained. 'Optional' training can be a contentious subject if it's not treated with care. Everybody needs to know that that they will not be negatively judged if they opt not to train, or even stay in their room and rest, because rest is as important as exercise. But it said a lot about the attitude of the squad that everybody wanted to be there, even if they didn't do much physical work.

Mick and I decided on two tactical changes. Wayne Parnell would open the bowling and Roelof would play as an extra spinner. There was an element of risk to both decisions but we had confidence that 'Parnie' would be a handful – especially if the ball swung – and Roelof was on his home ground and knew conditions well. It was increasingly clear that he was a cricketer with an 'unknown' quality, an ability to make something happen. He is a fighter. In Australia they would say he had some mongrel in him, a quality both Mickey and I enjoyed.

Steyntjie and Parney were incredible up front with the new ball: pace and swing from both ends at over 140 kilometres per hour, and different angles of attack, too. Sometimes, as a captain, you have to make the best use of your resources in difficult conditions and you need to try and be clever. On other days, much rarer days, you can stand at slip with two heavy artillery guns blazing and the hardest decision you have to make for the first hour is what you're going to have at the drinks break. They were a brilliant combination.

Australia were bowled out for 131 after they'd won the toss and batted first. It was the coach, Tim Nielsen, who had persuaded Ricky to bat. He said the pitch would 'probably do a bit' for the first hour and then calm down. He was right. The trouble is, his team were 40-6 by the time it calmed down.

We eased our way to 132-3 in reply without alarms. I made another 40 and felt good once again before falling to another soft dismissal. A little bit of disappointment – but heavily outweighed by the satisfaction of levelling the series in such convincing fashion.

We stuck with the same team for the third game at Newlands and confidence was high. You could almost sense how much more easily everybody was breathing. Everybody enjoys playing in Cape Town – and I mean purely the cricket – although it is also a popular destination. I managed to win a toss, which made a pleasant change, and we batted first on a very, very slow pitch which we knew would be even more awkward under lights.

It is possible to attack and score boundaries, but only in the last 10 overs when there is a good foundation laid and there are wickets in hand. Early on, however, you need to graft and make sure the bowlers don't put you under pressure. As a result we may have been a touch more conservative than we needed to be in the first 15 overs, but nonetheless, we were being smart – reading conditions.

We set ourselves little targets throughout the innings and we kept hitting them. It was a superbly intelligent and efficient partnership between AB and Jakes in the middle overs which set up the final onslaught. They didn't score too many boundaries, but they placed the ball, they ran hard and maintained great intensity. I sometimes wonder how many people actually appreciate the skill required to add 130 at five an over, without taking a risk. I guess it's not as exciting as watching Albie Morkel score 40 from 20 balls, but the level of talent required is very similar. We set a big total for them to chase, in excess of 280, which would have been a record chase under lights at Newlands.

We took control of the game pretty early and never relinquished it. We 'only' won by 20 or 30 runs, but it was like a rugby game in which a team only loses 18-6 despite never entering the winning team's 22. We looked to be heading for victory by 100 or more until a floodlight failure and a couple of other stoppages took the wind out of our sails – James Hopes and Callum Ferguson scored 60s to add a bit of respectability to the scoreline. But Roelof had bowled beautifully in the middle overs and done a lot to put us in control with three well-earned wickets.

We moved to Port Elizabeth over Easter, which is a little like the Christmas period for the players – work and more work, while friends and family spend time together over the holiday season. It doesn't feel much like Easter. Mind you, after four or five years as a professional cricketer you tend to forget what Christmas and Easter used to feel like before they involved nets, team meetings and matches. No complaints, however. There are many, many more people who give up their holidays to perform more important duties than we do, and for less money!

We prepared well and discussed how important it was to produce an emphatic performance at St. George's, for two reasons. Obviously we wanted to win the series – but also, we hadn't done ourselves justice on the ground for the last few years and had lost more games than we'd won. Somebody mentioned in the team meeting that St. George's was in danger of becoming a 'bogey' ground for the team, which was a horrible thought because we love its unique atmosphere and it's one of our favourite venues in the country. Many people have asked me over the years whether the players enjoy the band or whether we find it distracting. The answer is a very definite 'yes – we enjoy it!'

Australia decided to chase, which surprised me a lot. In all the games and series I've played against them, and that I've seen them play against other teams, they have always adopted a simple strategy, especially for the 'big' games: 'Bat first, post a good total and create pressure.' They had always backed their ability to bat first and put runs on the board under pressure. Perhaps their mindset had shifted and maybe they weren't as confident as they had been in the past? I really was surprised and, to be honest, it gave me a bit of a boost. I felt as though Australia had taken a step backwards before the contest had even begun. I couldn't see a valid cricketing reason to bowl first.

Herschelle had scored his very first ODI century at St. George's over a decade earlier and now, with so much on his mind and going on in his life, here he was again, scoring a century. A more emotional one than any before, perhaps, but like just about every Herschelle Gibbs century, it was to be a match-winning one.

He'd had a really tough year. He had made some very hard but very important decisions in his life and he'd shown fantastic discipline in sticking to them. He had mentioned the distance he had travelled as a person in the last six months compared to the preceding 10 years and the hundred obviously felt like a defining moment for him, the reward that made everything worthwhile. As much as he had occasionally frustrated me, I was willing him to succeed as much as I have ever wished anyone success. We all were. He is an immensely popular man.

AB once again played brilliantly – changing and adapting his role as the game situation changed, playing the foil to Hersch for a time and then taking over the lead role. He truly does have all the ingredients to become the best of his era. If he keeps progressing and learning as he has done for the last couple of years, he could even become one of the best of any era.

Between the two of them we put 317 on the board, which I felt was very convincing. Perhaps even 30 or 40 more than par.

But Australia made a flying start with a flurry of boundaries from Brad Haddin and some smart, run-chasing cricket from Michael Clarke. After 20 overs they were 120-0 and as well set as you could ever be for an assault on 300. They had a better platform than we'd had.

The asking rate was still six runs an over, however, and I made the point during drinks that a couple of partnerships with the ball, a spell of four or five overs at a cost of two or three runs each, and the resultant pressure would lead to a mistake. They couldn't keep scoring at six an over for the next 30. You have to have the courage of your convictions in situations like that and concentrate your energy on the next over, even the next ball. But if you look at the finish line and say 'they'll never chase 300' – that's when things can go wrong.

Again it was the spinners who bowled so well in the next session. Roelof picked up another three wickets and both he and Botes bowled their 10 overs for less than five an over, outstanding effort. It was further justification for our decision to play the extra front-line spinner and take the pace off the ball as much as possible. Unusually, Australia hadn't played spin well at all in either one-day series and I often felt fortunate in being able to dictate the pace of the game for much of the time with specific field settings. The credit for that, of course, does not go to the captain – it goes to the spinners.

It was mostly a new experience for me. It had happened once or twice before, but never consistently. But I'd been on the receiving end enough times, particularly on the subcontinent. Well-set batsmen being tied up in the middle overs by spinners at both ends ... I've sat and watched many a South African innings founder in that situation. But now it was happening the other way around. Who would have believed it, a South African captain controlling a one-day match – and much of the series – using three spinners. Wow.

The pressure resulted in boundary shots from the batsmen rather than steady accumulation and they succumbed pretty quickly to 250 all out.

Another series win against Australia. That made it three in as many months. But it felt absolutely magnificent. There was something very special about having the dressing room celebration with all the new faces, seeing how much it meant to them. They'd also grown up with Australia's domination of world cricket as a central theme in their development, and now they were playing a part in dismantling it. I looked around the room often at the players as they celebrated and thought how perfect the balance was between senior, middle and junior players.

An important realisation struck me. As hard as we had tried to maintain continuity in the last 18 months, many players had forced their way into both squads – especially the ODI squad – and I took that as a sign of great health in our game. The new ball options were good with Parnell and Tsotsobe competing hard, amongst others; we had spinners to choose from and South Africa's traditional strength – all-rounders – was also well catered for.

Mickey and I had spent so much time talking about the future, and about planning and preparing for the months, tours, competitions and years ahead, and we'd already started doing that once again. But that moment was a time to enjoy the present and to reflect back on how far we had come as a team, in both forms of the game, in the last 18 months.

There were good structures in place around the team, too, which had been critical. The support from Gerald Majola had been fantastic and deeply reassuring. On the occasions we had needed him most, he had been there for us, even when it was uncomfortable or difficult for him to fight our corner.

Mickey and I had gelled so well together and the input of Vinnie and Jeremy Snape on the coaching side had been world class. The management team had taken care of so much but, importantly, under the influence of Doc Moosajee, the players had been encouraged to avoid selfishness, take personal responsibility and not behave like sheep and follow the crowd. We had played well, against good teams, on every continent for a year and a half and achieved so much success, both individually and as a team. It was time to savour the memories and cherish the moment. It was a time to be satisfied.

But there was still one game to go!

It hadn't been the easiest week, with the IPL drawing ever closer to South Africa and with the marketing and enormous advertising campaign proving to be an understandable distraction. The IPL teams were also trying to organise the guys' travel schedules and integrate them, as much as possible, into the rest of the squad. Many of us were due to play in the double-header on the opening day of the tournament in Cape Town, the day after the final one-dayer against Australia at the Wanderers, so it was a hectic time. Thank goodness we'd won the series already.

The least we could do in the way of preparation was to change hotels from the Sandton Sun, which was awash with IPL fever, to the Montecasino where life was much quieter. Throughout the series we had stressed our desire to remain the hunters rather than become the hunted, and we wanted to finish the series on a high note. We'd achieved that, in a sense, by winning the series – but we still wanted to repeat the 4:1 score line of the series in Australia.

We chased 303, which was about 20 runs too many. Nonetheless we were on target for much of the time, but lost our way towards the business end of the innings. Herchelle made another wonderful 80 and Jakes a near run-a-ball 60, but we lost by 47 runs and Australia deserved the consolation.

Both teams had competed with an incredible camaraderie and spirit. There was mutual respect in the field and the teams were a credit to the game – I felt that much of the summer of competition had been almost ambassadorial for cricket.

The Test series, in particular, had placed the highest and most important form of the game back on the pedestal it deserved. It had been riveting to play in – and, from what everyone has told me, equally compelling to watch. The crowds in both countries were evidence of that.

I won't ever forget the last 18 months, but particularly the year of 2008. It is not the end of an era, however – far from it. The majority of the team are in their twenties and we are all very, very excited about the future and what we may still achieve.

I'd prefer to think of this as the beginning of an era.

Appendix by Andrew Samson

South Africa in International cricket

1 October 2007 – 30 April 2009

Test Results

VERSUS PAKISTAN IN PAKISTAN

Karachi, 1-5 Oct 2007: SA 450 (HH Gibbs 54, GC Smith 42, HM Amla 71, JH Kallis 155, AG Prince 36, AB de Villiers 77; Abdur Rehman 4-105) and 264-7* (JH Kallis 100*, AG Prince 45, A Nel 33; Abdur Rehman 4-105, Danish Kaneria 3-85). **Pak** 291 (Mohammad Hafeez 34, Kamran Akmal 42, Shoaib Malik 73; PL Harris 5-73) and 263 (Younis Khan 126, Faisal Iqbal 44, Shoaib Malik 30; DW Steyn 5-56). **South Africa won by 160 runs.**

Lahore, 8-12 Oct 2007: SA 357 (GC Smith 46, JH Kallis 59, AG Prince 63, AB de Villiers 45, MV Boucher 54, PL Harris 46; Umar Gul 3-103, Danish Kaneria 4-114) and 305-4* (GC Smith 133, JH Kallis 107*). **Pak** 206 (Salman Butt 40, Kamran Akmal 52, Misbah-ul-Haq 41; M Ntini 3-42, PL Harris 3-57) and 316-4 (Kamran Akmal 71, Younis Khan 130, Mohammad Yousuf 63*). **Drawn.**

South Africa won the series 1-0.

VERSUS NEW ZEALAND AT HOME

Johannesburg, 8-11 Nov 2007: SA 226 (HH Gibbs 63, AB de Villiers 33, MV Boucher 43; SE Bond 4-73, CS Martin 3-67) and 422-3* (HM Amla 176*, JH Kallis 186). NZ 118 (SP Fleming 40; DW Steyn 5-34, M Ntini 3-47) and 172 (JDP Oram 40, DL Vettori 46*; DW Steyn 5-59). **South Africa won by 358 runs.**

Centurion, 16-18 Nov 2007: NZ 188 (CD Cumming 48*, L Vincent 33, SP Fleming 43; DW Steyn 4-42) and 136 (SP Fleming 54; DW Steyn 6-49).

SA 383 (HM Amla 103, JH Kallis 131, AB de Villiers 33; MR Gillespie 5-136). **South Africa won by an innings and 59 runs.**

South Africa won the series 2-0.

VERSUS WEST INDIES AT HOME

Port Elizabeth, 26-29 Dec 2007: WI 408 (CH Gayle 66, D Ganga 33, RS Morton 33, MN Samuels 94, S Chanderpaul 104, DJG Sammy 38; M Ntini 3-100, A Nel 3-85) and 175 (D Ganga 45, MN Samuels 40; DW Steyn 3-67, PL Harris 4-35). SA 195 (AB de Villiers 59; DB-L Powell 3-58, JE Taylor 3-46, DJ Bravo 4-24) and 260 (JH Kallis 85, AB de Villiers 60, A Nel 34, DW Steyn 33*; FH Edwards 3-37, JE Taylor 3-66). **West Indies won by 128 runs.**

Cape Town, 2-5 Jan 2008: WI 243 (CH Gayle 46, MN Samuels 51, S Chanderpaul 65*; DW Steyn 4-60, A Nel 3-61) and 262 (D Ramdin 32, S Chanderpaul 70*, CH Gayle 38; A Nel 3-62, DW Steyn 4-44). SA 321 (HM Amla 32, JH Kallis 36, AG Prince 98, MV Boucher 59; DJ Bravo 4-82) and 186-3 (GC Smith 85, HM Amla 37). **South Africa won by 7 wickets.**

Durban, 10-12 Jan 2008: WI 139 (D Ramdin 30; SM Pollock 4-35, A Nel 3-45) and 317 (RS Morton 37, MN Samuels 105, DJ Bravo 75; DW Steyn 6-72). SA 556-4* (GC Smith 147, HM Amla 69, JH Kallis 74, AG Prince 123*, AB de Villiers 103*). **South Africa won by an innings and 100 runs.**

South Africa won the series 2-1.

VERSUS BANGLADESH IN BANGLADESH

Mirpur, 22-25 Feb 2008: Ban 192 (Mohammad Ashraful 34, Aftab Ahmed 44, Shakib Al Hasan 30; DW Steyn 3-27, M Morkel 5-50) and 182 (Junaid Siddique 74; DW Steyn 4-48, JH Kallis 5-30). SA 170 (AB de Villiers 46; Shahadat Hossain 6-27) and 205-5 (GC Smith 62, HM Amla 46, AG Prince 38; Shahadat Hossain 3-70). **South Africa won by 5 wickets.**

Chittagong, 29 Feb-3 Mar 2008: SA 583-7* (ND McKenzie 226, GC Smith 232, HM Amla 38, JH Kallis 39*; Shahadat Hossain 3-107). Ban 259 (Shahriar Nafees 69, Abdur Razzak 33, Shakib Al Hasan 40; DW Steyn 4-66, M Ntini 4-35) and 119 (Shahriar Nafees 31, Abdur Razzak 32*; DW Steyn 3-35, RJ Peterson 5-33). **South Africa won by an innings and 205 runs.**

South Africa won the series 2-0.

VERSUS INDIA IN INDIA

Chennai, 26-30 Mar 2008: SA 540 (GC Smith 73, ND McKenzie 94, HM Amla 159, AB de Villiers 44, MV Boucher 70, M Morkel 35; Harbhajan Singh 5-164) and 331-5* (ND McKenzie 155*, GC Smith 35, HM Amla 81; Harbhajan Singh 3-101). **Ind** 627 (W Jaffer 73, V Sehwag 319, RS Dravid 111, VVS Laxman 39; DW Steyn 4-103, M Ntini 3-128, PL Harris 3-203). **Drawn.**

Ahmedabad, 3-5 Apr 2008: Ind 76 (DW Steyn 5-23, M Ntini 3-18) and 328 (VVS Laxman 35, SC Ganguly 87, MS Dhoni 52, IK Pathan 43*; DW Steyn 3-91, M Ntini 3-44). **SA** 494-7* (GC Smith 34, ND McKenzie 42, JH Kallis 132, AB de Villiers 217*; Harbhajan Singh 4-135). **South Africa won by an innings and 90 runs.**

Kanpur, 11-13 Apr 2008: SA 265 (ND McKenzie 36, GC Smith 69, HM Amla 51; I Sharma 3-55, Harbhajan Singh 3-52) and 121 (GC Smith 35; Harbhajan Singh 4-44, V Sehwag 3-12). **Ind** 325 (VVS Laxman 50, SC Ganguly 87, Yuvraj Singh 32, MS Dhoni 32; DW Steyn 3-71, M Morkel 3-63, PL Harris 3-101) and 64-2. **India won by 8 wickets.**

The series was drawn 1-1.

VERSUS ENGLAND IN ENGLAND

Lord's, 10-14 Jul 2008: Eng 593-8* (AJ Strauss 44, AN Cook 60, KP Pietersen 152, IR Bell 199, SCJ Broad 76; M Morkel 4-121, PL Harris 3-129). **SA** 247 (ND McKenzie 40, AG Prince 101, AB de Villiers 42; MS Panesar 4-74) and 393-3* (GC Smith 107, ND McKenzie 138, HM Amla 104*). **Drawn.**

Leeds, 18-21 Jul 2008: Eng 203 (KP Pietersen 45, IR Bell 31; DW Steyn 4-76, M Morkel 4-52) and 327 (AN Cook 60, JM Anderson 34, TR Ambrose 36, A Flintoff 38, SCJ Broad 67*; DW Steyn 3-97, M Morkel 3-61). **SA** 522 (GC Smith 44, HM Amla 38, AG Prince 149, AB de Villiers 174, MV Boucher 34; JM Anderson 3-136, MS Panesar 3-65) and 9-0. **South Africa won by 10 wickets.**

Birmingham, 30 Jul-2 Aug 2008: Eng 231 (AN Cook 76, IR Bell 50, A Flintoff 36*; A Nel 3-47, JH Kallis 3-31) and 363 (KP Pietersen 94, PD Collingwood 135; M Morkel 4-97). **SA** 314 (ND McKenzie 72, JH Kallis 64, AG Prince 39, MV Boucher 40; RJ Sidebottom 3-81, JM Anderson 3-72, A Flintoff 4-89) and 283-5 (GC Smith 154*, MV Boucher 45*). **South Africa won by 5 wickets.**

The Oval, 7-11 Aug 2008: SA 194 (GC Smith 46, HM Amla 36, AB de Villiers 39; JM Anderson 3-42) and 318 (HM Amla 76, AB de Villiers 97, PL Harris 34; SCJ Broad 3-44). Eng 316 (AN Cook 39, KP Pietersen 100, PD Collingwood 61, SJ Harmison 49*; M Ntini 5-94, JH Kallis 3-51) and 198-4 (AJ Strauss 58, AN Cook 67). England won by 6 wickets.

South Africa won the series 2-1.

VERSUS BANGLADESH AT HOME

Bloemfontein, 19-22 Nov 2008: SA 441 (GC Smith 157, ND McKenzie 42, HM Amla 112, AG Prince 59*; Shakib Al Hasan 5-130). Ban 153 (Mushfiqur Rahim 48; M Ntini 3-20) and 159 (Mehrab Hossain 43*; DW Steyn 5-63). South Africa won by an innings and 129 runs.

Centurion, 26-28 Nov 2008: Ban 250 (Tamim Iqbal 31, Junaid Siddique 67, Shakib Al Hasan 30, Mushfiqur Rahim 65; M Ntini 4-32, M Morkel 4-73) and 131. SA 429 (HM Amla 71, AG Prince 162*, MV Boucher 117; Shakib Al Hasan 6-99). South Africa won by an innings and 48 runs.

South Africa won the series 2-0.

VERSUS AUSTRALIA IN AUSTRALIA

Perth, 17-21 Dec 2008: Aus 375 (SM Katich 83, MJ Clarke 62, A Symonds 57, BJ Haddin 46, JJ Krejza 30*; M Ntini 4-72) and 319 (SM Katich 37, RT Ponting 32, A Symonds 37, BJ Haddin 94, JJ Krejza 32; PL Harris 3-85, JH Kallis 3-24). SA 281 (GC Smith 48, HM Amla 47, JH Kallis 63, AB de Villiers 63; MG Johnson 8-61) and 414-4 (GC Smith 108, HM Amla 53, JH Kallis 57, AB de Villiers 106*, J-P Duminy 50*; MG Johnson 3-98). South Africa won by 6 wickets.

Melbourne, 26-30 Dec 2008: Aus 394 (SM Katich 54, RT Ponting 101, MJ Clarke 88*, BJ Haddin 40; DW Steyn 5-87) and 247 (RT Ponting 99, MG Johnson 43*; DW Steyn 5-67). SA 459 (GC Smith 62, J-P Duminy 166, PL Harris 39, DW Steyn 76; PM Siddle 4-81, NM Hauritz 3-98) and 183-1 (GC Smith 75, ND McKenzie 59*, HM Amla 30*). South Africa won by 9 wickets.

Sydney, 3-7 Jan 2009: Aus 445 (ML Hayden 31, SM Katich 47, MEK Hussey 30, MJ Clarke 138, BJ Haddin 38, MG Johnson 64, NM Hauritz 41; DW Steyn 3-95, PL Harris 3-84) and 257-4* (ML Hayden 39, SM Katich 61, RT Ponting 53, MEK Hussey 45*, MJ Clarke 41). SA 327 (GC Smith

30*, HM Amla 51, JH Kallis 37, MV Boucher 89, M Morkel 40; PM Siddle 5-59) and 272 (HM Amla 59, AB de Villiers 56; PM Siddle 3-54). **Australia won by 103 runs.**

South Africa won the series 2-1.

VERSUS AUSTRALIA AT HOME

Johannesburg, 26 Feb-2 Mar 2009: Aus 466 (RT Ponting 83, MJ Clarke 68, MJ North 117, BJ Haddin 63, MG Johnson 96*; DW Steyn 4-113, M Morkel 3-117) and 207 (PJ Hughes 75, BJ Haddin 37; M Ntini 3-52, JH Kallis 3-22). **SA** 220 (ND McKenzie 36, AB de Villiers 104*; MG Johnson 4-25, PM Siddle 3-76) and 291 (ND McKenzie 35, GC Smith 69, HM Amla 57, JH Kallis 45; MG Johnson 4-112, PM Siddle 3-46). **Australia won by 162 runs.**

Durban, 6-10 Mar 2009: Aus 352 (PJ Hughes 115, SM Katich 108, MEK Hussey 50, MJ North 38; DW Steyn 3-83) and 331-5* (PJ Hughes 160, SM Katich 30, RT Ponting 81). **SA** 138 (J-P Duminy 73*; MG Johnson 3-37, AB McDonald 3-25) and 370 (HM Amla 43, ND McKenzie 31, JH Kallis 93, AB de Villiers 84; PM Siddle 3-61, SM Katich 3-45). **Australia won by 175 runs.**

Cape Town, 19-22 Mar 2009: Aus 209 (PJ Hughes 33, SM Katich 55, BJ Haddin 42, MG Johnson 35; DW Steyn 4-56, PL Harris 3-34) and 422 (PJ Hughes 32, SM Katich 54, MEK Hussey 39, MJ Clarke 47, AB McDonald 68, MG Johnson 123*; DW Steyn 3-96, PL Harris 6-127). **SA** 651 (AG Prince 150, HM Amla 46, JH Kallis 102, AB de Villiers 163, JA Morkel 58; MG Johnson 4-148). **South Africa won by an innings and 20 runs.**

Australia won the series 2-1.

South Africa won 15, lost 6 and drew 3 of the 24 Tests played in this period.

Test Averages

BATTING & FIELDING

Name	M	Inns	NO	Runs	HS	Avg	100	50	Ct	St
GC Smith	23	39	4	2057	232	58.77	7	7	39	0
AB de Villiers	24	37	6	1801	217*	58.09	6	7	34	0
JA Morkel	1	1	0	58	58	58.00	0	1	0	0
AG Prince	19	30	7	1274	162*	55.39	5	3	13	0
JH Kallis	24	39	4	1847	186	52.77	7	7	42	0
HM Amla	24	40	3	1844	176*	49.83	5	10	19	0
J-P Duminy	6	10	2	389	166	48.62	1	2	9	0
ND McKenzie	17	29	3	1225	226	47.11	3	3	17	0
MV Boucher	24	33	3	844	117	28.13	1	4	77	6
J Botha	1	1	0	25	25	25.00	0	0	1	0
HH Gibbs	6	10	0	224	63	22.40	0	2	9	0
I Khan	1	1	0	20	20	20.00	0	0	1	0
DW Steyn	22	24	2	313	76	14.22	0	1	7	0
A Nel	9	11	1	137	34	13.70	0	0	4	0
PL Harris	20	26	3	278	46	12.08	0	0	10	0
M Morkel	16	20	0	205	40	10.25	0	0	3	0
M Ntini	24	27	18	69	28	7.66	0	0	5	0
RJ Peterson	1	1	0	4	4	4.00	0	0	1	0
M Zondeki	1	1	0	0	0	0.00	0	0	0	0
SM Pollock	1	0	0	0	0	-	0	0	0	0
Totals	264	380	56	12614	232		35	47	291	6
			Extras	776				subs	1	
			Total	13390		41.32			292	

Test Averages

BOWLING

Name	Overs	Mdns	Runs	Wkts	Avg	BB	5I	10M
M Zondeki	14.4	4	42	3	14.00	2-10	0	0
RJ Peterson	29	4	94	6	15.66	5-33	1	0
SM Pollock	28	6	85	5	17.00	4-35	0	0
DW Steyn	772.4	141	2704	128	21.12	6-49	9	3
JH Kallis	457.1	104	1265	45	28.11	5-30	1	0
M Ntini	764.4	166	2544	80	31.80	5-94	1	0
PL Harris	729.3	151	2001	60	33.35	6-127	2	0
A Nel	282.3	62	896	26	34.46	3-45	0	0
M Morkel	492.5	64	1809	52	34.78	5-50	1	0
J Botha	18	0	75	2	37.50	2-57	0	0
J-P Duminy	35	5	125	2	62.50	1-14	0	0
JA Morkel	32	4	132	1	132.00	1-44	0	0
ND McKenzie	3	0	5	0	-	-	0	0
AG Prince	3	0	16	0	-	-	0	0
HM Amla	6	0	24	0	-	-	0	0
GC Smith	9	1	51	0	-	-	0	0
Totals	3677	712	11868	410		6-49	15	3
		b/lb/pen	486	11	run outs			
		Total	12354	421	29.34			

Limited Overs International Results

VERSUS PAKISTAN IN PAKISTAN

Lahore, 18 Oct 2007: SA 294-5 in 50 overs (HH Gibbs 102, GC Smith 34, AB de Villiers 103*). Pak 249 in 46.3 overs (Mohammad Yousuf 53, Kamran Akmal 35, Shahid Afridi 47; M Ntini 4-69). **South Africa won by 45 runs.**

Lahore, 20 Oct 2007: Pak 265-9 in 50 overs (Younis Khan 32, Mohammad Yousuf 117, Shoaib Malik 56). SA 240 in 49.3 overs (GC Smith 65, AB de Villiers 35, SM Pollock 37, JA Morkel 31; Umar Gul 3-59, Iftikhar Anjum 3-43). **Pakistan won by 25 runs.**

Faisalabad, 23 Oct 2007: SA 197 in 49.2 overs (GC Smith 48, JM Kemp 42; Shahid Afridi 3-37, Iftikhar Anjum 3-33). Pak 202-4 in 48.1 overs (Shahid Afridi 32, Mohammad Yousuf 58*, Shoaib Malik 42). **Pakistan won by 6 wickets.**

Multan, 26 Oct 2007: Pak 230-9 in 50 overs (Younis Khan 82, Shoaib Malik 45, Abdur Rehman 31). SA 233-3 in 37.4 overs (GC Smith 81, HH Gibbs 39, SM Pollock 90). **South Africa won by 7 wickets.**

Lahore, 29 Oct 2007: SA 233-9 in 50 overs (HH Gibbs 54, JH Kallis 86, J-P Duminy 44; Shoaib Akhtar 4-43, Iftikhar Anjum 3-45). Pak 219 in 46.3 overs (Younis Khan 58, Mohammad Yousuf 53; M Ntini 4-61, JA Morkel 4-44). **South Africa won by 14 runs.**

South Africa won the series 3-2.

VERSUS NEW ZEALAND AT HOME

Durban, 25 Nov 2007: NZ 248-6 in 50 overs (BB McCullum 40, JM How 90, SB Styris 40, MS Sinclair 32*; A Nel 3-46). SA 249-8 in 50 overs (GC Smith 44, AB de Villiers 87, J-P Duminy 46, MV Boucher 35*; KD Mills 5-25). **South Africa won by 2 wickets.**

Port Elizabeth, 30 Nov 2007: SA 209-9 in 50 overs (MV Boucher 48, SM Pollock 52, A Nel 30*; KD Mills 3-43, MR Gillespie 3-55). NZ 210-3 in 38.4 overs (BB McCullum 81, JM How 76). **New Zealand won by 7 wickets.**

Cape Town, 2 Dec 2007: NZ 238-8 in 50 overs (SB Styris 60, MS Sinclair 73, JDP Oram 34). SA 242-5 in 45.2 overs (GC Smith 51, HH Gibbs 119, JH Kallis 30; DL Vettori 3-33). **South Africa won by 5 wickets.**

South Africa won the series 2-1.

VERSUS WEST INDIES AT HOME

Centurion, 20 Jan 2008: WI 175 in 35.5 overs (RS Morton 41, DJG Sammy 51). SA 176-4 in 34 overs (J-P Duminy 79*). **South Africa won by 6 wickets.**

Cape Town, 25 Jan 2008: SA 255-9 in 50 overs (GC Smith 86, AB de Villiers 45, J-P Duminy 68; JE Taylor 4-34). WI 169 in 48.2 overs (S Chattergoon 34, S Chanderpaul 54; M Morkel 4-36). **South Africa won by 86 runs.**

Port Elizabeth, 27 Jan 2008: WI 252-7 in 50 overs (S Chattergoon 52, PA Browne 35, MN Samuels 98). SA 256-3 in 48.4 overs (GC Smith 56, JH Kallis 121*, J-P Duminy 36*). **South Africa won by 7 wickets.**

Durban, 1 Feb 2008: WI 263-9 in 50 overs (BA Parchment 48, S Chattergoon 48, PA Browne 34, JE Taylor 43*). SA 266-5 in 47.5 overs (GC Smith 50, HH Gibbs 39, AB de Villiers 77, J-P Duminy 44). **South Africa won by 5 wickets.**

Johannesburg, 3 Feb 2008: WI 295-7 in 50 overs (DS Smith 91, S Chanderpaul 51, PA Browne 49*, DJ Bravo 40; CK Langeveldt 3-61). SA 211-2 in 28.5 overs (HH Gibbs 102, JH Kallis 74*). **South Africa won by 8 wickets (D/L method), target revised to 211 in 31 overs.**

South Africa won the series 5-0.

VERSUS BANGLADESH IN BANGLADESH

Chittagong, 9 Mar 2008: Ban 178 in 48.2 overs (Tamim Iqbal 82; A Nel 3-24). SA 180-1 in 36.5 overs (HH Gibbs 57, GC Smith 103*). **South Africa won by 9 wickets.**

Mirpur, 12 Mar 2008: Ban 173 in 48.2 overs (Shakib Al Hasan 52, Raqibul Hasan 63; A Nel 4-27, CK Langeveldt 3-31). SA 179-3 in 48.1 overs (AB de Villiers 69*, J-P Duminy 49*). **South Africa won by 7 wickets.**

Mirpur, 14 Mar 2008: Ban 143 in 42.5 overs (JA Morkel 4-29, J Botha 3-34). SA 147-3 in 34.2 overs (GC Smith 68*, AB de Villiers 40). **South Africa won by 7 wickets.**

South Africa won the series 3-0.

VERSUS ENGLAND IN ENGLAND

Leeds, 22 Aug 2008: Eng 275-4 in 50 overs (IR Bell 35, MJ Prior 42, KP Pietersen 90*, A Flintoff 78). SA 255 in 49.4 overs (HH Gibbs 37, JH Kallis 52). **England won by 20 runs.**

Nottingham, 26 Aug 2008: SA 83 in 23 overs (SCJ Broad 5-23, A Flintoff 3-29). Eng 85-0 in 14.1 overs (MJ Prior 45*). **England won by 10 wickets.**

The Oval, 29 Aug 2008: Eng 296-7 in 50 overs (IR Bell 73, MJ Prior 33, A Flintoff 78*, SR Patel 31). SA 170 in 42.4 overs (HM Amla 46; SR Patel 5-41). **England won by 126 runs.**

Lord's, 31 Aug 2008: SA 183-6 in 32.1 overs (HH Gibbs 74, HM Amla 34; A Flintoff 3-21). Eng 137-3 in 17.4 overs (OA Shah 44*, KP Pietersen 40, A Flintoff 31*). **England won by 7 wickets (D/L method), target revised to 137 in 20 overs.**

Cardiff, 3 Sep 2008: SA 6-1 in 3 overs . Eng did not bat. **No result.**

England won the series 4-0.

VERSUS KENYA AT HOME

Bloemfontein, 31 Oct 2008: SA 336-7 in 50 overs (HH Gibbs 44, JH Kallis 71, J-P Duminy 90, MV Boucher 57*; NN Odhiambo 3-59). Ken 177 in 49.1 overs (A Obanda 38, DO Obuya 35; J-P Duminy 3-31, J Botha 4-19). **South Africa won by 159 runs.**

Kimberley, 2 Nov 2008: Ken 222-9 in 50 overs (S Waters 74, TM Odoyo 32; JA Morkel 3-47). SA 224-3 in 35.3 overs (HM Amla 78, JH Kallis 92*). **South Africa won by 7 wickets.**

South Africa won the series 2-0.

VERSUS BANGLADESH AT HOME

Potchefstroom, 7 Nov 2008: SA 283-8 in 50 overs (HM Amla 35, JH Kallis 50, AB de Villiers 35, J-P Duminy 36, JA Morkel 31*; Naeem Islam 3-59). **Ban** 222 in 44.2 overs (Mohammad Ashraful 73, Shakib Al Hasan 51; DW Steyn 4-16, JA Morkel 3-40). **South Africa won by 61 runs.**

Benoni, 9 Nov 2008: SA 358-4 in 50 overs (HM Amla 140, GC Smith 65, JH Kallis 49, AB de Villiers 54*, JA Morkel 37*). **Ban** 230 in 49.2 overs (Tamim Iqbal 41, Junaid Siddique 47, Mashrafe Mortaza 34; DW Steyn 3-48, J Botha 3-27). **South Africa won by 128 runs.**

East London, 12 Nov 2008: Match abandoned without a ball bowled.

South Africa won the series 2-0.

VERSUS AUSTRALIA IN AUSTRALIA

Melbourne, 16 Jan 2009: Aus 271-8 in 50 overs (SE Marsh 79, RT Ponting 46, DJ Hussey 52). SA 272-7 in 49.3 overs (JH Kallis 41, J-P Duminy 71, ND McKenzie 63, JA Morkel 40*). **South Africa won by 3 wickets.**

Hobart, 18 Jan 2009: Aus 249-9 in 50 overs (SE Marsh 78, RT Ponting 64; M Ntini 3-39). SA 244-6 in 50 overs (JH Kallis 72, AB de Villiers 44, J-P Duminy 35, MV Boucher 37*). **Australia won by 5 runs.**

Sydney, 23 Jan 2009: Aus 269 in 49.2 overs (SE Marsh 43, DA Warner 69, DJ Hussey 36, JR Hopes 33; J Botha 3-32). SA 270-7 in 46.3 overs (HH Gibbs 64, JH Kallis 60, MV Boucher 31*, JA Morkel 40). **South Africa won by 3 wickets.**

Adelaide, 26 Jan 2009: Aus 222 in 48 overs (RT Ponting 63, CL White 30, JR Hopes 42; DW Steyn 3-49, M Ntini 3-52). SA 223-2 in 38.1 overs (HM Amla 80*, HH Gibbs 38, AB de Villiers 82*). **South Africa won by 8 wickets.**

Perth, 30 Jan 2009: SA 288-6 in 50 overs (HM Amla 97, AB de Villiers 60, J-P Duminy 60*; JR Hopes 3-44). Aus 249 in 49 overs (MEK Hussey 78, DJ Hussey 32, BJ Haddin 63; LL Tsotsobe 4-50). **South Africa won by 39 runs.**

South Africa won the series 4-1.

VERSUS AUSTRALIA IN SOUTH AFRICA

Durban, 3 Apr 2009: Aus 286-7 in 50 overs (BJ Haddin 53, RT Ponting 37, MEK Hussey 83*, JR Hopes 38). **SA** 145 in 33.1 overs (GC Smith 52, HH Gibbs 33; NM Hauritz 4-29). **Australia won by 141 runs.**

Centurion, 5 Apr 2009: Aus 131 in 40.2 overs (CJ Ferguson 50, MG Johnson 30; DW Steyn 4-27, WD Parnell 4-25). **SA** 132-3 in 26.2 overs (GC Smith 40, JH Kallis 31, AB de Villiers 36*). **South Africa won by 7 wickets.**

Cape Town, 9 Apr 2009: SA 289-6 in 50 overs (JH Kallis 70, AB de Villiers 80, J-P Duminy 32; MG Johnson 4-34). **Aus** 264-7 in 50 overs (MJ Clarke 35, CJ Ferguson 63, JR Hopes 63*; RE van der Merwe 3-37). **South Africa won by 25 runs.**

Port Elizabeth, 13 Apr 2009: SA 317-6 in 50 overs (HH Gibbs 110, AB de Villiers 84, J-P Duminy 40). **Aus** 256 in 45.5 overs (BJ Haddin 78, MJ Clarke 50, RT Ponting 53, JR Hopes 31; DW Steyn 4-44, RE van der Merwe 3-46). **South Africa won by 61 runs.**

Johannesburg, 17 Apr 2009: Aus 303-7 in 50 overs (BJ Haddin 62, MJ Clarke 66, RT Ponting 40, CJ Ferguson 41, MEK Hussey 49*; J-P Duminy 3-48). **SA** 256 in 45.5 overs (HH Gibbs 82, JH Kallis 64, AB de Villiers 38; MG Johnson 3-58). **Australia won by 47 runs.**

South Africa won the series 3-2.

South Africa won 24, lost 10 and had 1 'No Result' in the 35 Limited Overs Internationals played in this period.

Limited Overs International Averages

BATTING & FIELDING

Name	M	Inns	NO	Runs	HS	Avg	SR	100	50	Ct	St
HM Amla	16	15	3	574	140	47.83	85.79	1	3	6	0
J-P Duminy	32	26	7	866	90	45.57	80.70	0	5	9	0
AB de Villiers	34	31	6	1135	103*	45.40	84.01	1	8	24	0
JH Kallis	30	30	5	1095	121*	43.80	75.93	1	10	5	0
GC Smith	24	24	2	955	103*	43.40	79.78	1	9	14	0
HH Gibbs	31	31	0	1149	119	37.06	87.64	4	5	16	0
MV Boucher	30	24	10	483	57*	34.50	85.94	0	1	34	3
SM Pollock	13	11	4	240	90	34.28	87.59	0	2	1	0
A Nel	14	5	3	66	30*	33.00	146.66	0	0	4	0
ND McKenzie	5	4	0	108	63	27.00	65.45	0	1	2	0
AN Petersen	3	1	0	24	24	24.00	44.44	0	0	0	0
JL Ontong	5	3	0	69	27	23.00	79.31	0	0	2	0
J Louw	3	1	0	23	23	23.00	328.57	0	0	0	0
JA Morkel	28	18	4	302	40*	21.57	116.15	0	0	8	0
JM Kemp	3	3	0	51	42	17.00	52.04	0	0	2	0
VD Philander	2	2	0	33	23	16.50	84.61	0	0	1	0
J Botha	32	16	6	146	26	14.60	82.02	0	0	15	0
CK Langeveldt	11	4	2	18	12	9.00	78.26	0	0	2	0
RE van der Merwe	4	2	1	9	6*	9.00	112.50	0	0	1	0
M Ntini	15	8	5	25	9*	8.33	83.33	0	0	1	0
M Morkel	15	5	1	29	15	7.25	80.55	0	0	4	0
DW Steyn	22	6	3	16	6	5.33	64.00	0	0	5	0
VB van Jaarsveld	2	2	0	9	5	4.50	60.00	0	0	1	0
MN van Wyk	1	1	0	0	0	0.00	0.00	0	0	0	0
PL Harris	3	0	0	0	0	-	-	0	0	2	0
WD Parnell	4	0	0	0	0	-	-	0	0	1	0
LL Tsotsobe	1	0	0	0	0	-	-	0	0	2	0
M Zondeki	2	0	0	0	0	-	-	0	0	0	0
Totals	385	273	62	7425	140			8	44	162	3
			Extras	476					subs	1	
			Total	7901		37.44	82.93			163	

Limited Overs International Averages

BOWLING

Name	Overs	Mdns	Runs	Wkts	Avg	RpO	BB	4I
LL Tsotsobe	9	1	50	4	12.50	5.55	4-50	1
RE van der Merwe	35	0	149	8	18.62	4.25	3-37	0
CK Langeveldt	93.2	4	449	19	23.63	4.81	3-31	0
DW Steyn	186.2	14	934	34	27.47	5.01	4-16	3
PL Harris	30	4	83	3	27.66	2.76	2-30	0
A Nel	101.5	7	476	17	28.00	4.67	4-27	1
M Zondeki	17	1	90	3	30.00	5.29	2-40	0
J-P Duminy	70.1	1	330	11	30.00	4.70	3-31	0
M Ntini	126	5	747	24	31.12	5.92	4-61	2
WD Parnell	36	4	188	6	31.33	5.22	4-25	1
JA Morkel	198.4	8	1024	32	32.00	5.15	4-29	2
J Botha	262	5	1114	34	32.76	4.25	4-19	1
M Morkel	125.2	3	653	19	34.36	5.21	4-36	1
SM Pollock	125	20	381	10	38.10	3.04	2-13	0
JH Kallis	105	3	546	14	39.00	5.20	2-25	0
J Louw	26	1	148	2	74.00	5.69	1-45	0
AN Petersen	1	0	7	0	-	7.00	-	0
VD Philander	13	0	80	0	-	6.15	-	0
Totals	1560.4	81	7449	240			4-16	12
	b/lb/pen	204	33		run outs			
	Total	7653	273		28.03	4.90		

T20 International Results

VERSUS NEW ZEALAND AT HOME

Johannesburg, 23 Nov 2007: NZ 129-7 in 20 overs (SB Styris 30, KD Mills 33*; SM Pollock 3-28, JA Morkel 2-29). SA 131-7 in 19.5 overs (J-P Duminy 33, AB de Villiers 52*; JS Patel 2-17). **South Africa won by 3 wickets.**

VERSUS WEST INDIES AT HOME

Port Elizabeth, 16 Dec 2007: SA 58-8 in 13 overs (J Botha 28*; JE Taylor 3-6). WI 60-5 in 9.5 overs (DW Steyn 4-9). **West Indies won by 5 wickets.**
Johannesburg, 18 Jan 2008: WI 131-7 in 20 overs (M Ntini 2-22). SA 134-6 in 19.2 overs (AB de Villiers 25, SM Pollock 36*, JA Morkel 28*; JE Taylor 2-29, DJG Sammy 3-21). **South Africa won by 4 wickets.**

VERSUS ENGLAND IN ENGLAND

Chester-le-Street, 20 Aug 2008: Match abandoned without a ball bowled.

VERSUS BANGLADESH AT HOME

Johannesburg, 5 Nov 2008: SA 118-7 in 14 overs (LL Bosman 28, AB de Villiers 36; Abdur Razzak 4-16, Shakib Al Hasan 2-21). Ban 109-8 in 14 overs (Tamim Iqbal 25; DW Steyn 2-18, J Botha 2-15). **South Africa won by 12 runs (D/L method), target revised to 122 in 14 overs.**

VERSUS AUSTRALIA IN AUSTRALIA

Melbourne, 11 Jan 2009: Aus 182-9 in 20 overs (DA Warner 89; M Ntini 2-40, DW Steyn 3-38, JA Morkel 2-30). SA 130 in 18 overs (J-P Duminy 78; NW Bracken 2-18, SW Tait 2-36, BW Hilfenhaus 2-15, DJ Hussey 3-25). **Australia won by 52 runs.**

Brisbane, 13 Jan 2009: SA 157-5 in 20 overs (HM Amla 26, J-P Duminy

69*; JR Hopes 2-29). **Aus** 161-4 in 18.5 overs (RT Ponting 38, MEK Hussey 53*, CL White 40*; M Morkel 2-32). **Australia won by 6 wickets.**

VERSUS AUSTRALIA IN SOUTH AFRICA

Johannesburg, 27 Mar 2009: Aus 166-7 in 20 overs (DA Warner 38, DJ Hussey 88*; WD Parnell 2-29, RJ Peterson 3-30). **SA** 168-6 in 19.2 overs (HM Amla 26, MV Boucher 36*, JA Morkel 37; B Geeves 2-35, DJ Hussey 2-21). **South Africa won by 4 wickets.**
Centurion, 29 Mar 2009: SA 156-5 in 20 overs (RJ Peterson 34, RE van der Merwe 48; SM Harwood 2-21). **Aus** 139-8 in 20 overs (MJ Clarke 27, DJ Hussey 27; J Louw 2-36, J Botha 2-16). **South Africa won by 17 runs.**

South Africa won 5, lost 3 of the 8 T20 Internationals played in this period.

T20 International Averages

BATTING & FIELDING

Name	M	Inns	NO	Runs	HS	Avg	SR	100	50	Ct	St
RE van der Merwe	1	1	0	48	48	48.00	160.00	0	0	0	0
J Botha	8	5	4	47	28*	47.00	123.68	0	0	5	0
J-P Duminy	8	8	1	243	78	34.71	137.28	0	2	7	0
RJ Peterson	2	1	0	34	34	34.00	125.92	0	0	1	0
LL Bosman	1	1	0	28	28	28.00	155.55	0	0	0	0
HM Amla	2	2	0	52	26	26.00	104.00	0	0	0	0
SM Pollock	3	3	1	44	36*	22.00	125.71	0	0	0	0
JA Morkel	8	8	2	126	37	21.00	144.82	0	0	4	0
MV Boucher	6	6	2	82	36*	20.50	98.79	0	0	2	0
AB de Villiers	7	7	1	120	52*	20.00	106.19	0	1	7	1
JL Ontong	3	2	0	20	14	10.00	71.42	0	0	0	0
HH Gibbs	7	7	0	63	20	9.00	110.52	0	0	1	0
GH Bodi	1	1	0	8	8	8.00	32.00	0	0	0	0
GC Smith	2	2	0	11	7	5.50	55.00	0	0	1	0
VB van Jaarsveld	3	3	0	15	12	5.00	65.21	0	0	0	0
JH Kallis	2	2	0	8	4	4.00	72.72	0	0	2	0
VD Philander	2	2	0	6	4	3.00	37.50	0	0	0	0
DW Steyn	6	2	1	2	1*	2.00	66.66	0	0	1	0
LL Tsotsobe	1	1	0	1	1	1.00	14.28	0	0	0	0
MN van Wyk	1	1	0	1	1	1.00	25.00	0	0	0	0
M Ntini	3	1	0	0	0	0.00	0.00	0	0	1	0
ND McKenzie	1	1	1	7	7*	-	87.50	0	0	0	0
RK Kleinveldt	1	1	1	3	3*	-	100.00	0	0	0	0
J Louw	2	1	1	1	1*	-	100.00	0	0	0	0
YA Abdulla	1	0	0	0	0	-	-	0	0	0	0
CK Langeveldt	1	0	0	0	0	-	-	0	0	0	0
M Morkel	3	0	0	0	0	-	-	0	0	0	0
WD Parnell	2	0	0	0	0	-	-	0	0	0	0
Totals	88	69	15	970	78			0	3	32	1
			Extras	82					subs	0	
			Total	1052		19.48	112.13			32	

T20 International Averages

BOWLING

Name	Overs	Mdns	Runs	Wkts	Avg	RpO	BB	4I
DW Steyn	21	0	145	11	13.18	6.90	4-9	1
SM Pollock	10	0	66	5	13.20	6.60	3-28	0
RJ Peterson	6	0	46	3	15.33	7.66	3-30	0
YA Abdulla	3	0	16	1	16.00	5.33	1-16	0
LL Tsotsobe	2	0	16	1	16.00	8.00	1-16	0
M Morkel	9.5	0	69	4	17.25	7.01	2-32	0
M Ntini	11	0	78	4	19.50	7.09	2-22	0
RK Kleinveldt	1	0	20	1	20.00	20.00	1-20	0
J Botha	26	0	133	6	22.16	5.11	2-15	0
JL Ontong	2	0	25	1	25.00	12.50	1-25	0
J Louw	7	0	54	2	27.00	7.71	2-36	0
RE van der Merwe	4	0	30	1	30.00	7.50	1-30	0
JA Morkel	24	0	189	6	31.50	7.87	2-29	0
WD Parnell	8	0	73	2	36.50	9.12	2-29	0
J-P Duminy	1	0	8	0	-	8.00	-	0
VD Philander	0.5	0	10	0	-	12.00	-	0
JH Kallis	2	0	25	0	-	12.50	-	0
CK Langeveldt	4	0	33	0	-	8.25	-	0
Totals	142.4	0	1036	48			4-9	1
		b/lb/pen	41	7	run outs			
		Total	1077	55	19.58	7.54		

Team Highlights

At the beginning of the period South Africa were ranked 5th in Test cricket with 102 points. They improved to 2nd with 119 points at the end of the period.

In Limited Overs Internationals South Africa were ranked 2nd with 102 points. They improved to 1st with 126 points at the end of the period, and gained the ICC prize money of US$175 000 for being the leading team as at 1 April 2009.

South Africa became the 3rd team from outside the subcontinent to win both the Test and Limited Overs International series on a tour of Pakistan:

Team	Season	Tests P	W	L	D	LOIs P	W	L	NR
West Indies	1980/81	4	1	0	3	3	3	0	0
Australia	1998/99	3	1	0	2	3	3	0	0
South Africa	2007/08	2	1	0	1	5	3	2	0

Hashim Amla and Jacques Kallis added three consecutive partnerships of 150 or more, becoming the 4th pair to do this in Test cricket:

Garry Sobers and Charlie Davis (West Indies)
170* (4th wkt) v India (Georgetown), 167 (4th) v India (Bridgetown) and 177 (5th) v India (Port-of-Spain) 1970/71
Matthew Hayden and Justin Langer (Australia)
158 (1st) v England (The Oval) 2001, 224 (1st) v New Zealand (Brisbane) 2001/02 and 223 (1st) v New Zealand (Hobart) 2001/02
Matthew Hayden and Ricky Ponting (Australia)
182 (2nd) v South Africa (Sydney), 154 (2nd) v South Africa (Cape Town) and 201 (2nd) v South Africa (Durban) 2005/06
Hashim Amla and Jacques Kallis (South Africa)
170 (3rd) v Pakistan (Karachi) 2007/08, 330 (3rd) v New Zealand (Johannesburg) and 220 (3rd) v New Zealand (Centurion) 2007/08

South Africa's 2-1 series win over West Indies was the third time that they had won a three-Test series after losing the first match. They had previously done this against New Zealand in 1994/95 and India in 2006/07 both at home.

Neil McKenzie and Graeme Smith broke the record for the highest opening partnership in Test cricket when they added 415 against Bangladesh at Chittagong. This passed the previous record of 413 that had stood since 1955/56.

Highest Test opening partnerships

Runs	By	Match	Season
415	ND McKenzie and GC Smith	South Africa v Bangladesh (Chittagong)	2007/08
413	MH Mankad and Pankaj Roy	India v New Zealand (Madras)	1955/56
410	V Sehwag and RS Dravid	India v Pakistan (Lahore)	2005/06
387	GM Turner and TW Jarvis	New Zealand v West Indies (Georgetown)	1971/72
382	WM Lawry and RB Simpson	Australia v West Indies (Bridgetown)	1964/65

In the process McKenzie and Smith became the 4th opening pair to bat through the full first day of a Test without being separated:

Batsmen	Total	Match	Season
MH Mankad and P Roy	234-0	India v New Zealand (Madras)	1955/56
WM Lawry and RB Simpson	263-0	Australia v West Indies (Bridgetown)	1964/65
GR Marsh and MA Taylor	301-0	Australia v England (Nottingham)	1989
ND McKenzie and GC Smith	405-0	South Africa v Bangladesh (Chittagong)	2007/08

South Africa bowled India out for 76 at Ahmedabad. This is the 4th lowest total made against South Africa in Test cricket.

Lowest Test totals against South Africa

Total	By	Against	Venue	Season
54	Zimbabwe	South Africa	Cape Town	2004/05
66	India	South Africa	Durban	1996/97
75	Australia	South Africa	Durban	1949/50
76	England	South Africa	Leeds	1907
76	India	South Africa	Ahmedabad	2007/08

South Africa's 2-1 series win in England was their first there since 1965 and 3rd overall. South Africa won 1-0 in England in both 1935 and 1965.

Neil McKenzie and Graeme Smith set a world record with a fifty opening partnership in 10 consecutive Tests. The sequence was as follows:
52 v Bangladesh at (Mirpur) 2007/08;
415 v Bangladesh at (Chittagong) 2007/08;
132 & 53 v India (Chennai) 2007/08;
78 v India (Ahmedabad) 2007/08;
61 & 26 v India (Kanpur) 2007/08;
13 & 204 v England (Lord's) 2008
51 & 9* v England (Lord's) 2008;
17 & 65 v England (Birmingham) 2008;
56 & 0 v England (The Oval) 2008 and
102 v Bangladesh (Bloemfontein) 2008/09.

The previous record was 8 held by Gordon Greenidge and Roy Fredericks against England and Pakistan in 1976 and 1976/77.

Ashwell Prince and Mark Boucher set a South African 6th wicket part-nership record when they added 271 against Bangladesh at Centurion. The record was previously held by Graeme Pollock and Tiger Lance who added 200 against Australia at Durban in 1969/70.

South Africa's win against Australia at Perth was the 2nd highest success-ful 4th innings run-chase in Test cricket history.

Highest 4th innings total to win a Test

Total	By	Against	Venue	Season
418-7	West Indies	Australia	St John's	2002/03
414-4	South Africa	Australia	Perth	2008/09
406-4	India	West Indies	Port-of-Spain	1975/76
404-3	Australia	England	Leeds	1948
387-4	India	England	Chennai	2008/09

South Africa managed to win the Test against Australia at Melbourne after being in serious trouble in their first innings. When the 6th wicket fell at 141, South Africa were still facing a deficit of 253. Only six teams have won a Test from a worse position.

Teams winning a Test having the highest deficit when they lost their 6th wicket in the first innings

Deficit	6th wkt	Result	Venue	Season	Team1	Totals	Team 2	Totals
392	98-6	West Indies won by 1 wicket	Bridgetown	1998/99	Aus	490 & 146	WI	329 & 311-9
375	211-6	England won by 10 runs	Sydney	1894/95	Aus	586 & 166	Eng	325 & 437
353	92-6	India won by 171 runs	Kolkata	2000/01	Aus	445 & 212	India	171 & 657-7*
334	93-6	Australia won by 3 wickets	Fatullah	2005/06	Ban	427 & 148	Aus	269 & 307-7
289	112-6	England won by 18 runs	Leeds	1981	Aus	401-9* & 111	Eng	174 & 356
266	45-6	Australia won by 5 wickets	Durban	1949/50	SA	311 & 99	Aus	75 & 336-5
253	141-6	South Africa won by 9 wickets	Melbourne	2008/09	Aus	394 & 247	SA	459 & 183-1

JP Duminy and Dale Steyn's partnership of 180 against Australia at Melbourne is the 3rd highest for the 9th wicket in Test cricket. South Africa now have two of the top three partnerships for this wicket.

Highest Test 9th wicket partnerships

Runs	By	Match	Season
195	MV Boucher and PL Symcox	South Africa v Pakistan (Johannesburg)	1997/98
190	Asif Iqbal and Intikhab Alam	Pakistan v England (The Oval)	1967
180	J-P Duminy and DW Steyn	South Africa v Australia (Melbourne)	2008/09
163*	MC Cowdrey and AC Smith	England v New Zealand (Wellington)	1962/63
161	CH Lloyd and AME Roberts	West Indies v India (Calcutta)	1983/84
161	Zaheer Abbas and Sarfraz Nawaz	Pakistan v England (Lahore)	1983/84

The win against Australia at Melbourne was South Africa's 119th in Test cricket. This meant that South Africa had won more Tests than they had lost for the first time in their Test history. At that point South Africa had won 119 and lost 118 of their 340 Tests with 103 draws.

South Africa won 11 of their 15 Tests in the 2008 calendar year, losing 2 and drawing 2. This equaled the record for most Test wins in a calendar year. West Indies won 11 of their 14 Tests in 1984 and England won 11 of their 13 Tests in 2004.

The 2-1 series win in Australia was South Africa's first in that country. Australia had won five of the eight series between the teams in Australia prior to this. Three series were shared: 1952/53, 1963/64 and 1993/94. The result meant that South Africa became the first country to win Test series at home and away against all nine Test opponents (excluding one-off Tests).

South Africa twice had sequences where they played the same eleven players for 5 consecutive Tests: v Pak (2), NZ (2) & WI (1) 2007/08 and v Aus in Aus (3) & Aus in SA (2) 2008/09. This equalled the South African record set in 1905/06 in a 5-Test series against England. Only England (6 v New Zealand and South Africa) in 2007/08 and 2008 have had the same team for more consecutive matches.

South Africa's 651 at Cape Town was their highest Test total against Australia and 3rd highest overall. The previous best against Australia was 622-9* at Durban in 1969/70.

Highest Test totals by South Africa

Total	By	Against	Venue	Season
682-6*	South Africa	England	Lord's	2003
658-9*	South Africa	West Indies	Durban	2003/04
651	South Africa	Australia	Cape Town	2008/09
622-9*	South Africa	Australia	Durban	1969/70
621-5*	South Africa	New Zealand	Auckland	1998/99

Australia's win in the series in South Africa brought to an end to a run of 10 consecutive Test series without a loss by South Africa. Excluding one-off Test matches this was the third time South Africa had gone 10 series without a loss. Only five teams have had longer runs.

Consecutive Series without defeat

Series	By	From	Until
27	West Indies	1980	1994/95
16	Australia	2001	2004/05
14	England	1950/51	1958
11	Australia	1934	1952/53
11	Australia	1956/57	1964/65
10	South Africa	1965	1995/96
10	England	1967	1971
10	Australia	1972	1976/77
10	Pakistan	1985/86	1989/90
10	South Africa	1998/99	2001/02
10	South Africa	2006/07	2008/09

Player Highlights

The highlights for the 35 players who represented South Africa between 1 October 2007 and 30 April 2009 were as follows:

Yusuf Abdulla
Made his T20 International debut against Australia at Centurion in March 2009, taking 1-16 in 3 overs. His first international wicket was Ricky Ponting.

Hashim Amla
Scored 1 161 runs (avg 52.77) in 15 Tests in 2008, including 3 centuries and 6 fifties.

Passed both 1 000 and 2 000 Test runs during this period and collected a career best of 176* against New Zealand at Johannesburg in 2007/08 along the way.

Made his mark in Limited Overs Internationals for the first time with scores of 140 against Bangladesh and 80* and 97 against Australia.

Gulam Bodi
Made 8 in the T20 International against West Indies at Port Elizabeth in his only appearance during this period.

Loots Bosman
Made 28 off 18 balls in the T20 International against Bangladesh at Johannesburg in his only appearance during this period.

Johan Botha
Captained South Africa in eight Limited Overs Internationals, winning 7 and losing 1, including the 4-1 series win in Australia. He was also captain for five T20 Internationals.

Took a Limited Overs International best of 4-19 v Kenya at Bloemfontein.

Reappeared in the Test team against Bangladesh at Mirpur, scoring 25 and taking 2-57 in the first innings.

Mark Boucher
Passed the record for most dismissals in a Test career twice in the period. First he went past Ian Healy's 395 when he stumped Umar Gul off Paul

Harris against Pakistan at Karachi in 2007/08. He thus became the first South African to hold any major Test career aggregate record.

Later in that series he became the first wicket-keeper to take 400 Test dismissals when he caught Danish Kaneria off Makhaya Ntini.

After Adam Gilchrist passed him and retired on 416 dismissals Boucher reclaimed the record when he caught Mushfiqur Rahim off Jacques Kallis against Bangladesh at Mirpur in 2007/08.

Out of his 475 Test dismissal, Boucher has taken 84 catches off Makhaya Ntini, 79 off Shaun Pollock, 68 off Jacques Kallis and 53 off Allan Donald.

He also became the 2nd wicket-keeper to reach 400 Limited Overs International dismissals during the period and passed the 4 000 run milestone in both Tests and Limited Overs Internationals during the period.

AB de Villiers
Made a maiden Test double-century when he scored 217* against India at Ahmedabad. It was the first Test double-century for South Africa against India.

Was dismissed for a duck for the first time in Test cricket when he was stumped by Mushfiqur Rahim off Shakib Al Hasan against Bangladesh at Centurion. It was his 77th Test innings and set a world record for most Test innings before making a first duck, passing the 75 by Sri Lanka's Aravinda de Silva.

Scored 1 061 runs (avg 58.94) in 15 Tests in 2008, including 4 centuries and 2 fifties.

Passed 2 000 and 3 000 runs in Tests during the period. On each occasion he became the 2nd youngest South African to reach the milestone after Graeme Smith. He also passed 2 000 Limited Overs International runs during the period.

Became the 4th South African to appear in 50 consecutive Tests when he played against Australia at Johannesburg, and the 2nd after Gary Kirsten to do so from debut.

J-P Duminy
Made his Test debut against Australia at Perth following a thumb injury to Ashwell Prince. He had previously appeared in a South African record of 37 Limited Overs Internationals before making his Test debut. Up to that time Fanie de Villiers and Nicky Boje held the record with 23.

Made an immediate impact in Test cricket with 50* against Australia at Perth to help AB de Villiers complete the run-chase and then 166 at Melbourne. He also dismissed Michael Clarke at Sydney with the 4th ball he bowled in Test cricket.

Passed 1 000 Limited Overs International runs during the period.

Herschelle Gibbs

Although he lost his Test place to Neil McKenzie he continued to perform in Limited Overs Internationals with 4 centuries during the period.

Became the 2nd South African after Jacques Kallis to reach 8 000 Limited Overs International runs and extended his South African record for most Limited Overs International centuries to 2.

In addition, he passed Jonty Rhodes' South African fielding record in Limited Overs Internationals when he caught Australia's James Hopes off Wayne Parnell at Port Elizabeth to collect his 106th catch.

Paul Harris

Became the first spin bowler to take five wickets in an innings in a home Test since Harry Bromfield took 5-88 against England at Cape Town in 1964/65 when he took 6-127 against Australia at Cape Town. 98 Test matches were played in South Africa between these Tests without a South African spinner taking 5 wickets in an innings. These were his best Test bowling figures. He also made a Test best score of 46 against Pakistan at Lahore.

Made his Limited Overs International debut and played three matches during the series in Bangladesh, but remained the Test specialist spinner, with Johan Botha and Roelof van der Merwe playing the limited overs games.

Jacques Kallis

Passed 10 000 runs in both Tests and Limited Overs Internationals during the period. He reached the milestone in Tests during the match against Australia at Johannesburg and the Limited Overs International milestone against Australia at Sydney. In both forms of the game he became the 8th batsman and first South African to reach 10 000 runs.

He is the first all-rounder to score 10 000 runs and take 200 wickets in Tests and the 2nd after Sanath Jayasuriya to perform the same double in Limited Overs Internationals.

Became the 4th South African to score two centuries in a Test, and the 2nd since re-admission when he made 155 and 100* against Pakistan at Karachi.

Name	Scores	Against	Venue	Season
A Melville	189 & 104*	England	Nottingham	1947
B Mitchell	120 & 189*	England	The Oval	1947
G Kirsten	102 & 133	India	Calcutta	1996/97
JH Kallis	155 & 100*	Pakistan	Karachi	2007/08

Scored three centuries in the Test series in Pakistan, joining Aravinda de Silva (twice) as the only players to have done this in a 2-Test series.

Captained South Africa for the 2nd time in Tests against Australia at Cape Town. The circumstances were identical to his only other Test as captain. In both cases it was a dead rubber at home against Australia with the series already lost 2-0. Fortunately for him the result was different this time around as South Africa won, having lost his previous match as captain in Johannesburg in 2005/06.

Justin Kemp
His only appearances in this period were three Limited Overs Internationals in Pakistan. He then made himself unavailable for selection. His final innings was a score of 42 against Pakistan at Faisalabad.

Imraan Khan
Made his Test debut against Australia at Cape Town, following a successful domestic season for Dolphins. He was the leading run-scorer for the season in the SuperSport Series with 835 runs at an average of 55.66 in 10 matches including 4 centuries and 2 fifties. He also made 100 for the Board President's XI against Australians in Potchefstroom. In all, he scored 961 first-class runs (avg 53.38) in the season.

Rory Kleinveldt
Made his T20 debut against Bangladesh at Johannesburg in November 2008, taking 1-20 in his only over and scoring 3*.

Charl Langeveldt
Performed well in the 14 Limited Overs Internationals that he played during the period, taking 22 wickets at an average of 24.72 and an economy rate of 4.84. He then made himself unavailable for further selection.

Johann Louw
Made his debt in the Limited Overs International against Kenya at Bloemfontein and played three Limited Overs Internationals.and two T20 Internationals.

Neil McKenzie
Re-appeared in the Test team against West Indies at Cape Town having missed 38 Tests in the nearly 4 years since his previous Test appearance. This is the 3rd most Test matches missed between appearances for South Africa. Only Justin Kemp (47) and Clive Eksteen (43) have more.

Had great success opening the batting with fellow former King Edward VII pupil Graeme Smith and scored 1 073 runs (avg 53.65) in 14 Tests in 2008, including 3 centuries and 3 fifties. His only previous experience as an opener in first-class cricket was when he opened against Sri Lanka in 2000, his first 3 Test matches.

Passed 3 000 Test runs and made a career best 226 against Bangladesh at Chittagong. This was his maiden first-class double-century.

He also re-appeared in the Limited Overs International team in Australia, having missed 113 matches between appearances.

Albie Morkel

Was a regular member in the Limited Overs and T20 International teams, impressing most with a Man of the Series award for the Limited Overs Internationals in Australia. He scored his Limited Overs International runs at a strike-rate of 116.15 during the period and collected career best Limited Overs International figures of 4-29 against Bangladesh at Mirpur.

Made his Test debut against Australia at Cape Town after 35 Limited Overs International appearances. He scored 58 and claimed Ricky Ponting as his first Test wicket. He and Morne became the 2nd pair of brothers to appear for South Africa in Tests since re-admission after Peter and Gary Kirsten.

Morne Morkel

Claimed his first five-wicket haul in Tests with 5-50 against Bangladesh in Mirpur, and also took career best Limited Overs International figures of 4-36 against West Indies at Cape Town.

Opened the batting in the 2nd innings of the Test against Australia at Sydney after the injury to Graeme Smith, having made a Test best of 40 in the 1st innings.

Andre Nel

Took his 100th Test wicket during the match against Pakistan at Karachi and made a Test best 34 against West Indies at Port Elizabeth.

Also passed 100 Limited Overs International wickets and made a career best Limited Overs International score of 30* off just 13 balls against New Zealand at Port Elizabeth.

Made himself unavailable for selection after the 2008/09 season.

Makhaya Ntini

Took 54 wickets at an average of 28.46 in 15 Tests in 2008.

During the match against Bangladesh at Chittagong he took his 331st Test wicket to pass Allan Donald and move into 2nd place on the list of

South African Test wicket-takers, behind only Shaun Pollock's 421. He also passed Ian Botham's 383 wickets to move into 11th place on the all-time list of Test wicket-takers.

Played his longest Test innings when he batted for 103 minutes (75 balls) for 28* against Australia at Sydney in the vain attempt to save the match.

Justin Ontong

Played five Limited Overs Internationals and three T20 Internationals in this period.

Wayne Parnell

Came to light during the Under-19 World Cup in Malaysia in 2008. He captained South Africa to the final at the tournament, taking 18 wickets at an average of just 8.38 and an economy rate of 3.04. He also contributed 134 runs at an average of 26.80 and strike-rate of 85.35. In the quarter-final against Bangladesh he scored 57 off 59 balls and then took 6-8 in 5 overs.

Became the 3rd youngest player to play Limited Overs Internationals for South Africa when he made his debut against Australia at Perth aged 19 years and 184 days. He also made his T20 International debut on that tour.

His best international performance came when he took 4-25 helping to reduce Australia to 40-6 at Centurion. At 19 years, 249 days, he is the youngest bowler to take four wickets in a Limited Overs International for South Africa. Vernon Philander previously held this record, having taking 4-12 on his 22nd birthday against Ireland at Belfast on his debut in 2007.

Alviro Petersen

Played all three Limited Overs Internationals in Bangladesh, his only appearances in this period. He only batted in the 3rd match, scoring 24.

Set a record for the most first-class runs in a South African season by a home player with 1 376 (avg 57.33), passing the 1 373 by HD Ackerman in 1997/98.

Robin Peterson

Remained in and around the squad, but only appeared in one Test and two T20 Internationals in the period.

Collected a first Test five wicket-haul in the match against Bangladesh at Chittagong when he took 5-33.

Vernon Philander

Played two T20 Internationals in the home season of 2007/08 and toured England playing two Limited Overs International matches. His best contribution was 23 off 27 balls in the Limited Overs International against England at Leeds.

Shaun Pollock

Ended his career after the West Indies tour to South Africa and was Man of the Series in the Limited Overs Internationals, his final series.

Finished as the leading wicket-taker for South Africa in Tests with 421, and the 8th highest overall. He also retired as South Africa's leading wicket-taker in Limited Overs Internationals with 387 and 5th on the all-time list with 393.

Is one of six players to score 3 000 runs and take 300 wickets in Tests and one of three to perform the same double in Limited Overs Internationals.

Bowled the most maidens in Limited Overs with 313 and is 7th on the list in Tests with 1222. Only Glenn McGrath has bowled more Test maidens amongst fast bowlers.

Ashwell Prince

Scored 900 runs at an average of 64.28 in 13 Tests in 2008 with 4 centuries and 2 fifties, including a career best 162* against Bangladesh at Centurion.

Missed the series in Australia as a result of a thumb injury and only regained his place for the final Test of the return series at Cape Town. He opened the batting for the first time in a Test match and scored 150. The previous weekend he scored a first-class best 254 opening for Warriors against Titans in a SuperSport Series match at Centurion.

Had a run of 371 runs without being dismissed in Tests with 59* and 162* against Bangladesh and then 150 against Australia at Cape Town. Only Jacques Kallis (456) and Daryll Cullinan (427) have had longer runs for South Africa.

Of batsmen with 15 or more scores over fifty he has the 3rd best conversion rate to centuries:

Name	Team	50+	100	%
DG Bradman	Aus	42	29	69.04
GA Headley	WI	15	10	66.66
AG Prince	SA	19	11	57.89
AJ Strauss	Eng	31	17	54.83
KP Pietersen	Eng	30	16	53.33

Graeme Smith

Passed Hansie Cronje's South African record for most Test captaincies of 53 and is now 4th on the list for most Test captaincies overall with 69 (68 for South Africa and 1 for ICC World XI).

His 154* v England at Birmingham is the highest 4th innings score for a winning team in Test cricket for South Africa and 7th highest overall:

Score	Name	Match	Season
214*	CG Greenidge	West Indies v England (Lord's)	1984
182	AR Morris	Australia v England (Leeds)	1948
173*	DG Bradman	Australia v England (Leeds)	1948
173*	MA Butcher	England v Australia (Leeds)	2001
168	SM Nurse	West Indies v New Zealand (Auckland)	1968/69
160	J Darling	Australia v England (Sydney)	1897/98
154*	GC Smith	South Africa v England (Birmingham)	2008

When he and Neil McKenzie broke the world record opening partnership in Tests, he became the first player to be involved in 4 triple-century partnerships for the 1st wicket, having previously shared 3 with Herschelle Gibbs.

His 108 against Australia at Perth was his 3rd century in a match-winning 4th innings in Tests. He now has the most career runs for a winning team in the 4th innings of Tests with 919 at an average of 83.54 including 3 centuries and 5 fifties in 16 innings. He passed Matthew Hayden's record of 913.

His 1 656 Test runs in 2008 are the 3rd most in a calendar year in Tests:

Name	Team	M	Inns	NO	Runs	HS	Avg	100	50	Year
Mohammad Yousuf	Pak	11	19	1	1788	202	99.33	9	3	2006
IVA Richards	WI	11	19	0	1710	291	90.00	7	5	1976
GC Smith	SA	15	25	2	1656	232	72.00	6	6	2008

Passed 5 000 and 6 000 runs in Tests during the period, in each case becoming the 2nd youngest to reach the milestone behind Sachin Tendulkar.

Also passed 5 000 Limited Overs International runs during the period.

Dale Steyn

Became the 2nd South African after Makhaya Ntini to take ten wickets in consecutive Tests when he took 10-93 and 10-91 in the two Tests against New Zealand at Johannesburg and Centurion. His took his 20 wickets in that series at an average of 9.20, the 7th lowest average by a bowler taking 20 wickets in series.

His 76 against Australia at Melbourne is the highest score by a number 10 batsman for South Africa in Test cricket, passing the 73* that Chud Langton made against England at The Oval in 1935.

Took 74 wickets at an average of 20.01 in his 13 Tests in 2008.

Was named as the ICC Test player of the year for 2007.

Took his 100th Test wicket in his 20th match, the quickest for South Africa beating the record of 22 held by Hugh Tayfield and Allan Donald and later equalled Tayfield's South African record for the quickest to 150 in 29 Tests.

Lonwabo Tsotsobe

Made his T20 and Limited Overs International debuts on the tour of Australia. He took 4-50 v Australia on his Limited Overs International debut at Perth. These are the 5th best Limited Overs International debut bowling figures for South Africa:

Bowling	Name	Against	Venue	Season
5-29	AA Donald	India	Calcutta	1991/92
4-12	VD Philander	Ireland	Belfast	2007
4-34	SM Pollock	England	Cape Town	1995/96
4-42	DB Rundle	Australia	Brisbane	1993/94
4-50	LL Tsotsobe	Australia	Perth	2008/09

Roelof van der Merwe

Was selected for the home T20 and Limited Overs International series against Australia after two successful MTN Championship campaigns. He made a superb start to his international career with a score of 48 off 30 balls in the T20 match against Australia at Centurion and 8 wickets at an average of 18.62 and an economy rate of 4.25 in four matches in the Limited Overs International series.

Vaughn van Jaarsveld

Made his Limited Overs and T20 International debuts against Australia, but did not have much impact.

Morne van Wyk

Played one Limited Overs and one T20 International during the period without success.

Monde Zondeki
Played two Limited Overs Internationals against Kenya and reappeared in the Test team against Bangladesh at Centurion, 3 and a half years and 34 Tests since his previous appearance.

All statistics are as at 30 April 2009.